Shorebirds

of North America, Europe, and Asia

A Guide to Field Identification

Stephen Message & Don Taylor

Princeton University Press
Princeton and Oxford

Published in the United States, Canada, and the Philippine Islands by Princeton University Press, 41 William Street, Princeton, New Jersey 08540

Published in the United Kingdom and European Union by Christopher Helm, an imprint of A&C Black Publishers Ltd, 38 Soho Square, London W1D 3HB

Library of Congress Control Number 2005936128

ISBN-13: 978-0-691-12671-5 (cloth)
ISBN-10: 0-691-12671-2 (cloth)
ISBN-13: 978-0-691-12672-2 (paperback)
ISBN-10: 0-691-12672-0 (paperback)

nathist.princeton.edu

Printed in Slovenia on behalf of Compass Press Limited.

10 9 8 7 6 5 4 3 2 1

CONTENTS

Colour plates: Waders in flight

PREFACE

WADER IDENTIFICATION REMAINS A CHALLENGE to even the most experienced birders and there is still much to learn. Early field guides were of huge benefit, but for wader enthusiasts the publication of *Shorebirds: An identification guide to the waders of the world* by Peter Hayman, John Marchant and Tony Prater in 1986 was a ground-breaking event. Of this impressive guide Roger Tory Peterson said "We owe a debt to the artist and authors who have so painstakingly and skilfully portrayed and described the many plumages of the world's waders, some of which had never been illustrated before. If you are not already addicted to shorebirds, you will be after studying this landmark volume".

Another important publication for wader enthusiasts was *Shorebirds of the Pacific Northwest*, written by Dennis Paulson in 1993, with illustrations by Jim Erckman and numerous excellent photographs. It may sound limited in its scope but that is far from the truth; it is extremely comprehensive. The author describes it as a 'fact book' that increases the observer's knowledge base rather than serving as a sole reference. He continues to say that its purpose will have been fulfilled if it both increases the reader's interest in and appreciation of shorebirds and enables him or her to go into the field and correctly identify them. It certainly does that and has been an invaluable source of information, as has his most recent book *Shorebirds of North America: the photographic guide*.

Individual birders have different approaches to identification, most often determined by their experience, and many will argue that 'jizz' still has an important role to play. When you find a wader, its 'jizz' – size, shape, posture, plumage and flight or feeding actions – helps to quickly reduce the choice of species. With experience, simply looking at the habitat and knowing the time of year and where you are will help you to focus on an even shorter list of possible species. It is often then that the techniques described in *The New Approach to Identification*, published by the late Peter Grant in 1989 and illustrated by Killian Mullarney, will come into play. *The New Approach* is based on a thorough knowledge of bird topography and moult, as well as other related subjects and the use of new optical equipment. It places emphasis on plumage detail and firm structural differences. Close views, often with the aid of a telescope, are essential. The same approach can be applied to good photographs and illustrations of problematic birds.

The concept of this book was to produce plates of confusing species, particularly when in flight, irrespective of family; Ruff is included with Pectoral, Sharp-tailed, Baird's and Buff-breasted Sandpipers, for example, with the texts adjacent to the illustrations. Wader identification probably concerns birds at rest more frequently than in flight, so one section of the book concentrates on waders at rest, with only a few species to each plate, enabling as many plumage variations as possible to be included, with large-scale illustrations clearly depicting feather and structural detail. Being able to identify waders in flight is another challenge, so a second section of the book deals purely with waders in flight and includes, where possible, similarly plumaged species on the same plate. As an identification guide the texts are concise, often supplementing the illustrations, as far as the plumage descriptions are concerned. However, considerably more than plumage detail can aid identification and various subheadings, such as Behaviour, Habitat and Flight action, were chosen carefully to cover these other characteristics, where applicable. Some aspects of display are included and these can be spectacular and a pleasure to witness, but for more comprehensive information on any one species or family of waders, we recommend that you consult the wide range of monographs and other books available, many of which are listed in the Bibliography.

A similar concept was used by Richard Fitter and Richard Richardson in their 1952 *The Pocket Guide to British Birds*, in which the plates were arranged in three broad habitat groups and the birds within these groups in ascending order of size, also grouping those with similar colours. One plate, for example, included Black and Bar-tailed Godwits, Ruff, Curlew Sandpiper, Knot and Dotterel, all in their summer plumages. So, in the British Isles, a medium to large wader with some orange plumage would be found on that page. If it were that easy, we doubt that there would be so much interest in studying this fascinating group of species. It still does not surprise us when we hear birders say of waders, "but they all look the same", particularly those that have drab winter plumages. There are also some groups, like snipe, within which the separation of individual species remains a daunting challenge, particularly when they occur away from their known breeding or wintering grounds. But for many others, identification is relatively straightforward once basic principles are learned and followed. We hope the carefully considered selection of species, especially for the 'In Flight' plates, will aid the separation of a number of those that can cause confusion. Further tables are included for quick reference regarding in-flight upperpart and underpart features.

ACKNOWLEDGEMENTS

I AM MOST GRATEFUL to Nigel Redman, for commissioning me to produce the text to accompany the excellent colour plates that Stephen Message has painted. It has been a challenging and rewarding experience. The individual species are so well illustrated that in many cases few descriptive words are needed. However, Stephen Message and I have worked closely together to ensure that the words and all his illustrative work complement each other.

My knowledge of this fascinating and challenging group of birds developed during numerous field trips with Tony Prater and David Rosair, and the latter was instrumental in initiating this book. I thank them both for the many pleasurable hours spent studying waders across four continents. I also thank Dennis Paulson, Ernest Garcia and Ray Tipper, whose critical comments on early drafts have helped to improve the texts. Thanks, too, are extended to all those other authors of books and numerous articles describing crucial identification criteria. In their various different ways they have formed an invaluable resource. Numerous photographers, whose photographs in many cases are now so readily accessible, have also provided an important source of information and I also express my gratitude to them.

Don Taylor

I would like to thank Robert Kirk for commissioning me as sole artist for this book, and both Nigel Redman and Jim Martin of Christopher Helm for their comments and advice. Thanks, too, to Tina Tong for her contribution to the design of the book. The assistance of Robert Prys-Jones and Mark Adams, at The Natural History Museum, Tring, has been invaluable, as have the constructive comments received from Steve Broyd, Mark Edgeller, Richard Millington, Alan Pavey, David Rosair and Ray Tipper. Keith Betton, Paul Doherty and Gehan de Silva Wijeyeratne provided important photographic and video references. I thank my parents for their continual support, and finally Libby, for her tireless help at Tring and for her endless encouragement throughout the long gestation of this book.

Stephen Message

The publishers would like to thank Edward Dickinson for permission to base distribution information in the systematic list on material in Dickinson, E. C. (2003), *The Howard and Moore Complete Checklist of the Birds of the World* (Christopher Helm, London). We would also like to thank Josep del Hoyo for allowing us to use and, where appropriate, update the distribution maps of waders in del Hoyo, J., Elliott, A. and Sargatal, J. (1996), *Handbook of the Birds of the World*, Volume 3, Hoatzin to Auks (Lynx Edicions, Barcelona).

WADERS, AS THEY ARE KNOWN IN EUROPE, or shorebirds, as they are more widely referred to, comprise some 222 species in 14 families within the Charadriiformes order, including sheathbills (according to Clements, 2000). This book includes 124 species from ten of those families. The descriptive terms for these birds are both, in certain respects, misleading; some waders never wade and some shorebirds never visit a shoreline! However, they are ground-living, and in the main ground-nesting, birds, usually found associated with water, either inland or by the sea, and a few occur up to 5,000 metres above sea level. Most prefer open areas, relying for safety on cryptic plumage colours. They can fly strongly and run swiftly, while the phalaropes habitually swim. Their bills are of particular interest; each has evolved to exploit a certain source of food, so bills are amazingly varied. A long-billed wader usually has long legs, but not always. Some have webbing between the front toes, on others the hind toe is small or absent, except in the case of jacanas. A number of species are sexually dimorphic, and, while the male Ruff takes this to one extreme, it is the females of the Dotterel, Painted Snipe and phalaropes that have the more brightly coloured plumages and their respective breeding roles are virtually reversed. Waders are often remarkably gregarious, feeding, roosting and migrating in large flocks, but they are usually more solitary when breeding, although here too there are exceptions, such as Pied Avocet. Many are migratory; a few fly annually from the Arctic to the southern tip of South America. This inevitably leads to individuals turning up in the most unexpected places, even on the 'wrong' side of the Pacific or Atlantic oceans, or Asia. However you classify this remarkable group of birds, there will always be an exception and it is probably this diversity, as well as the distances they migrate, that make them so fascinating.

The sequence and nomenclature, particularly for the 'At rest' plates, follows that used in Clements (2000) closely. However, a number of preferred English names are used and artistic licence also influences the sequence occasionally. The sequence of the 'In flight' plates is less rigid, and species are grouped according to plumage characteristics that they share.

Overview of wader families

The notes that follow highlight a few distinctive characteristics of the ten families with species that occur within the region. The bracketed figures show the number of species within that family that are included in this book, followed by the number of species worldwide.

Jacanas (Jacanidae) (2: 8) A most distinct family, with extremely long toes and claws. The birds' large feet spread their weight and allow them to walk on floating plants, from which they pick food items, hence the name 'Lily-trotter', which is more often associated with the African species.

Painted Snipe (Rostratulidae) (1: 2)
A snipe-like family, with shorter bills and more rounded wings. The female has the more brightly coloured plumage; she leaves the incubation and care of the brood to the male.

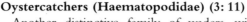

Crab Plover (Dromadidae) (1: 1) In a family of its own, this unique species, found mainly on Indian Ocean coasts, is quite unmistakable. It is the only wader to nest underground in a burrow.

Oystercatchers (Haematopodidae) (3: 11) Another distinctive family of waders, with long, stout and generally orange bills, and either all black or black and white plumages.

Ibisbill (Ibidorhynchidae) (1: 1) A unique species in a family of its own, which inhabits stony rive valleys in the mountains of southern Asia.

Stilts and avocets (Recurvirostridae) (4: 10) Tall, elegant and unmistakable, stilts and avocets often wade in deep water, often picking for prey items or sweeping their long bills side-to-side through the water.

Thick-knees (Burhinidae) (5: 9) A distinctive family of largely nocturnal medium to large waders, characterised by large eyes, a broad head and a stout bill. The long legs have an enlarged 'knee' joint that gives them their name.

Coursers and pratincoles (Glareolidae) (7: 17) The elegant coursers frequent grassland and sub-desert habitats. Several species are crepuscular or nocturnal. Pratincoles, too, are elegant, particularly in flight when they appear tern-like, with their long wings and, in most cases, deeply forked tails.

Lapwings and plovers (Charadriidae) (27: 66) The second-largest group of small to medium-sized waders, with rounded heads, thick necks, rather thick and short bills, and medium-length legs. Lapwings have broad, round wings, while plovers have long, narrow, sharply pointed wings suited for long-distance flight. A very distinctive 'run-and-pause' visual foraging technique is typical of this group. Unique among the plovers, the female Dotterel has the brighter plumage. This is because the males are responsible for the incubation of the eggs, and therefore require a more cryptic plumage.

Sandpipers, snipe & allies (Scolopacidae) (71: 89) By far the largest of the wader families, the Scolopacidae can be divided into seven groups of species. Many are long-distance migrants, undertaking some of the most prodigious journeys of any bird species.

Woodcocks (2: 8) are adapted to woodland environments, with long bills, short legs and cryptically coloured brown plumages.

Snipe and dowitchers (11: 22) are small to medium-sized waders, almost all with very long straight bills and short legs. Snipe, like woodcocks, look similar from season to season but dowitchers have very distinct breeding, non-breeding and juvenile plumages; they feed by continually probing deeply into soft mud.

Godwits, curlews and *Upland Sandpiper* (13: 13) are large, long-legged and long-billed waders (apart from the last) that usually feed by probing deeply in soft mud.

The *Tringa* and related *sandpipers* (16: 20) include the 'shanks', yellowlegs, tattlers and Willet; they are small to medium-sized waders, elegant, delicately built, in most instances, with generally medium–length, straight bills, long necks and medium-long legs, with a small amount of webbing between the toes.

The two *turnstones* (2: 2) are similar species, with very different distributions; the Ruddy Turnstone is cosmopolitan, while the Black Turnstone is restricted to the rocky shores of the North American Pacific coast; they are medium-small, short-legged sandpipers, with short pointed bills and striking white and dark upperparts visible when the bird is in flight.

The *calidrines and allies* (24: 24) include the Surfbird, the 'stints', commonly called 'peeps' in North America, the rare, extraordinary spatulate-billed Spoon-billed Sandpiper and the Ruff – the male of which is the only wader to develop elongated neck feathers in the breeding season, which give it its English name.

The *phalaropes* (3: 3) include the Red-necked and Grey Phalaropes, which are the only pelagic waders, spending their non-breeding seasons at sea. Phalaropes' different feeding habits have led to differences in leg length and bill shape; all three species have lobed toes to aid swimming and the females are polyandrous and leave incubation and care of the young to the male.

There are four wader families with no species present in the region. These are **Magellanic Plover (Pluvianellidae)** (0: 1), **Plains Wanderer (Pedionomidae)** (0: 1), **Seedsnipes (Thinocoridae)** (0: 4) and **Sheathbills (Chionididae)** (0: 2).

How to use this guide

The area covered in this field guide is as shown in the maps below – the Holarctic zoogeographical region. This vast area, covering most of the northern hemisphere north of the Tropic of Cancer, is divided by zoologists into the Palearctic, which consists of Europe plus North Africa and Asia north of the Himalayas; and the Nearctic, which consists of North America including the Mexican Plateau.

Figure 1. Map of the Palearctic zoogeographical region.

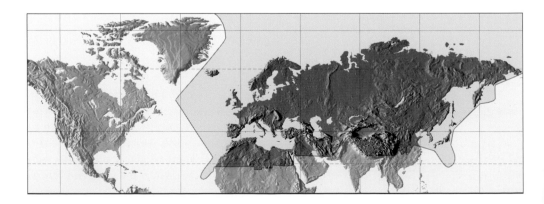

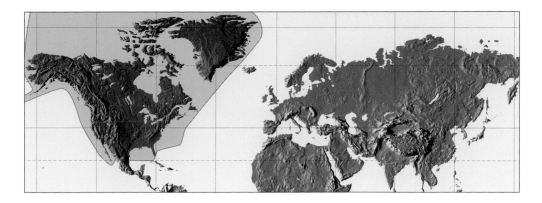

Figure 2. Map of the Nearctic zoogeographical region.

As a wader family may have a global distribution, the plates of waders at rest sometimes link east with west – whether either side of an ocean or a continent. For example, Solitary Sandpiper is included with Wood and Green Sandpipers, while three large curlew species, Eurasian, Far-eastern and Long-billed all appear on the same plate. Although it is highly unlikely that Caspian and Mountain Plovers will ever occur together, they do look remarkably similar in their juvenile plumages. As with many other species, distribution can be a key to identification.

Following sections that deal with wader topography, bills, feet and legs, structure, size and colour, moult, feather patterns, plumage variation and behaviour, the main text opposite each plate of 'waders at rest' provides a summary of the principal identification features and habitat, and describes those identification characters which aid the separation of confusingly similar species. Adjacent to the 'waders in flight' plates the text includes descriptions of calls as well as manner of flight and key flight identification features. The distribution maps are included in this section (see p. 127 for the key to the distribution maps).

Appendices at the end of the book include tables that are designed to provide a quick key for identifying waders in flight, either from above or below.

Waders can often be tantalisingly difficult to identify positively, but we hope that our approach to their identification will remove some of the frustration and that birders will have greater confidence when trying to confirm the identity of individuals of this most enigmatic group of birds.

How to identify waders at rest

An important starting point to wader identification is deciding on the age of the bird. This involves an understanding not only of the terminology associated with the various tracts of feathers but also the moult sequences. When confronted by a puzzling wader, it is important to remember that it is more likely to be a common species than a rarity, possibly in a hitherto unfamiliar plumage. Getting to know the different plumages of the common waders is therefore invaluable.

Topography of waders at rest

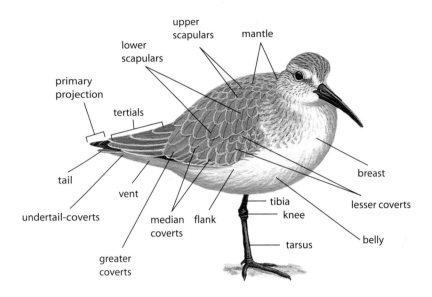

Figure 3. Topography of a typical wader at rest – a Curlew Sandpiper.

An essential key to identification is an understanding of the topography and the terminology used. When looking at a wader feeding or at rest note that the secondaries and all the outerwing except the tips of the primaries are concealed. The scapulars are extensive and when patterned will be an obvious separate group, or tract, of feathers. The most important tracts to be aware of are the mantle, upper and lower scapulars, tertials and the three tracts of innerwing-coverts, as these usually provide most identification and ageing features.

Figures 3–6 clearly illustrate the names given to the various feather tracts, as well as the bare parts, such as legs and bill. More general terms are sometimes used to describe groups of these feathers: the visible feathers of the 'upperparts' include the mantle, scapulars, greater, median and lesser coverts, and tertials. The primaries and secondaries are largely hidden.

Whenever possible it is good practice to follow a standard procedure on each occasion. For example, work forward from the tail end, noting (a) by how much the primaries project beyond the tail tip and (b) the 'primary projection', *i.e.* how many, if any, projecting tips of *primaries* are visible beyond the *tertials*. On the different stints, for example, the primary-projection can be long, short or entirely lacking and this can be an important identification pointer. In front of the tertials are the three, rather horizontal tracts of innerwing–coverts: one row of *greater coverts*, then a row of *median coverts* and several rows of *lesser coverts*. However, on the closed wing these are invariably overhung by the two rows of *lower scapulars*. To separate the roughly horizontal division between the scapulars and coverts, note the larger size of the former compared with the much smaller lesser coverts and narrower median and greater coverts. The three rows of *upper scapulars*, the upper one small and often concealed by the overlapping mantle feathers, are between the lower scapulars and the mantle.

If you study a range of photographs to test your understanding of the described feather tracts, you will find that limitations are caused by plain or worn plumage. Disarranged or missing feathers can also complicate the otherwise neat feather arrangement. Note in particular that the scapulars may be positioned anywhere between fully spread and fully raised, concealing a variable number of the innerwing-coverts (see figure 16).

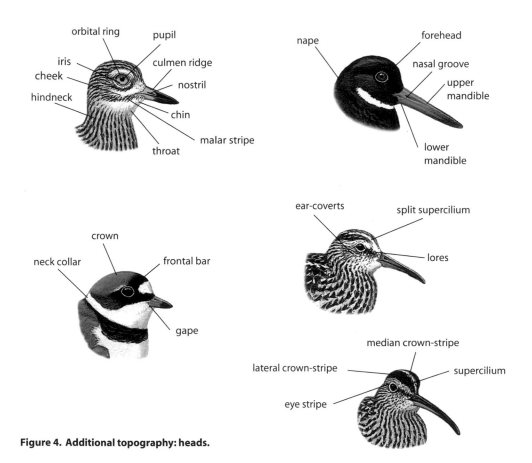

Figure 4. Additional topography: heads.

The illustrations in figure 4 clearly show the main parts of the heads of waders that are referred to when describing features that aid identification. The *crown* usually refers to that part of the head between the *forehead* and the *nape* and the usually dark *frontal bar* is a frequent feature on *Charadrius* plovers. The *median crown-stripe* runs over the centre of the crown and the *lateral crown-stripe* is between the *median* crown-stripe and the *supercilium*, which is the pale stripe immediately above the eye, on occasions reaching from the base of the bill to the nape, but usually shorter. The Broad-billed Sandpiper shows a characteristic *split supercilium* that sandwiches the lateral crown-stripe. The *eye-stripe* is the usually narrow dark line in front of but mainly behind the eye; the narrow area between the base of the bill and the eye is known as the *lores* or the *loral line*, and the *ear-coverts* describes the area just below and behind the eye. A usually darker *malar stripe*, which a few species have, runs from the bill base below the cheek to below the ear-coverts. In some species, when only a minute area under the bill is a different colour, this is referred to as the *chin*; if it is larger the area is described as the *throat*.

The top ridge of the *upper mandible* is known as the *culmen* and the bottom half of the bill is referred to as the *lower mandible*. Two features on the bill can be significant: variations in the shape of the *nostril* and the length of the *nasal groove* on the bill can help to separate similar groups, such as the pratincoles and tattlers.

The unfeathered, or bare, parts can be significant in identification; the colours in particular can help not only in identifying a bird but also in ageing it. The *orbital ring* and *eye-ring* are sometimes confused. The orbital ring is the bare skin immediately surrounding the eye, whereas the *eye-ring* is composed of tiny feathers immediately surrounding the *orbital ring*. In the field and in the text the term *eye-ring* is commonly used to describe both features.

Bills

Bills have evolved to deal with particular foods; the wide range of foods that waders eat is matched by an extraordinary variety of bill shapes and sizes.

Crab Plover Marsh Sandpiper Terek Sandpiper

Long-billed Curlew Spoon-billed Sandpiper

Figure 5. A variety of wader bills.

At the extremes there are the short-billed stints, which pick food items from surfaces, to the incredibly long-billed curlews, that probe deeply for their prey items. In between there is the unique powerful bill of the Crab Plover, capable of breaking open crab shells; the long delicate bill of the Marsh Sandpiper, which enables it to pick prey more easily while wading; the upturned bill of the Terek Sandpiper, which is sometimes used in a scything action to filter prey; and the extraordinary bill of the Spoon-billed Sandpiper, which is constantly swept from side to side in water to collect its prey like a vacuum cleaner.

Feet and legs

Certain features of the feet and legs can provide keys to the identification of a number of species. There are considerable variations in the sizes of the three front and single rear toes. The jacanas have particularly long toes, including the hind one, suited to walking on pond leaves.

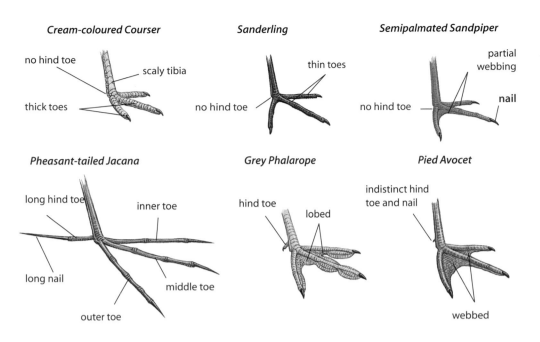

Figure 6. Additional topography: feet (the right foot is illustrated in each case).

In contrast, the Sanderling and small plovers have no hind toes, enabling them to run fast. All waders are capable of swimming but some, such as phalaropes, do so more habitually. Their lobed toes help them to be more effective swimmers. Avocets have webbed toes, and a few species have partially webbed toes – hence the names Semipalmated Plover and Semipalmated Sandpiper – the presence of which is another diagnostic identification feature. To confirm the presence of partial webbing in the field can be difficult and the circumstances need to be favourable; ideally dry terrain – sticky mud may form apparent palmations. Muddy legs can also make the assessment of leg colour extremely difficult and this needs to be borne in mind, particularly when leg colour is crucial to identification.

Structure

Judging shape and structure can be an important aid to identification. When the differences are obvious, like the fairly thick, slightly upturned bill of a Greenshank, compared with the needle-thin, straight one of a Marsh Sandpiper, no special technique is required.

Figure 7. Differences of bill morphology between Greenshank (a) and Marsh Sandpiper (b).

For similar species, slight differences in bill shape and length, for example, are notoriously prone to incorrect assessment, which may lead to misidentification. Experience and knowledge help to minimise errors that occur through such subjective judgements. It is also important to be aware that all birds are able to alter the shape of their head and body by holding the plumage either sleek, or puffed up for warmth. This means of temperature control is a reflex, so birds are more likely to look slim in a warm climate and fluffed up in cold or windy conditions. However, this may not apply to all birds in a flock at the same time: one or two may look fluffed up and the others slim.

Remember, too, that there are differences, sometimes quite marked, between the sexes of individual species, not only in overall size but, for example, in bill length. In a flock of Eurasian Curlews, a shortest male bill of 83mm compared with a longest female one of 192mm might certainly make you wonder whether individuals from the same species are involved. There are also racial variations; the difference in bill lengths of Greater and Lesser Sand Plovers can be quite marked, but sometimes there is little variation, depending on the races compared.

Some of the pitfalls of judging structural differences can be avoided by using objective measurement techniques, such as the primary projection already described for variations in wing structure. These techniques can be applied to other features. For example, the tibia can be compared with the length of the tarsus. Also the length of tail that projects beyond the wing-tips can help separate pairs of similar species, such as Spotted and Common Sandpipers.

a b

Figure 8. Diagnostic differences between the tail lengths of Spotted (a) and Common (b) Sandpipers.

Size and colour

Size is particularly difficult to judge accurately, and misjudgement of size is often a cause of misidentification. Against a featureless sky assessing size is impossible, likewise on an open mudflat. Of two Dunlins a short distance apart the farthest will appear too large for a Dunlin. An observer, unaware of size-illusion, would understandably believe that his judgement had been correct. Through binoculars or a telescope, comparative sizes can only be judged correctly when two birds are exactly the same distance from the observer, and relatively close to each other. The contrast between the bird and its background may also affect the impression of size. For example, a dark wader flying against a light, calm sea will look larger than against a dark, stormy sea, while the opposite is true for a pale wader. Looking into or against the light can also affect the impression regarding the shape of a bird, which will appear slimmer, as 'the light eats the edges'.

As well as size and proportion, light can also affect colour. The type of light and the weather alter the perception of colour, not only by creating contrasts. Low morning or evening sunlight can completely change the apparent tonal colour of a bird – a neutral grey can become a warm grey-brown, or the neutral grey against a dark background can look very pale. Bright sunlight at noon will create marked contrasts between the upperparts and the underparts, which will be in deep shadow, and subtle differences in tones will be difficult to judge. In overcast but clear conditions, the contrasts decrease and truer colours can be seen.

Moult

Moult is the process through which old feathers are shed and replaced by new ones. It is necessary for keeping plumage in good condition and for waders, as in other species, produces different juvenile, non-breeding and breeding plumages, as well as some distinct first-winter plumages and perplexing transitional ones. Understanding moult is an important aspect of identification. It explains how different plumages are acquired, which is essential when trying to age waders. In separating similar species diagnosing the age often provides a key starting point, so that comparisons can be made with similar birds in the equivalent plumage.

All feathers are generally renewed at least once a year and, in the case of body feathers, twice. Most adults have a complete, uninterrupted moult during the autumn or winter. The timing of moult is dependent on a wide range of interrelated factors, including the bird's age, the latitudes of the breeding and wintering areas, the timing of the breeding season, length of migration and the availability of food concentrations. Consequently, there are many exceptions to the general pattern of moult strategies and also to the duration of the moult, which not only varies between species, but also within races of one species, from as few as 40 days to as many as 135. Three races of Red Knot provide examples of two different strategies; the Siberian race *canutus* uses the Waddenzee in Holland as a stopover site, where they feed for a few weeks before continuing their migration to the wintering grounds in west Africa, where they have a complete moult. The more western Canadian race *rufa* has a similar strategy, with refuelling posts along the Massachusetts coast, before the long flight to South America. A third race *islandica*, which breeds in NE Canada and Greenland, has a different strategy, again visiting the Waddenzee, but remaining there for a complete moult, before flying to Britain and Ireland

Table 1. Wader plumages

Plumage	Alternative Names	Usual Season	Duration
Juvenile	juvenal	July – September	first autumn of life
First-winter	first non-breeding first basic	October – April	first winter of life
First-summer	first breeding first alternate	May – July	first full summer of life
Non-breeding	basic/adult winter	August/October – March	from first or second winter throughout life
Breeding	alternate/adult summer	April – September	from first or second summer throughout life

Figure 9. Downy feathers on the tail-tip ages this Killdeer as a newly fledged juvenile.

for the winter. Species such as the Bar-tailed Godwit and the Grey Plover also moult at staging posts. A third strategy is used by the *pacifica* race of Dunlin, which breeds in western Alaska and winters south to Mexico: they commence the wing moult while breeding and complete the moult on the breeding grounds, before migrating. Most waders that have a complete moult on the breeding grounds are sedentary species or short-distance migrants, like the Killdeer, or the three woodcocks. Several long-distance migrants, such as Pacific Golden Plover and Wood Sandpiper, have a partial wing moult on the breeding grounds, replacing the outer primaries and inner secondaries only, and then suspending the moult until they reach their wintering areas, while others, such as Greater Yellowlegs and Long-billed Dowitcher will complete their wing moult at a staging post, before flying to their wintering grounds to moult the rest of their feathers. However, some birds, such as Least Sandpiper, fly direct from Canada to their South American wintering quarters and undertake a complete primary moult there, in preparation for the return migration in the spring. During their first summer, many migrant waders either remain on their southerly wintering grounds, or return only part way north. This may explain the occurrence of birds, summering in the northern hemisphere, that look like non-breeding adults.

The newly fledged *juvenile* will still have some loose downy feathers during the first few weeks (see figure 9). The Thick-knees retain down streamers on the tail for a slightly longer period, and this can be one of the few means of ageing them as juveniles. In other species, once these fall away the full juvenile plumage will be characterised by rather small, neat and

breeding   juvenile

Figure 10. Comparison of breeding adult and juvenile scapular lengths in Semipalmated Sandpiper.

often strikingly patterned feathers. In most, if not all, species, juvenile primaries are shorter and narrower than those of an adult, but beware comparing them, when at rest, with the juvenile tertials, which will also be shorter, thus, in some species, making the juvenile primaries look longer than those of the adults. In many species, the rows of juvenile innerwing–coverts are more visible, below the smaller scapulars. In contrast, the large, rather loose adult scapulars frequently overhang the lesser, median and greater coverts. Adults of both turnstone species have unusually large median coverts that look more like additional scapulars and tend to droop from the wings, when the birds are at rest.

Typically, the wing coverts and mantle feathers in juvenile *Calidris* species are fringed with whitish-buff or whitish; in *Tringa* species they are spotted buff or whitish; and in *Charadrius* species they are finely fringed pale buff, with a fine subterminal band of a darker colour. The Jack Snipe and American Woodcock, however, have plumages that are almost identical at all ages. The post-juvenile moult is generally a partial one, and usually involves most of the

juvenile to first-winter

juvenile

breeding

non-breeding

Figure 11. Sequence of Dunlin plumages.

body feathers and a variable number of wing-coverts and tertials. The juvenile primaries, secondaries and tail feathers are usually retained. A number of species, the Common Snipe for example, lose most of their juvenile wing-coverts during the post-juvenile moult and grow feathers similar to those of the adults. Only coursers and pratincoles replace all their feathers during the post-juvenile moult. As a result of post-juvenile moult, the appearance of most waders is changed significantly. In contrast to the juvenile feathers that are usually quite bright and fairly strongly patterned, the newly acquired first non-breeding feathers are often comparatively dull and featureless, so that by the time the moult is complete the bird often appears a plainer, drabber individual. In many instances, the first-winter bird can be distinguished from the otherwise very similar non-breeding adult by the unmoulted but worn feathers retained from its juvenile plumage. The particular feather tracts to examine are the wing-coverts and tertials, though the number of these feathers that are lost at the post-juvenile moult varies between species, and also between races of the same species. The feathers that are not moulted during that first autumn have to survive considerably longer and will be extremely worn by the following summer, prior to the first complete moult. Some flight feathers, usually tail feathers and some tertials and coverts, will be at least a year old.

Leading up to the first breeding season, a partial moult takes place to produce the full breeding plumage, though larger waders will generally not acquire this until their second summer, having spent the first on their wintering grounds, where they will rarely attain full adult breeding plumage and either retain first-winter plumage or gain a mixture of winter and summer plumages. In many migrant species the change into breeding plumage can be dramatic, with pale underparts becoming bright red, black or barred. During the latter part of the breeding season, first-year birds will complete a full moult to attain the adult non-breeding plumage.

Figure 12. Curlew Sandpipers. The brightest breeding plumage is achieved by abrasion.

The complete moult of adults in the late summer and autumn produces the non-breeding plumage, which may be retained for as long as eight months, while in spring the adult body feathers are moulted to produce the full breeding plumage. In some species, such as Curlew Sandpiper, the newly acquired white-tipped body feathers abrade to produce uniform rich chestnut underparts. Later, when the birds start moulting into winter plumage, they appear more blotchy (see figure 12).

Figure 13. Broad-billed Sandpiper looks darker in late summer in 'worn' breeding plumage.

Once the breeding season is over adult birds will again undergo a complete moult – occasionally commencing during breeding – and migrant species that commence this moult on the breeding grounds will generally follow the juveniles south a few weeks later, as occurs with the *pacifica* race of the Dunlin and shorter-distance migrants like the Killdeer. However, for the majority of waders breeding within the Arctic Circle the adults commence their southerly migration before the juveniles. In Europe, the adult Curlew Sandpipers, for example, will appear about two to three weeks before the juveniles.

Moult sequences are not the only factors to alter appearances. The environment immediately affects new feathers and the effects become more pronounced as time passes. Friction and particles in the air cause wear, which most affects the edges of feathers. Wear is particularly evident on the scapulars, tertials, coverts and primaries. As dark pigment protects feathers from wear, lighter areas wear more rapidly. Bleaching of feather colour can be caused by relentless strong sunshine, so that brown fades to pale brown. Bright sunlight may also make a bird appear pale, and as the feathers fade they become weaker and abrade more quickly. The overlapping scapulars and tertials help to protect most of the wing feathers, but they will therefore abrade faster than the other feather tracts. The pale areas, usually the fringes or tips of all feathers, are lost first in early summer. For example, the tips of fresh primary feathers often have pale fringes, but those primaries become all dark as the fringes wear off.

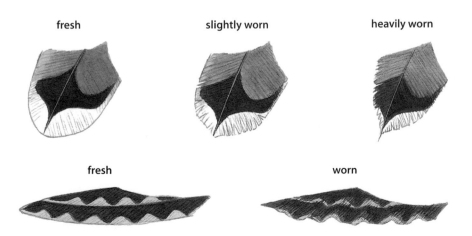

Figure 14. Feather wear – Red-necked Stint lower scapulars (top row) and Pacific Golden Plover tertial feathers (bottom row).

Wear on the upperpart breeding plumage feathers – often dark-centred, brightly-edged and paler-tipped – is particularly interesting, as in the Broad-billed Sandpiper (see figure 13). In this species the paler tips create a frosty appearance in spring. As these abrade the appearance is more brightly patterned, followed by a darker plumage as the buff edges abrade.

Feather patterns

In general terms, wader upperparts are dark, with varying amounts of lighter markings and the underparts light, with variable dark markings. However, there are always exceptions and the markings often vary in distinctiveness, even between birds in the same plumage. The range of

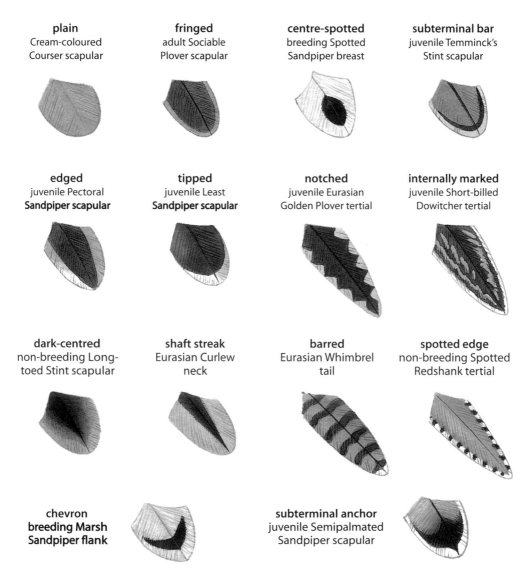

Figure 15. Feather pattern terminology.

complex feather markings grouped in tracts of feathers produces certain patterns of wader plumage. These details can be seen in the field, with the aid of good optics. Different species in each taxonomic group frequently share feather patterns, but their arrangement and colour creates the distinct differences in appearance. The understanding of these basic feather patterns is another identification tool. Though markings usually occur singly on feathers, some like dots, notches and bars can be repeated to create a distinctive pattern.

As examples, the lower white-edged feathers of the mantle and scapulars link to produce the white lines typical of juvenile Little Stints and Pectoral Sandpipers; and the dark subterminals and pale fringes will produce the scalloped appearance of the juveniles of Baird's Sandpiper and White-tailed Plover.

Plumage variations

The typical variety of plumages, involving variation according to age, sex, season and moult, has already been outlined. There is also geographic variation, which may simply be clinal, leading to differences in colour tones of feathers, like the more rufous upperparts of Killdeer in the south of their range or the variation in colour of the underparts of Kittlitz's Plovers. When different populations of one species become geographically isolated the genetic divergence may become sufficient for a subspecies to be recognised. This may involve differences in size, as in Rock Sandpiper, or bill length and upperpart colours, as in Dunlin.

Partial and complete albinism occurs in waders, producing individuals which either have several feather tracts white or are completely white, with pale legs and bill and pink eyes. A far scarcer extreme is melanism, when the feathers are all dark or even black. More frequent is the incidence of leucistic plumages, when the feathers are all a very pale fawn.

Hybrid waders have posed and still can produce considerable challenges and though they are relatively rare, the possibility of hybridisation is worth considering when it is proving a struggle to identify an individual. 'Cox's Sandpiper', a hybrid between Curlew and Pectoral Sandpipers, was initially described as a separate species, *Calidris paramelanotos*. Other hybrid *Calidris* sandpipers have been described and proving their parentage can be a considerable challenge. Other hybrids are more straightforward, like those of the American and Black Oystercatchers, which do hybridise, where their ranges overlap, and reference to them is made in the species' texts. Similarly, when a Black-necked Stilt hybridises with an American Avocet the parentage is obvious.

Behaviour

The term 'jizz' is frequently used in the context of identification. It means a combination of characters, including behaviour, stance, overall size and shape. The manner of behaviour can provide important clues to assist wader identification, though it is rarely diagnostic and may occasionally be atypical, particularly with a vagrant out of its normal range and habitat. The teetering (bobbing or tail pumping) of some *Tringa* and *Actitis* waders are useful aids. However, be aware, for example, that when a bird is alarmed its posture can alter dramatically (see figure 16). When alert it will appear slim and may seem long-necked while it scans for the cause of the alarm, and it may also appear long-legged since the tibiae are more exposed. As the scapulars are often raised when the bird is alert, a fuller range of wing-coverts will be visible. When relaxed, the scapulars of the bird will overhang more of the wing-coverts; the bird will appear more compact with a shorter looking neck, and it will appear to have shorter tibiae, since these will be partially hidden by the belly feathers.

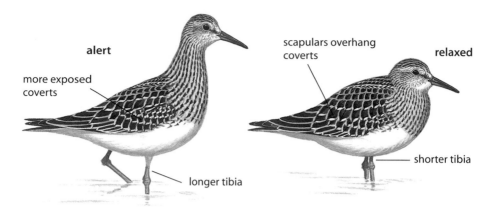

Figure 16. **Variations in appearance of a juvenile Pectoral Sandpiper – alert and relaxed.**

Feeding

The two basic feeding methods, described most simply as 'picking' and 'probing', can help assign a bird to the correct family. Waders find their prey by sight or touch, or sometimes a combination of both. Each shape and size of bill is designed for particular prey items, as discussed under the section on bills. It is generally safe to say that shorter bills are used for picking and longer ones for probing. However, there is nothing to stop a Grey Plover from probing mud for a worm, a Whimbrel from picking a crustacean from the surface, or an Eurasian Curlew from picking insects from vegetation.

When feeding by sight, waders tend to be well spaced, to prevent loss of time and energy when two compete for the same prey. Plovers and lapwings are sight feeders and all species use the 'run–and–pause' method. They sprint forward, pause and turn their heads rapidly to catch

Figure 17. **Semipalmated Plovers 'picking' and 'foot trembling'.**

sight or sound of their prey. These families also use the 'foot-trembling' method: tapping rapidly on the ground disturbs the prey, and the movement discloses its whereabouts. 'Foot-trembling' also brings invertebrates to the surface. Eurasian Dotterels are known to use this method. Sanderlings also find food by sight, running along the tideline like mechanical toys. They have no hind toe, which enables them to run faster.

Probing, the immersion of the bill beneath the surface, or into existing hollows, may be shallow or deep, slow or fast, regular or intermittent, and either to pursue detected prey, or to explore tactilely for prey. The term 'stitching' describes a rapid series of probes (like the action of a sewing machine), and a species like the Dunlin may use three feeding methods: picking at the mud's surface, probing the mud or stitching. The feeding habits of Dunlin, several other *Calidris* species and larger probers like Bar-tailed Godwit will be dictated by the tides. They feed during both night and day, mostly on the intertidal flats but also on saltmarsh. Waders using the probing method often do so in close-knit flocks.

Figure 18. Greenshanks dashing after fish.

Shingle beaches and rocky coastlines will attract waders with different feeding habits. The Wandering Tattler and Rock and Purple Sandpipers have become specialist rock feeders, with no apparent differences in their bills from the probing sandpipers. Oystercatchers, however, have bills especially adapted to capture and break through the defences of bivalve molluscs, which are exposed at low tide on rocky shores as well as on mudflats. Oystercatchers also use their heavy bills to hammer limpets, dislodge them and suck out the contents. The Black Oystercatcher is primarily a rock species, with rocky shores being the predominant coastal habitat within its range. The Surfbird is another rock specialist, as are the aptly named turnstones, whose short, pointed, fairly stout bills are ideal for sliding beneath stones to flick them over, revealing sandhoppers and other small invertebrates of the shore. Surfbirds feed by plucking young mussels, barnacles and limpits with a sideways tug of the head; they later regurgitate the shells.

Figure 19. Pied Avocet feeding methods – picking, scything and stirring.

Greenshanks use a dash-and-lunge method to hunt small fish and will also chase fish by dashing after them with their bills half-submerged (see figure 18). Common, Spotted and Terek Sandpipers are largely insectivorous, catching low-flying insects by sight, or stalking them with head held low, even looking up at the undersides of leaves to pick insects from their surfaces. Their large eyes and acute hearing enable Stone Curlews to catch nocturnal insects, like moths, which they may catch by jumping into the air. Ruffs eat beetles and insects such as grasshoppers, which they find by walking steadily across wet grassland and pecking at the surface. They will also follow the plough and take invertebrates or wade and take insects from

Figure 20. Red-necked Phalaropes spinning and picking.

the water's surface. Pratincoles feed more like swallows, hunting in flocks and catching flying insects in the air, though they will also pick them from the ground, dashing after their prey. Coursers are also insectivorous, usually hunting on foot. Avocets have three main feeding techniques. One involves sight feeding, as they pick insects from the surfaces of water or mud. The other methods include scything and stirring with the bill, both of which locate prey by touch (see figure 19). Scything avocets may work in groups in a line. Aquatic insects are also favoured by the stilts, which snatch beetles from the water's surface, immerse their heads beneath the water to take dragonfly nymphs, and also take flying insects that are about to land.

Waders with partially webbed feet swim occasionally and others do so habitually, like the phalaropes, which have lobed feet (see figure 6). Red-necked Phalaropes feed while swimming, simply picking insects from the surface, or from slightly submerged vegetation. They also spin rapidly to bring food items to the surface (see figure 20). Spotted Redshanks often swim together in small flocks to disturb and catch shoals of small fish.

Display

Much display involves variations in the manner of flight and is dealt with in the section on flight behaviour. Whether the display is on the ground or in the air it essentially serves two purposes, advertising territory or attracting a mate. As oystercatchers form pair bonds, which last from year to year, their 'piping' display, involving both sexes, is used against trespassers.

Figure 21. Oystercatchers 'piping' to defend territory.

The dramatic behaviour of Ruffs at a lek is almost unique among waders, as is their breeding plumage. At the lek the dominant males spar with other males, seeing them off before performing a wing fluttering display to greet females. Great Snipes also have communal displays at leks, at dusk and after dark, whereas Ruffs lek mainly in the early morning. The male Great Snipe attracts the attention of females by performing an extravagant movement of the neck, stretching it until it is almost touching the back, simultaneously rattling the bill to produce continuous clicking noises. They also adopt an erect posture, puffing out the

Figure 22. Male Buff-breasted Sandpiper displaying to females.

chest and cocking and fanning the tail, while they sing, often leaping high into the air. A third species, the Buff-breasted Sandpiper, also displays at a lek; the males of this species perform a series of spectacular 'wing-flashing' displays, exposing the silvery-white undersides of the wings to impress watching females. Most waders, including plovers, godwits, curlews, and the *Calidris* and *Tringa* sandpipers, have a courtship display that involves wing-lifting. The display of each species is characteristic, sometimes within a family, or with the emphasis often relating to plumage features, such as the black-and-white tail of Black-tailed Godwits. Male Pectoral Sandpipers are able to expand their streaked breasts by inflating their throat sacs (see figure 26) – yet another method of attracting potential mates.

Feigning injury

A majority of waders nest on the ground, often with little more than a scrape for their eggs, which tends to make them vulnerable. When a predator approaches too closely, plovers, including Killdeers (see figure 23) and Northern Lapwings, will try to slip away from the nest unnoticed and, when a short distance away from the nest, will drop one wing and hobble further away, as if injured. The predator, assuming that these are easy-to-catch adult birds, will generally follow them away from the nest. Once a safe distance away the adults will fly off. Species like Dunlin, Purple Sandpiper, Red Knot, Ruff and the various curlews will jump into the air, as if trying unsuccessfully to take off. Other strategies, employed by Black-winged and Black-necked Stilts, for example, involve moving away from the nest and either pecking at the ground for food, or preening, as if busy doing anything other than incubating eggs; or, alternatively, giving the false impression that they are incubating or brooding in full view of predators.

Figure 23. A Killdeer feigns injury to draw a predator away from the nest.

How to identify waders in flight

There is little more impressive than the synchronised, swirling flocks of small to medium-sized waders flying to roost. Many migrate from the northern to the southern hemisphere and are capable of flying long distances at one stretch. However, the majority of observations probably concern birds flying short distances between roosts and feeding areas, or when disturbed by predators, rather than flocks on migration. In general their long wings and rapid flight distinguish them from other groups, and in a number of cases the manner of flight can aid in the identification of a species. However, there can be variation within a species or family, especially between the manner of flying short and long distances. The short-distance 'wing-flicking' flight of Common and Spotted Sandpipers, low over water, is probably the best example; this is very different from their wing action when migrating.

Smaller waders tend to fly in compact flocks, while large ones often fly in lines, or long Vs. Several characteristics can be used to aid identification of waders in flight, including size, the relative length and shape of the bill and the relative length of the legs. The upper- and under-wing patterns, even in poor light when colours can't be seen, may often provide vital clues. Noting the presence or absence of wingbars, from obscure to obvious, as well as rump and tail patterns, and any underpart markings, will all be of assistance in establishing correct identification (see Appendices A and B).

Size is always difficult to judge but there is one important aid to remember – generally the larger the bird the slower the wing beat. Certain waders have plumage characteristics that make them easy to identify, like the black-and-white upperparts of turnstones, or the black axillaries of the Grey Plover. If they are seen in the vicinity of other waders in flight, a comparison of size can be made. Like all skills, judgement of size will improve with experience and it will make possible an approximate estimation as to whether the birds are large: American Oystercatcher or Eurasian Curlew to Willet size; medium-sized: Grey Plover or Greater Yellowlegs to Redshank; or small: Rock Sandpiper or Ringed Plover to Least Sandpiper.

The relative proportions of wader body parts have been mentioned above and can be judged well in flight. The length of bill can be compared with that of projecting legs and feet, for example. The shape of the wings is also an important aid to identification; for example, whether they are rounded as in the Northern Lapwing, or pointed as in the American Golden Plover. The length of leg can be judged by the amount that is visible beyond the tip of the tail and whether or not the feet project beyond the tail-tip can help separate similar species. It can also cause confusion: Spotted Redshanks have been mistaken for dowitchers, as long-legged waders do sometimes retract their legs in flight, most often in cold weather.

Topography of waders in flight

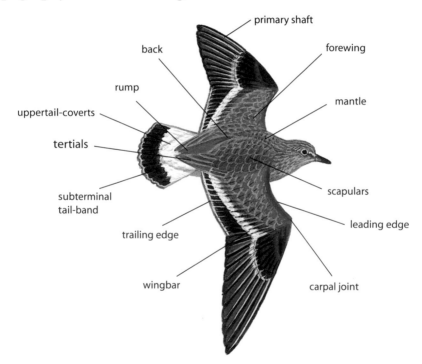

Figure 24. Upperpart topography of a typical wader in flight – a Surfbird. Note the tertials are exposed in this topographical study. Sometimes, these feathers are partially concealed by the lower scapulars.

As when studying waders at rest, an understanding of the topography and terminology used for those parts visible in flight is equally important. Figures 24 and 25 illustrate the names given to the various feather tracts. Wing feathers, virtually hidden when the bird is at rest, can clearly be seen in flight. Nevertheless, the best opportunity to see underwing-feather detail is invariably when birds raise their wings at rest, or when they stretch, when the upperwing can be best seen. More general terms are sometimes used to describe groups of these feathers:

Flight feathers – primaries and secondaries

Innerwing-coverts – lesser, median and greater coverts

Outerwing-coverts – lesser, median and greater primary coverts

Underwing-coverts – lesser, median and greater underwing-coverts

When waders are disturbed and fly directly away, the obvious areas to concentrate on are the upperparts – essentially the mantle and back but also the scapulars, rump and tertials – plus the wings and tail. Note the colour of the upperparts and decide whether it extends over the wings, or whether there are distinct areas of different colours or tones. A dark *leading edge* may be created by darker *lesser coverts*; a pale innerwing panel may be formed by paler markings on some or parts of the *innerwing-coverts*. If there is a contrasting white *wingbar*, it will either be formed by white tips to the *greater coverts*, or occasionally by white bases to the underlying *secondaries*, as on the Common Sandpiper (Plate 70). A white *trailing edge* to the wing is formed by varying amounts of white on the tips of the secondaries, sometimes extending onto the tips of the inner *primaries*. The term *rump*, often used incorrectly to include the uppertail-coverts, is a narrow tract of feathers between the *back* and the *uppertail-coverts*. One or both may be a contrasting colour; quite a number of waders have white rumps and/or white uppertail-coverts. The tail pattern may often provide a key to identification. The tail may be dark-centred, with white sides, or it may have a dark *subterminal tail-band*, with white tips.

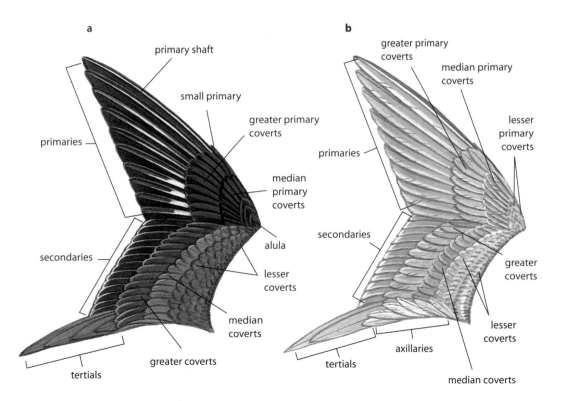

Figure 25. Topography of Caspian Plover upperwing (a) and underwing (b).

Another feature sometimes visible on the upperwing is a noticeably pale *primary shaft*, more often restricted to the longest primary, as on the pratincoles, for example. It is present in Wood Sandpipers but not on either Solitary or Green Sandpipers. For some species, the underwing may provide a key identification feature: the colour of the *axillaries*, noticeably black in the case of a Grey Plover in non-breeding plumage; or the *lesser underwing-coverts*, either black or chestnut on the pratincole species, for example. There may be a noticeable contrast between the underwing-coverts and the flight feathers, as in Wood Sandpiper, or they may be uniformly dark, as in Solitary and Green Sandpipers. More information on both upper- and underwings may be found in the Appendices.

Figure 26. Display flights of Pectoral Sandpiper (a), Temminck's Stint (b) and Northern Lapwing (c).

Behaviour

Different aspects of behaviour result in different patterns of flight, most notably during display. Certain species can sometimes be identified by their manner of flight when flushed. The zigzag flight of Common Snipes, for example, or the towering flights of Temminck's and Long-toed Stints and Solitary Sandpiper.

Song flights, the principal function of which invariably is to attract a mate, are also performed by most waders. Territorial males usually restrict their display flights to their territories, while species such as Redshank and Eurasian Curlew perform all over the breeding area. The aim of this is to encourage an unmated female into the air and occasionally the pair will perform together. During the song flight the wings may be quivered rather than beaten normally and the flight action varies. Others, such as Temminck's Stints, hover while they display. In some species, such as Redshank and Greenshank, the wings are held below the horizontal and in others, such as Red Knot, they are held in a V above the horizontal. A few display flights are described by name: for example the 'drumming' or 'winnowing' of snipe and 'roding' of woodcock. In a few sexually dimorphic species, such as Painted Snipe, these display flight roles are reversed and it is the females that perform them. A number of these displays are spectacular, like the tumbling sequence performed by Northern Lapwings.

THE MAJORITY OF THESE PLATES are arranged systematically, following Clements (2000), but there are a few exceptions. Vagrants that reach Europe and Asia from Africa and the Orient respectively have been grouped to produce two plates (44 and 45), while 'North American rarities' (plate 43) includes vagrants from Central or South America, and the almost certainly extinct Eskimo Curlew. There are two other plates where the species have been grouped regionally, rather than systematically – 'Asian Plovers and Lapwings' (16), and 'Asian specialities' (32) – Spoon-billed Sandpiper, Asian Dowitcher and Nordmann's Greenshank.

Plate annotation has been kept as simple as possible. Illustrations are of the nominate race unless otherwise stated. The choice of plumages illustrated was determined by variations that exist within each species. The plumage of male and female waders varies little in some of the species shown; full-grown birds in which there is no seasonal change are labelled adult (**ad**), or breeding (**br**) and non-breeding (**non-br**) for species in which change takes place. Juvenile (**juv**) plumages are often retained for only a few months, before moulting into a first-winter (**1st-w**) plumage – a mixture of juvenile and fresh winter feathers that creates a different appearance. This is well illustrated, for example, on the phalarope plate (42). Moult and feather wear can cause considerable changes to plumage and a few examples have been illustrated: the 'fresh' and 'worn' breeding plumages of Broad-billed Sandpiper (40), for example. A Semipalmated Sandpiper (34) is shown as moulting from breeding to non-breeding plumage (**br to non-br**), whereas Pacific Golden Plover (10) is illustrated moulting from non-breeding to breeding (**non-br to br**). All species on any one plate are to scale, unless otherwise labelled.

Explanation of the species accounts

The reference to another plate in each species header enables the 'in flight' views to be quickly checked, while the cross-referencing in the 'Confusion species' section refers to similar species on other 'at rest' plates.

This is essentially a field guide concentrating on identification. Therefore, not all of the sections described below appear for every species, but they occur whenever there is relevant identification text to be included. Selected other information, particularly regarding display behaviour, is occasionally mentioned.

Key ID features – this section concentrates on features common to all plumages (i.e. general characteristics of the species), or to key features by which breeding adult males can usually be identified. For comparison, the overall lengths (L) are always included first. Length is the total body length from tail-tip to bill-tip; as the lengths of tail, neck and bill vary considerably in waders and size is difficult to judge, these measurements need to be used with caution.

Behaviour – elements of behaviour that may aid identification are included, with occasional mention of other behavioural features that are of particular interest.

Habitat – both breeding and non-breeding habitats are usually described.

Plumage – a summary of the more salient features, subdivided under 'adult' (where there is no seasonal variation), or 'breeding' and 'non-breeding', and 'juvenile'. Sexual differences are also detailed where relevant. As relatively few species have a different plumage in their first winter, this is only rarely commented on. The text is designed to complement the illustrations, and include sufficient detail to separate similar species. For the sake of brevity, this section may avoid repetition of the Key ID features.

Racial variation – included when obvious differences are visible on the birds at rest.

Confusion species – includes those that may cause identification difficulties. The characteristics that separate them at rest will have been mentioned in other parts of the text and are either referred to, or may be repeated here for emphasis. Similar species that occur just outside the region are sometimes mentioned for comparison.

Plate 1 PAINTED SNIPE, CRAB PLOVER AND IBISBILL

Painted Snipe
Rostratula benghalensis   See also plate 46

Key ID features L 230–260mm. Like a short-billed *Gallinago* snipe, with a quite unmistakable plumage. The golden crown-stripe and the white or buffish eye-ring extending behind the eye are both distinct. From the white underparts a white line separates the wing from the breast, neck and mantle.
Behaviour A strong sexual dimorphism exists: the female initiates courtship and the male is primarily responsible for incubation and chick-care. Generally crepuscular, even fully nocturnal on moonlit nights, this species is secretive and unobtrusive, and can be difficult to flush, preferring to freeze when disturbed. In addition to a display flight performed by the female, both sexes perform frontal 'spread-wing' displays on the ground.
Habitat Favours wetlands, especially swamps and wet grassland, in tropical and subtropical lowlands.
Plumage: Breeding female The crown is greenish-brown, with a golden median-stripe; a white ring surrounds the large eye and reaches the upper ear-coverts; the remainder of the head, neck and breast are a rich reddish-brown, with a dark border extending round onto the mantle. The upperparts are mainly glossy-green, with an intricate patterning of dark brown and rufous. Several narrow, tapering white scapulars form a mantle V. The bill is a pale reddish-brown, decurved towards the tip.
Breeding male Smaller, with a much duller plumage. Head and neck are grey-brown, with whitish streaks; extensive golden buff on the upperparts, includes spots and crescents on the wing-coverts. **Juvenile** Very similar to adult male, with a different wing-covert pattern, initially having whitish tips and paler buff spots on greyish feathers.

Crab Plover
Dromas ardeola   See also plate 47

Key ID features L 380–410mm. A highly distinctive black-and-white wader, with a disproportionately heavy bill and head, and long bluish-grey legs.
Behaviour Highly gregarious and noisy, forming large flocks during high-tide roosts. Gait similar to *Charadrius* plovers, especially as they pursue crabs, when they adopt a more rapid, dashing walk. When not feeding they regularly stand with hunched shoulders, or squat on their tarsi. Uniquely among waders they nest in burrows, which they excavate.
Habitat Subtropical and tropical coastlines of the Indian Ocean. Mud and sandflats, beaches, lagoons and exposed coral reefs.
Plumage: Adult Head white, with small blackish areas in front of and behind the eye. Some adults show dark streaks on the rear crown and hindneck; mantle feathers, upper scapulars, greater coverts and the flight feathers are black; the lower scapulars, lesser and median coverts are white; the tertials vary from white to silver-grey; and the tail is greyish. **Juvenile** Lacks the distinctive adult black-and-white upperparts, much of the white being replaced by greys. Shows extensive streaking on the crown and hindneck; the mantle is a dark, silvery-grey; the scapulars, wing-coverts and tertials are a pale grey.

Ibisbill
Ibidorhyncha struthersii   See also plate 46

Key ID features L 380–410mm. Another unmistakable wader with a long decurved crimson bill, crimson legs, and a contrasting grey and black-and-white plumage.
Behaviour Feeding behaviour varies according to temperature. In warmer conditions will pick insects from the surface of the water. At colder times will either probe amongst submerged stones, or rake, tilting the head to one side and sliding the bill sideways through the pebbles.
Habitat Breeds in shingle-beds in high mountain river valleys, usually devoid of any vegetation and where the water is relatively slow-moving. Winters in similar habitat, although usually at lower altitudes.
Plumage: Breeding The crown, front of face, chin and throat are black, bordered by a narrow white line, which does not join on the nape. Rest of the head, neck and breast are a bluish-grey; the upperparts are a uniform brownish-grey. The underparts are white, with a black breast band beneath a narrow white line bordering the bluish-grey breast. **Non-breeding** As breeding adult but the duller black face has white feathering around the base of the bill. **Juvenile** Pattern as adult but face brownish, mottled white; the upperpart feathers are greyish-brown, with indistinct warm buff fringes. The breast band is dark brown, without the white line above. The bill and legs are a dull pinkish-grey.

Painted Snipe

♀ ad

juv

♂ ad

ad variant

Crab Plover

ad

juv

Ibisbill

br

non-br

juv

Plate 2 OYSTERCATCHERS

Ageing of oystercatchers: in all three species the iris is dull in juveniles, becoming brighter in first winter and breeding-plumaged birds. This also applies to the eye-ring. Similarly, the juvenile bill is duller, becoming brighter orange-red with age, losing the dark tip.

Black Oystercatcher
Haematopus bachmani   See also plate 47

Key ID features L 430–450mm. An unmistakable all-dark oystercatcher, with a bright orange-red straight bill, stout pink legs, and a yellow eye with red eye-ring.

Behaviour When resting with their bills hidden, Black Oystercatchers can be difficult to see among dark rocks. They move slowly and methodically while foraging, when they lever limpets from rocks and open mussels with a stab of the bill. They are usually seen in pairs or family groups, though small non-breeding flocks do occur.

Habitat A strictly coastal, sedentary species, favouring rocky outcrops.

Plumage: Adult Head, neck and upper breast are black, shading into dark brown on the belly. The upperparts are dark brown. **Juvenile** The upperparts are dark brown, with indistinct buff fringes to the upperpart feathers, including the coverts, which also have subtle dark subterminal bars.

Confusion species The range overlaps with American Oystercatcher, with which it may occasionally interbreed, but the white underparts of that species are quite distinct.

American Oystercatcher
Haematopus palliatus   See also plate 47

Key ID features L 400–440mm. This species appears black–and–white at a distance, with a long straight orange-red bill. It is the only pied oystercatcher with a yellow eye and a red eye-ring.

Behaviour This species does not flock in such large numbers as its Eurasian relation and usually occurs in scattered pairs or small groups. Feeds on limpets and mussels, like the Black Oystercatcher.

Habitat A predominantly coastal species at all seasons, though it does occur as a vagrant inland. Nests and feeds in a variety of coastal habitats, including rocky outcrops and on sandy or shell beaches. The nominate race *palliatus* feeds mainly on mudflats and beaches, while the western race *frazari* shows a strong preference for rocky shorelines, though frequents sandy beaches in Mexico.

Plumage: Adult Dark brown above and white below, with a distinct black head, neck and breast. **Juvenile** Similar to the adult but the upperpart feathers are paler brown, with buff fringes. Also has pale-spotted fringes to the blackish feathers of the head, neck and breast, when fresh. The soft parts are duller.

Racial variation The western race *frazari* usually shows some speckling on the lower edge of the black breast, lacking the clean division between the black and white of *palliatus*. Those with speckling may have evolved through hybridisation with Black Oystercatchers.

Confusion species Eurasian Oystercatcher, which has black rather than dark brown feathers on the upperparts, in adult plumage.

Eurasian Oystercatcher
Haematopus ostralegus   See also plate 47

Key ID features L 400–460mm. A strikingly black-and-white oystercatcher, with a bright orange-red bill and pink legs; also has a red eye and a red eye-ring.

Behaviour The only oystercatcher that habitually occurs and breeds inland, as well as on the coast. Known to pair for up to 20 years and use the same territory. When not breeding, this species forms large feeding and roosting flocks in coastal estuaries. Feeds on mussels and cockles by levering open the shell or hammering through it.

Habitat Breeds in a variety of coastal and inland habitats, often some distance from water, but winters almost exclusively on the coast.

Plumage: Breeding The head, neck, mantle, scapulars and tertials are glossy black; the greater coverts are largely white. The breast is black and the rest of the underparts are white. The bill is either chisel-shaped or pointed at the tip. **Non-breeding** As the adult breeding but with a white fore-neck collar. **Juvenile** As the non-breeding adult but lacks the white collar. The head and neck are a dull, sooty-black. The upperpart feathers are brownish-black, with narrow paler fringes.

Racial variation The bill length increases from west to east and the eastern race *longipes* is browner above, compared with the other two races, and the nasal groove extends more than halfway along the bill - *ostralegus* extends less than halfway.

Confusion species Any oystercatcher in non-breeding plumage showing a white foreneck collar will be of this species.

Black Oystercatcher

juv

1st-w

ad

American Oystercatcher

juv

1st-w
frazari

ad

Eurasian Oystercatcher

juv

1st-w

br

non-br

Plate 3 STILTS

Black-winged Stilt

Himantopus himantopus   See also plate 48

Key ID features L 350–400mm. An unmistakable, tall elegant black-and-white wader, with a long thin black bill and incredibly long, delicate pink legs.

Behaviour This species walks gracefully on its spidery legs and picks insects rapidly from the water's surface; will also probe, but does not use the scything action favoured by avocets. Its long legs enable it to feed in quite deep water, but this species rarely swims. It is gregarious, where common; forms large roosting flocks and will feed communally, sometimes with Pied Avocets.

Habitat Breeds in a wide variety of shallow, usually lowland wetlands, including freshwater marshes, lake edges and sewage ponds. Also in saltpans and brackish coastal lagoons and marshes, often in loose colonies. Also breeds around mountain lakes, up to about 2,000 metres in Turkey.

Plumage: Breeding male The head marking can be extremely variable, from pure white to extensively black, but the lower hindneck and all the underparts are white; some may show a pinkish flush on the breast. The upperparts are black, with a greenish sheen. **Breeding female** As the male, but the upperparts are blackish-brown rather than black, sometimes with a greyish wash on the nape and hindneck. **Non-breeding** The upperparts are a dull black, with varying amounts of greyish wash on the crown, nape and hindneck. **Juvenile** The crown, nape and hindneck are a pale greyish-brown; never white. The mantle, scapulars, tertials and coverts are a dull greyish-brown, fringed pale buff.

Confusion species Black-necked Stilt is very similar. Though their ranges have not as yet overlapped, the black hindneck of Black-necked Stilt joining the mantle is distinctive.

Black-necked Stilt

Himantopus mexicanus   See also plate 48

Key ID features L 350–400mm. The black of the crown extends onto the hindneck, down the sides of the neck and onto the mantle.

Behaviour As with the other stilts, this species feeds visually, picking invertebrates from, or from close to, the water's surface. Breeds colonially with little territorial aggression, but is extremely aggressive and noisy towards aerial and ground predators.

Habitat Breeds in similar habitat to the Black-winged Stilt and up to about 2,500 metres in Mexico.

Plumage: Breeding male The crown, nape, ear coverts, hindneck and adjacent mantle are all black; the forehead and spot above the eye are white. Otherwise the plumage is virtually the same as Black-winged. **Breeding female** As the male but, in good light, the mantle and scapulars are obviously dark brown, rather than black. **Non-breeding** Similar to plumage of breeding female. **Juvenile** The upperpart feathers, including the coverts and tertials, are dark brown with buff fringes; the legs are a pale pink.

Racial variation The Hawaiian Stilt *knudseni* is a larger bird overall, with a longer, heavier bill and considerably longer legs. The black on the sides of the neck is more extensive than on the nominate race *mexicanus*, extending to the cheeks and round the sides of the neck; the white spot above the eye tends to be smaller.

Confusion species The black plumage that some Black-winged Stilts exhibit on the hindneck never joins the black on the mantle. Also, a Black-winged Stilt with a black head will not show the white crescent of feathers above the eye that is typical of both *mexicanus* and *knudseni*.

Black-winged Stilt

non-br

♀ br

juv

♂ ♂ br

Black-necked Stilt

non-br

♀ br

juv

♂ br

♂ *knudseni*

♀ *knudseni*

Plate 4 AVOCETS

Pied Avocet
Recurvirostra avosetta   See also plate 48

Key ID features L 420–450mm. The characteristic upcurved bill, with the black crown and hindneck, distinguish this long-legged wader.

Behaviour   Both visual and tactile feeding methods are used. The typical 'scything' method involves the neck being stretched out, while the head and slightly opened bill are swept from side to side regularly through water or soft mud to filter out small food items. At times, will swim into deeper water to forage.

Habitat A colonial nesting species that favours salt and brackish lagoons with short vegetation. At other times of the year feeds, often in flocks, in estuaries and on tidal flats. Infrequently found on freshwater lakes and occasionally on agricultural land, particularly in the Netherlands.

Plumage: Adult male In addition to the black crown and hindneck, shows two distinct black bands on mantle and upper scapulars, lesser and median upperwing coverts, and outer primaries, which contrast with the rest of the brilliant white plumage. **Adult female** Very similar to adult male, but black generally duller and the bill is shorter and more strongly upcurved. **Juvenile** As adult, but the black is replaced by a dull brown or brownish-grey. Much of the white upperparts are initially mottled, with buff and grey-brown feather fringes, especially the tertials.

Confusion species There is little chance of confusing an adult Pied Avocet with any other species, but very young avocets, particularly at some distance, can cause considerable confusion, looking like a wide range of smaller wader species, such as Terek Sandpiper.

American Avocet
Recurvirostra americana   See also plate 48

Key ID features L 400–500mm. The rusty-orange head and neck, strongly upcurved bill and black-and-white plumage are characteristics that distinguish this long-legged wader. In non-breeding plumage at a distance, the American Avocet is strikingly pale-headed.

Behaviour   The feeding action is as for Pied Avocet, and this species also swims well.

Habitat Favours sparsely vegetated alkaline lakes for breeding, but also nests around saline lakes and beside estuaries. At other times of the year often forms large flocks, foraging in tightly-packed groups in freshwater habitats, as well as in estuaries and on tidal flats.

Plumage: Breeding male The white around the eye and at the base of the bill contrasts with the rusty-orange of the head and neck, which fades out on the mantle and the upper belly. Apart from the paler brownish-grey tertials, the upperpart feathers are predominantly blackish-brown, with white on the mantle feathers, lower scapulars and tips of the greater coverts. **Breeding female** As the breeding male but the bill is shorter and more strongly upcurved. **Non-breeding** The orange colour is lost by late summer and replaced with pearly-grey on the crown, the sides of the head and hindneck. **Juvenile** The crown of the bird is greyish, merging with the variable rusty-orange on the head, neck, breast and upper mantle, normally paler than that of the breeding adults; the brown upperpart feathers initially have buffy fringes.

Confusion species   Pied Avocet, though the ranges do not overlap.

Pied Avocet

ad ♂

ad ♀

juv

non-br

♂ br

♀ br

American Avocet

juv

Plate 5 **THICK-KNEES**

Thick-knees are large terrestrial waders, cryptically plumaged, with long legs and big heads. They have large eyes, essential for the crepuscular and nocturnal activities typical of this family.

Spotted Thick-knee
Burhinus capensis   See also plate 49

Key ID features L 400–430mm. The spotted pattern of the upperparts, the large yellow eye, the yellow-based black bill and the long yellow legs make this a most distinctive species.

Behaviour A sociable species; flocks of up to 50 can be seen together at daytime roosts outside the breeding season. Then they stand or squat among stones in the open, or under scattered bushes on bare ground. On hot days they may lie down with their legs stretched out behind them.

Habitat Generally prefer open, arid countryside, though often found in suburban areas, nesting on derelict ground.

Plumage: Adult The head, neck and breast are gingery or sandy-brown with dark streaks; there is a short white supercilium just above the eye; and the white lores and cheek, chin and throat contrast with a dark brown malar stripe that reaches the hindneck, close to a distinctive white spot behind the ear-coverts. The upperpart feathers, including the wing-coverts, are cinnamon-buff, with large dark subterminal marks and white tips, producing a bold, spotted appearance. The belly is white and the undertail coverts cinnamon. **Juvenile** Similar to adult but the wing-coverts have dark brown shaft streaks and narrower subterminal marks.

Racial variation Only *dodsoni* occurs in the region.

Confusion species Lacking spotted upperparts, both Senegal Thick-knee and Stone Curlew look different and have distinctive wing patterns.

Senegal Thick-knee
Burhinus senegalensis   See also plate 49

Key ID features L 320–380mm. A slightly smaller thick-knee with a distinct pale grey wing-panel; the heavy bill with yellow base has black extending onto the culmen ridge and a narrow white crescent under the eye, creating a spectacled appearance.

Behaviour Fairly tame and approachable. This species is known to nest on roof-tops in Cairo and often feeds among the various livestock. Outside the breeding season, flocks of 20 or more birds frequent the Nile Valley.

Habitat Often seen along riverbanks and on vegetated sandy islands in rivers, as well as open areas in towns and villages. Never far from water.

Plumage: Adult and **Juvenile** Both ages have extremely similar plumages; the lesser coverts are dark brownish-black; median coverts are grey with dark shaft streaks; greater coverts have subterminal black bands and white tips.

Confusion species The pale-grey wing-panel distinguishes this species from Spotted Thick-knee and Stone Curlew. In addition, the latter has a black-and-white wing-bar.

Stone Curlew
Burhinus oedicnemus   See also plate 49

Key ID features L 400–440mm. Large headed and short-necked, with big staring yellow eyes, a bicoloured bill, obvious black-and-white wingbars and long yellowish legs, making this another extremely distinctive species.

Behaviour When disturbed will crouch on bent legs or slink away into vegetation, rather than fly. Holds head down as it runs. Uses the plover-like stop, run and pick method of feeding, though catching moths requires a more stealthy action. Those breeding in temperate zones are strongly migratory. Flocks of up to 300 have been seen at diurnal roosts or pre-migration gatherings in Europe outside the breeding season.

Habitat Usually nests on arid or semi-arid heath and grassland. Also frequents stony, arable fields with bare patches, as well as coastal sand dunes and shingle.

Plumage: Adult Crown and nape feathers are a sandy-brown, streaked brown; the sandy-brown upperpart feathers have dark brown shaft streaks; the prominent black-bordered white wingbar is formed by a pattern of bars on the median coverts; the greater coverts show a black sub-terminal bar and white tips. **Juvenile** Similar to adult but the short supercilium is brownish-white. The tertials and median coverts usually show black subterminal bars and warm buff fringes; the wing-coverts lack the contrasting black-and-white of adult.

Racial variation The nominate race *oedicnemus* and *harterti* are the largest; the latter race is paler and less heavily streaked, with the patterning of the wing coverts more diffuse; *saharae* is smaller and more sandy coloured, with finer shaft streaks on the upperpart feathers.

Confusion species The black-and-white wing-bars separate Stone Curlew from the Spotted and Senegal Thick-knees. The Double-striped Thick-knee (plate 43) only occurs in the New World and is longer-legged, with a distinct long white supercilium bordered by a narrow black stripe.

Spotted Thick-knee
(not to scale)

ad *dodsoni*

juv
dodsoni

juv

**Senegal
Thick-knee**

ad

ad *saharae*

juv

Stone Curlew

ad

Plate 6 **EGYPTIAN PLOVER AND COURSERS**

Egyptian Plover
Pluvianus aegyptius   See also plate 50

Key ID features L 190–210mm. The Egyptian Plover is chunky and short-legged, with a striking plumage that makes this unique wader unmistakable.

Behaviour Has a unique method of incubation: the eggs are buried in warm sand and rarely kept warm by the adult's body. Feeds by pecking for insects, occasionally on the backs of Hippopotamus; also takes flying insects. May form small flocks when not breeding.

Habitat Nests on sandbars along the middle stretches of large rivers and is invariably found along rivers at other times.

Plumage: Adult The upperparts are a blue-grey, with glossy black bands on head, breast and mantle, which contrast with the white throat and supercilia. The underparts are a peachy-buff. **Juvenile** The plumage pattern is as the adult's, but the crown is a mixture of rusty-brown and black; the breast-band is duller and narrow; and the lesser and some median coverts are a rusty brown.

Cream-coloured Courser
Cursorius cursor   See also plate 50

Key ID features L 210–240mm. The short, thin decurved bill, contrasting black eye-stripes and white supercilia, which meet to form an obvious V on the nape, make this a most distinctive species.

Behaviour Runs rapidly while feeding, like other coursers, but also digs for food with its bill.

Habitat Nests on open, arid desert, in semi-desert areas and on sparsely vegetated plains.

Plumage: Adult Fore-crown and the rest of the upperparts are a uniform warm sandy-brown; the rear crown is blue-grey, bordered by a black lower nape and white supercilia. Underparts are a paler sandy-brown, fading to a buff-white on the rear belly and vent. **Juvenile** Has an indistinct creamy supercilium and brownish eye-line; the head and neck are spotted brown; the upperpart feathers have irregular, subterminal bars.

Racial variation The Cape Verde Island race *exsul* (not illustrated) has warmer buff underparts. The upperparts of the eastern race *bogolubovi* are a more pallid sandy-brown, including the fore-crown; the underparts are very similar to the nominate race *cursor*.

Confusion species The crown colour and plain underparts clearly separate this species from Temminck's Courser.

Temminck's Courser
Cursorius temminckii   See also plate 50

Key ID features 190–210mm. The long white supercilium contrasting with the black eye-stripe and rich chestnut crown and nape make this another most distinctive species.

Behaviour Feeds like other coursers, alternatively running and pecking. When not breeding may gather in small flocks.

Habitat Frequents short grasslands and semi-arid bush savannah, in particular favours newly burnt areas.

Plumage: Adult The forehead is cinnamon and the lores are pale. The sides of the neck and the upper breast are cinnamon, merging into chestnut on the lower breast and belly, which has a black central patch; the rest of the underparts are white. **Juvenile** The crown is brown with buffish-chestnut flecks; the eye-stripe a dark brown; and the breast is flecked brown. Upperpart feathers are a warm grey-brown, with dark brown bars and creamy-buff fringes.

Confusion species The pale lores of the Temminck's Courser distinguish it from the very similar Indian Courser (outside the region), and with its multi-coloured underparts it cannot be confused with the Cream-coloured Courser.

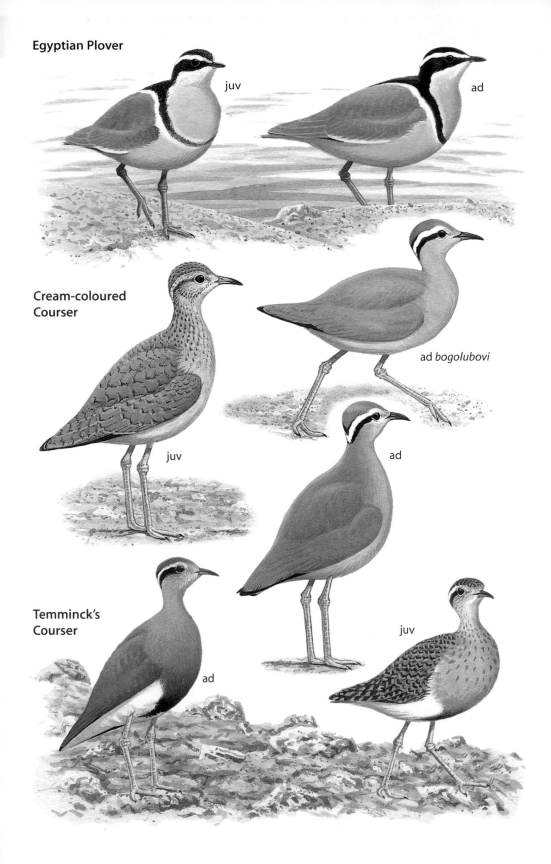

Egyptian Plover

juv

ad

Cream-coloured Courser

ad *bogolubovi*

juv

ad

Temminck's Courser

ad

juv

Plate 7 **PRATINCOLES**

The plumages of non-breeding and juvenile pratincoles vary considerably, with much overlap in coloration, at times making specific identification extremely difficult or virtually impossible.

Oriental Pratincole
Glareola maldivarum   See also plate 51

Key ID features L 230–240mm. Upperparts in spring are a dark tawny-brown, with an olive-tinge; orangey-buff wash to lower breast; very short tail streamers, tips falling approximately mid-way between tips of tertials and primaries; an oval-shaped nostril and long-looking dark legs; in summer dark lores prominent.
Behaviour Gregarious at all seasons, often forming large flocks. Largely crepuscular, with feeding behaviour as Collared Pratincole.
Habitat Summers on the Asian steppes, usually near water, but also nests by tidal mudflats and in rice stubble. Winters on open grasslands, muddy wetlands and intertidal mudflats.
Plumage: Breeding The warmer tones of a cinnamon tinge to the neck-sides is indicative of this species; inner and outer webs of primaries uniformly blackish-brown; amount of red at base of lower mandible, which becomes brighter when breeding, falls between that on Collared and Black-winged; the black line encircling a usually rich orange-buff throat may be marginally wider than in the other species. **Non-breeding** Upperparts dark olive-brown, with a slight olive-green cast. Pale buffy-grey fringes to dark brown centres of breast feathers sometimes create a scaly appearance; lower breast orangey-buff. Bill usually all-black. **Juvenile** As Collared, feathers of upperparts have dark subterminal bars and pale fringes.
Confusion species Typical Collared can be separated from Oriental by the Key ID features, supported by additional plumage characteristics; similarly from Black-winged Pratincole.

Collared Pratincole
Glareola pratincola   See also plate 51

Key ID features L 235–265mm. Upperparts in spring are a pale sandy or tawny-brown; adult tail streamers equal to or just projecting beyond wing-tips; inner webs of visible primary tips usually paler than outer webs; slit-shaped nostril, with parallel sides; short-looking dark legs.
Behaviour Nests in large colonies. Often feeds by running and lunging after insects on ground.
Habitat Favours flat, open areas, on the steppe plains of Eurasia and nests in short, patchy vegetation, usually near water. On migration often attracted to reservoirs, lakes or flooded fields.

Plumage: Breeding Black lores and white lower eye-ring; narrow black line encircles usually creamy-buff throat; crown and upperparts uniform tawny-brown contrasting with the blackish-brown primaries. Breast pale olive-brown, rest of underparts white. **Non-breeding** Lores pale; complete pale eye-ring; throat-line of fine dark streaks; breast mottled grey-brown. Upperpart feathers fringed buff. **Juvenile** Crown and nape streaked; pale feathers of upperparts have large dark subterminal bars and broad buff-white fringes, creating a scaly appearance. Underparts white, with brown streaks on the breast.
Confusion species In worn plumages Collared and Oriental Pratincoles can be extremely similar to each other – the former having short tail-streamers and little evidence of a white trailing edge to the secondaries. The safer months for correct identification are December to June or July. Typical Oriental can be separated from Collared by the Key ID features detailed below, supported by the additional plumage characteristics; similarly from Black-winged Pratincole.

Black-winged Pratincole
Glareola nordmanni   See also plate 51

Key ID features L 230–260mm. The dark upperparts show little contrast with the primaries, which show no contrast between inner and outer webs of visible primary tips; tail streamers usually fall short of folded wing-tips; red at base of the bill does not reach nostril; medium length dark legs.
Behaviour Very similar to Collared Pratincole, with which it may form large flocks where the ranges overlap.
Habitat Nests in large colonies on open steppes, often with tall vegetation, including grasslands and always near water.
Plumage: Breeding Crown tinged cinnamon; nape, sides of neck and ear coverts are a richer cinnamon; breast also more cinnamon-buff; upperparts dark olive-brown, showing less contrast with uniformly blackish-brown primaries. **Non-breeding** The crown and nape show broad pale fringes; the throat is streaked, with few streaks around the throat-band. **Juvenile** Very similar to the other species but the upperparts are generally darker.
Confusion species Typical Collared and Oriental can be separated, with care, from Black-winged by the Key ID features.

Oriental Pratincole

non-br

br

juv

Collared Pratincole

br

non-br

juv

Black-winged Pratincole

br

non-br

juv

Plate 8 **LAPWINGS**

Sociable Lapwing (Plover)
Vanellus gregarius　　　　　See also plate 52

Key ID features L 270–300mm. A striking Lapwing in breeding plumage, with contrasting head pattern and dark belly patch.
Habitat Breeds on dry terrain, between grassland and sagebrush or wormwood scrub, often associated with water. Forms post-breeding flocks, wintering on grassland, ploughed fields and burnt areas of steppe and desert. Vagrants often join flocks of Northern Lapwings.
Plumage: Breeding Black crown with striking broad white supercilium joining across forehead and on nape; uniform dull grey-brown upperpart feathers, with indistinct pale fringes rapidly wearing off. The underparts are grey-brown, tinged lilac, with a blackish belly patch shading to deep maroon, contrasting with white vent and undertail-coverts. **Non-breeding** Overall much duller, with a less clear-cut head pattern and brown-streaked crown; in fresh plumage the upperpart feathers are broadly fringed sandy-brown. The pale-fringed breast feathers produce a mottled appearance; rest of the underparts are white. **Juvenile** Resembles non-breeding adult, but brownish upperpart feathers have dark subterminal bars and broad buff fringes, creating a scaly appearance. The crown, face, neck and breast are heavily streaked, with distinct chevrons on the breast.
Confusion species Non-breeding and juvenile birds can be separated from juvenile White-tailed Lapwing by the streaked crown and breast, and blackish not yellow legs.

White-tailed Lapwing (Plover)
Vanellus leucurus　　　　　See also plate 52

Key ID features L 260–290mm. A graceful, slim, pale-faced and long yellow-legged *Vanellus* with longish, slender black bill.
Behaviour Unique among *Vanellus* species it persistently feeds in deep water, submerging its head. Gait is decidedly delicate.
Habitat Breeds in damp, vegetated areas near salt or fresh water, winters in the vicinity of water.
Plumage: Adult Whitish forehead, chin and cheeks and indistinct supercilia merge into a uniform brownish-grey neck; the greyish-brown upperpart feathers have a lilac tinge; along the closed wing, the black-and-white greater coverts and black primary feathers are often visible as contrasting panels. The breast is greyish; the belly a soft pinkish-buff and the undertail-coverts

are white. **Juvenile** The crown feathers are dark-centred, with buff fringes; the upperpart feathers have broad, dark subterminal bars and pale buffish-yellow fringes that create a chequered appearance.
Confusion species Juvenile similar to Sociable Lapwing.

Northern Lapwing
Vanellus vanellus　　　　　See also plate 52

Key ID features L 280–310mm. The distinctive long crest characterises this Lapwing, with glossy-green upperparts and unique orange undertail-coverts.
Habitat Breeds in a variety of open wetlands, heaths, moors, meadows and arable fields. Forms post-breeding flocks and winters on grassland and inter-tidal mudflats.
Plumage: Breeding male The black crest, crown, forehead, cheek bar, chin and throat expands into a broad breast-band; the upperpart feathers are glossy-green, with a purple sheen to the scapulars. Apart from the black breast and the orange undertail-coverts the rest of the underparts are white. **Breeding female** Has a shorter crest and the black of face, chin and throat is variably mottled white. **Non-breeding** Shorter crest; head and face mottled warm buff and black; upperpart feathers as breeding but fringed buff. **Juvenile** Very short crest; mantle, scapulars and wing-coverts clearly fringed buff, with buff notches on tertials and coverts.

Spur-winged Lapwing (Plover)
Vanellus spinosus　　　　　See also plate 52

Key ID features L 250–280mm. A striking 'pied' *Vanellus* with loose crest; the small curved black carpal spur is difficult to see.
Behaviour Performs complex ground displays featuring the spurs and the black-and-white plumage.
Habitat Inevitably associated with waterside habitats including lagoons, deltas, salt pans and marshes, also occurs on reservoir banks and flooded fields.
Plumage: adult Black nape feathers form a flat, loose crest; face and sides of neck brilliant white; broad black line extends from throat to centre of breast widening to form solid black belly and flanks. Upperpart feathers are a uniform pale brown. **Juvenile** Similar to adult but crown duller, tinged brown, with white flecks; scapulars and wing-coverts have dark subterminal bars with buff fringes.

Sociable Lapwing

non-br

br

juv

White-tailed Lapwing

ad

juv

juv

Northern Lapwing

♀ br

♂ br

♂ non-br

Spur-winged Lapwing

ad

juv

Plate 9 **EURASIAN GOLDEN AND GREY PLOVERS**

Eurasian Golden Plover
Pluvialis apricaria   See also plate 54

Key ID features L 260–290mm. A plump plover, with gold-spangled upperparts and black underparts in breeding plumage; the primary projection is shorter than American Golden and longer than Pacific Golden, but the folded primary tips align closely with the tail-tip. The bill is short.

Behaviour A highly gregarious species on migration and in winter, when flocks of many thousands assemble in western Europe. They often feed with Northern Lapwings but form segregated flocks when disturbed.

Habitat Nests in a variety of habitats, including highland moors and coastal tundra. In winter, favours open grassland, but are also found on cultivated fields, saltmarsh and intertidal mud.

Plumage: Breeding The crown and upperpart feathers are blackish, boldly streaked and notched with bright gold; the face and underparts are variably black, according to race, sex and moult; and a white dividing line from the forehead to the flanks creates a marked contrast. **Non-breeding** The upperpart feathers are brown, with yellowish-golden notches and spots, giving a spangled appearance; the breast is washed buff, with indistinct brown streaking spreading onto the flanks, and the rest of the underparts are whitish. **Juvenile** Like the non-breeding birds, but dark-brownish upperpart feathers show greater contrast initially, with golden-yellow spangling; the underparts appear marbled with indistinct barring; the belly is whitish.

Racial variation In breeding plumage, birds of the 'southern' race *apricaria* are generally paler, particularly around the head, than the 'northern' *altifrons*, but the validity of racial variation remains to be resolved.

Confusion species A non-breeding Grey Plover is larger and greyer. Pacific and American Plovers (plate 10) are longer winged and their folded primary tips project beyond and well beyond the tail-tip respectively; their legs are also longer, particularly the tibiae. In male breeding plumages, the undertail coverts of Eurasian are white, but blotchy-white on Pacific and black on American.

Grey (Black-bellied) Plover
Pluvialis squatarola   See also plate 54

Key ID features L 270–300mm. A large plover, with a big head, heavy bill and bulky body; the black, grey and white breeding plumage is distinctive and the primary tips extend just beyond the tail-tip. This is the only *Pluvialis* species with a hind toe.

Behaviour Feeding behaviour is typical of plovers, running, stopping and pecking, occasionally probing; sometimes wades and picks from the surface of water. Usually spreads out randomly and feeds at a distance from other waders, but forms large communal roosts, often with other species of wader.

Habitat Nests on lowland tundra and at other times favours intertidal mudflats, but also feeds and roosts on saltmarsh and grasslands.

Plumage: Breeding male The crown is greyish; the brilliant white of the forehead and supercilia extend round the neck onto the sides of the breast; the upperparts are spangled blackish-grey and silvery-white. The underparts are mainly black, with white from the rear belly to the undertail-coverts. **Breeding female** Black areas duller, showing a variable amount of white. **Non-breeding** The upperpart feathers are pale brownish-grey, notched and fringed off-white; the breast and flanks are suffused brownish-grey, with fine streaking. **Juvenile** Like non-breeding birds, but the upperpart feathers are darker grey-brown with pale buff notches, which give a spangled appearance. The underparts are washed buff, extensively barred and streaked brown.

Confusion species Grey Plover is larger and greyer, in all plumages, than the three species of Golden Plover, and also heavier billed. In non-breeding plumage it is superficially similar to Red and Great Knots (plate 33) but larger, with a proportionately shorter, thicker bill, and is not as uniformly grey.

Eurasian Golden Plover

♂ br *altifrons*

♀ br *apricaria*

non-br to br

♀ br *altifrons,*
♂ br *apricaria*

non-br

juv

Grey Plover

non-br to br

♂ br

♀ br

non-br

juv

Plate 10 **PACIFIC AND AMERICAN GOLDEN PLOVERS**

Similarities between these two species when in moult and in non-breeding plumages mean that specific identification in the field may not always be possible. Spangled upperparts separate the Golden Plover species from Charadrius *plovers.*

Pacific Golden Plover
Pluvialis fulva   See also plate 54

Key ID features L 230-260mm. Though similar in all plumages to American and Eurasian Golden Plovers, there are key structural differences (but beware the effect of moult on feather length) that can aid identification: just 2-3 primary tips are exposed beyond the tertials and the folded primaries only project a short distance beyond the tail-tip. The legs, particularly the tibiae are long.
Behaviour   Feeds in typical plover fashion, stop-run-pick, also probes in mud, sand and pasture.
Habitat   Nests in drier parts of typical tundra away from the coast and on stony, well-drained upland with moss and lichen. Away from the nesting zones favours intertidal mudflats, beaches and reefs; also feeds on short grasslands.
Plumage: Breeding male The white of the forehead extends through the supercilia and sides of neck to sides of breast and narrowly along flanks, forming a marked contrast with the black underparts. Upperpart feathers are dark brown, broadly notched and edged with golden and white. **Breeding female** Like male but duller, lacking the intensity of black. **Non-breeding** Distinct buffish supercilium; dark spot on ear-coverts; upperpart feathers grey-brown, finely notched and edged warm buff. Underparts suffused buffish-brown, with subtle brown streaking. **Juvenile** Similar to non-breeding adult; supercilium typically yellowish-buff; upperparts appear spangled, with dark brown feathers broadly notched and edged with golden-buff. Breast washed yellowish-buff, mottled brown; flanks indistinctly barred.
Confusion species Of the three Golden Plovers *P. fulva* is the smallest and slimmest. In breeding plumage, male Pacific usually has blotchy-white undertail coverts, which are usually all black on

American and predominantly white on Eurasian (plate 9). Upperparts of American generally have smaller notches and narrower edges, consequently appearing blacker than Pacific. In non-breeding and juvenile plumages Pacific and Eurasian are more buff compared with brownish-grey of American, which may lack any trace of yellow. Juvenile Eurasian is very similar but note shorter legs and a proportionately shorter bill.

American Golden Plover
Pluvialis dominica   See also plate 54

Key ID features L 240–280mm. Though similar to Pacific and Eurasian Golden Plovers, this species is the longest winged, with 4-5 primary tips exposed beyond the tertials and the folded primaries project well beyond the tail-tip.
Behaviour As Pacific, feeds in typical plover fashion, also probes in mud, sand and pasture.
Habitat Nests on high arctic tundra, on well-drained uplands with vegetation of moss and lichen.
Plumage: Breeding male Upperpart feathers are blackish, edged and notched golden and white; the continuous narrow area of white from the forehead, through the supercilium, broadens on the sides of the neck and breast to contrast with the all black underparts, which includes the flanks. **Breeding female** Like male, but duller, lacking the intensity of black. **Non-breeding** Prominent long off-white supercilium; dark smudges on ear-coverts and in front of eye. Upperpart feathers greyish-brown, notched and edged dull buff and whitish. Underparts whitish, with breast feathers mottled grey-brown. **Juvenile** Similar to non-breeding, but upperpart feathers darker brown, with small off-white or buff notches; supercilium usually white; breast, upper belly and flanks appear marbled and indistinctly barred grey.
Confusion species In non-breeding plumages in particular, the structural differences between the three Golden Plovers (see Key ID features) often provide a key to identification. The prominent supercilium when non-breeding might cause momentary confusion with Eurasian Dotterel (plate 15).

Pacific Golden
Plover

♂ br

juv

non-br

non-br to br

American
Golden Plover

♂ br

juv

non-br

non-br to br

Plate 11 **RINGED PLOVERS**

Little Ringed Plover
Charadrius dubius   See also plate 55

Key ID features L 140–170mm. Obvious white neck collar and yellow eye-ring; smaller and slimmer than Semipalmated and Ringed; the longer tail of Little Ringed projects beyond the wing-tips, giving a tapered appearance.

Behaviour Feeding actions are rather faster than Ringed Plover. Occasionally forms small flocks of 10-20 on migration, with larger numbers of 50 or more in autumn.

Habitat Mainly lowland, nesting on bare or sparsely vegetated sand or shingle, often in the vicinity of water. At other times favours freshwater areas but does occasionally occur along coasts.

Plumage: Breeding Thin white line separates black frontal bar from brown crown. Bill thinner than in Ringed Plover, black with a small pale base to the lower mandible. Legs usually dull, pinkish. **Non-breeding** Black is largely replaced by brown, with a buffy wash to supercilium. **Juvenile** Sandy-brown upperpart feathers show dark subterminal bars and warm buff fringes. Brown breast-band barely meets in centre. Orbital ring duller, legs yellowish.

Racial variation The only race that occurs in the region is *curonicus*.

Confusion species Long-billed Plover (plate 16) is larger, with proportionately longer bill, legs and tail. In juvenile plumage Little Ringed could be mistaken for Kentish (plate 13) but for pale legs and buffy supercilium. Differences in size and structure, and the presence of a more conspicuous eye-ring separate Little Ringed from Ringed in all plumages.

Semipalmated Plover
Charadrius semipalmatus   See also plate 55

Key ID features L 170–190mm. Obvious white neck collar; has a thin, complete yellow eye-ring and short stubby bill. Also has partial webbing between both outer and middle and inner and middle toes.

Behaviour Forages as other plovers, using run-stop-pick method; also uses 'foot-trembling'. Like Ringed may nest in small colonies.

Habitat Breeding and wintering habitats similar to Ringed Plover.

Plumage: Breeding The black on ear-coverts extends across lores over base of bill, leaving a thin wedge of white above gape-line (see Confusion species for additional characters). **Non-breeding** Black on head and breast replaced with brown; white forehead contiguous with obvious white supercilium. Breast-band barely meets at centre. **Juvenile** Upperpart feathers have narrow, dark subterminal bars and buff fringes.

Confusion species More compact than Ringed Plover, but a combination of differences from that species is the key to successful identification. The call is diagnostic; a breeding male (females are more variable) of this species usually shows a narrower black breast band; white patch to rear of eye is very small or absent; and invariably, in all plumages, there is a thin wedge of white between the gape and loral stripe; and a thin, complete yellow eye-ring is also obvious. Assessing the extent of palmations in the field is extremely difficult. In juvenile plumage similar to Wilson's Plover (plate 12) which is larger, with a longer, heavy bill. Piping Plover (plate 13) is much paler.

Ringed Plover
Charadrius hiaticula   See also plate 55

Key ID features L 180–200mm. A plump plover, with obvious white neck collar. Partial webbing only between outer and middle toes.

Behaviour Gregarious, forming flocks of several hundred at high-tide roosts. As with Semipalmated may nest in small colonies.

Habitat In south of range nests on shingle beaches, but extensively inland on arctic tundra and along river valleys, or by lakes. In winter occurs in a variety of habitats, including intertidal mudflats, along river valleys and on grassland or cultivated land.

Plumage: Breeding Black on ear-coverts extends across lores over base of bill; bold, white rear supercilium. Broad, black breast-band. **Non-breeding** and **Juvenile** Plumage changes as for Semipalmated.

Racial variation Nominate *hiaticula* generally has paler upperparts; *tundrae* is smaller and darker on upperparts, but there is considerable variation throughout the range.

Confusion species For Semipalmated and Little Ringed Plovers see above. Juveniles with incomplete breast bands may be confused with Kentish Plover (plate 13), which has black legs – beware the influence of mud – and usually just small dark patches at breast sides.

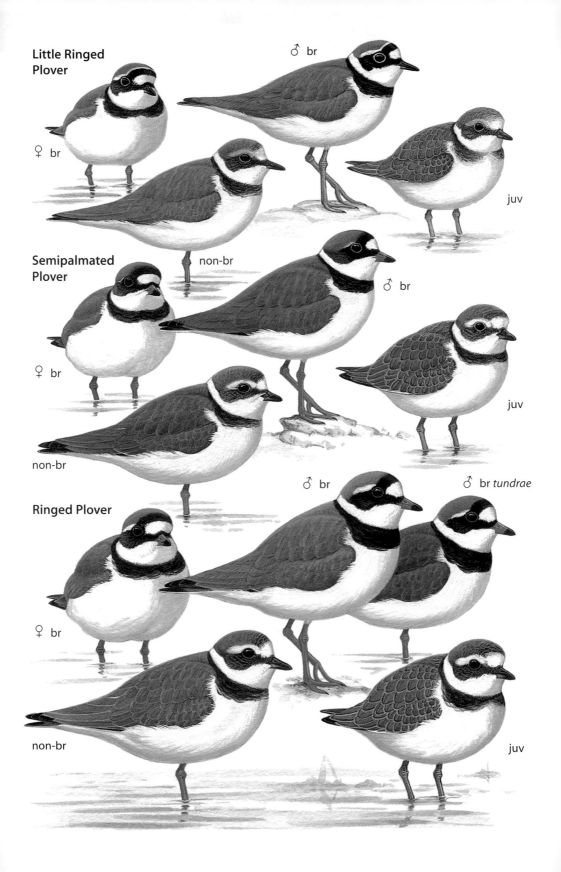

Little Ringed Plover

♂ br

♀ br

non-br

juv

Semipalmated Plover

♀ br

♂ br

non-br

juv

Ringed Plover

♂ br

♂ br *tundrae*

♀ br

non-br

juv

Plate 12 WILSON'S PLOVER AND KILLDEER

Wilson's Plover
Charadrius wilsonia   See also plate 56

Key ID features L 165–200mm. A banded plover with an unusually large and heavy black bill, both mandibles of which curve to a dagger-like point; legs are pink or pinkish-grey.
Behaviour The feeding action differs from other small plovers, being slow and deliberate as crabs form a major part of the diet.
Habitat An essentially coastal species that nests on sandy beaches and sandbars, or the edges of coastal lagoons. At other seasons visits estuarine mudflats and occasionally freshwater lagoons a short way inland.
Plumage: Breeding male White of forehead continues into a short supercilium; there is a distinctive black frontal bar; the rest of the head is grey-brown, apart from blackish lores; a white hindneck-collar is almost complete around the nape; the rest of the upperpart feathers are uniform grey-brown. The underparts are white, apart from a broad black breast-band. **Breeding female** Similar to male but the black on the head and breast is replaced by reddish-brown; the white supercilium is tinted with buff. **Non-breeding** Both sexes are like breeding female but grey-brown rather than reddish-brown breast; upperpart feathers are initially fringed pale buff. **Juvenile** Similar to non-breeding adult but the breast-band is less distinct and often incomplete; the upperpart feathers, with narrow dark subterminal lines and neat buff fringes, create a scaly effect.
Racial variation The nominate male *wilsonia* usually lacks any rufous coloration on the head; *beldingi* has rufous ear-coverts extending to the nape and crown; also has darker upperparts and usually, a broader breast band, and less white on the forehead. A female *beldingi* has a more rufous breast band than female *wilsonia*.
Confusion species Some confusion possible with fledgling Killdeer, which has only one breast band. Compared with Semipalmated and Ringed Plovers (plate 11), Wilson's is longer-legged and heavier-billed. Lesser Sand-plover (plate 14) is similar but lacks the white collar and heavy bill of Wilson's.

Killdeer
Charadrius vociferus   See also plate 56

Key ID features L 230–260mm. The largest of the banded plovers, and the most distinctive with its two breast bands; the long tail projects well beyond the wing tips, giving an elongated appearance; and a bright red orbital ring is distinctive.
Behaviour The most widespread North American shorebird which, when disturbed on its breeding grounds, announces its presence with its onomatopoeic calls. When feeding, forages in typical plover fashion, running intermittently, stopping and pecking at one prey item, or looking for another. Often makes use of 'foot-trembling' to attract prey. When nesting, exposes the bright rump and tail in a display to distract predators. Forms small flocks during the non-breeding season.
Habitat Nests in open, lowland areas, often on agricultural land and usually near water. Also breeds close to habitation, sometimes on flat roofs.
Plumage: Breeding The white of the forehead extends to below the eye; a narrow black band extends from eye to eye between the white forehead and the brown crown and nape. The upperparts are variable from uniform brown to rufous brown and the underparts white, apart from two black breast-bands, the upper one of which borders a white neck-collar. The thin black bill is longish, for a plover. **Non-breeding** The mantle feathers, scapulars, new wing-coverts and tertials are fringed rufous. The upperparts of extreme variants may appear more rufous than brown. **Juvenile** The facial mask and breast bands are dark brown; the upperpart feathers are buff-fringed, with indistinct dark subterminal bars.
Confusion species The only other double-banded species in our region, the Three-banded Plover (plate 45) is considerably smaller and really bears little resemblance to Killdeer.

Wilson's Plover

♀ br *beldingi*

♂ br

♀ br

♂ br
beldingi

juv

non-br

Killdeer

ad variant

br

non-br

juv

Plate 13 KENTISH AND PIPING PLOVERS

Kentish (Snowy) Plover
Charadrius alexandrinus   See also plate 57

Key ID features L 150–175mm. A small short-tailed plover, with a white hindneck collar and dark breast-side patches. The white forehead and supercilia separate the black frontal-bar from the eyes; the relatively long legs are usually dark grey and the thin bill is black.

Behaviour The feeding action is typically plover-like, but Kentish runs more rapidly than Ringed in between picking and the occasional probe; also forages by 'foot-trembling' in wet sand and soft mud. The Kentish Plover is one of the real runners of the wader-world, and when disturbed will invariably run rather than fly. Usually roosts in single-species flocks but is sociable and at other times mixes with flocks of other small waders.

Habitat Nests mainly on sandy, coastal beaches and by inland saline pools. Migrants may occur at inland freshwater sites, but brackish or saline wetlands are preferred and in winter most favour coastal localities.

Plumage: Breeding male Has a distinctive head pattern, with a white forehead and supercilium; the black frontal-bar, lores and ear coverts, with the grey-brown crown and variable rufous on nape, contrast with the white neck-collar and throat. The upperparts are a uniform grey-brown. The underparts are white, with distinct black breast-side patches (a complete breast-band is exceptionally rare). **Breeding female** Lacks the rufous on the nape and the black features of the male are replaced by brown, which is marginally darker than the uniform upperparts. **Non-breeding** Both sexes resemble a dull breeding female. The uniform grey-brown upperpart feathers are initially paler fringed. **Juvenile** As non-breeding adult but with a buffish wash to the supercilia and the upperpart feathers have neat buff fringes and dark subterminals, giving a scaly appearance at close range.

Racial variation The North American race *nivosus*, commonly known as 'Snowy' Plover, is shorter-legged and shorter-billed, with paler brown upperparts, lacking the warm rufous on the nape and crown of the nominate race *alexandrinus* and usually has white lores. The eastern race *dealbatus* (not illustrated) is very similar to the nominate but has a slightly longer and heavier bill. **Confusion species** Smaller than Ringed and Semipalmated Plovers (plate 11), plumper than Little Ringed (plate 11) and Long-billed (plate 16), with longer legs than the first three. Piping Plover has much paler upperparts and a distinct orange-based bill in breeding plumage.

Piping Plover
Charadrius melodus   See also plate 56

Key ID features L 170–190mm. A smallish plover, with a round-headed appearance, very pale sandy-grey upperparts and a variable black breast-band. In breeding plumage the orange legs and very short blunt orange-based bill contrast noticeably with the overall pale plumage.

Behaviour Forages by running, stopping and picking like other plovers, though individuals are often more widely-spaced over the sandy beaches.

Habitat The coastal population breeds on sandy beaches, in competition with human use, while birds of the Great Lakes prefer the sparsely vegetated sand or gravel edges of the shorelines; this habitat is also being lost. Vulnerable.

Plumage: Breeding male The forehead is white, with a black frontal-bar virtually reaching the eyes; the distinct white supercilium is mainly to the rear of the eye; and a narrow, complete or broken black breast-band, extends to form a narrow band, beneath the broader white neck-collar; remainder of underparts pure white. **Breeding female** As male, though frontal-bar and breast-band – browen or complete – may be browner. **Non-breeding** The upperparts are uniform sandy-grey; the breast-band and frontal-bar are grey-brown and the bill is all black. **Juvenile** Similar to non-breeding adult but has pale fringes to the upperpart feathers, producing a scaly effect. **Confusion species** The adult Piping Plover is distinctive but juvenile plumages may cause some confusion: Semipalmated Plover is darker and more scaly above, usually with a complete breast-band; 'Snowy' Plover is smaller, generally darker, with darker legs and a thinner, more pointed bill; and Collared Plover (plate 43) despite its name, lacks a white neck-collar.

Kentish Plover

non-br

♂ br

♀ br

juv

juv *nivosus*
'Snowy' Plover

♂ br *nivosus*
'Snowy' Plover

Piping Plover

non-br

♂ br

juv

♀ br

Plate 14 **SAND PLOVERS**

Lesser Sand Plover

Charadrius mongolus   See also plate 58

Key ID features L 190–210mm. A smallish plover, though there is considerable variation among the different races, with bright chestnut and black head and breast, and relatively short bill.
Behaviour Mixes freely, roosting in large flocks with other waders, including Greater Sand Plover. Forages like other plovers by running, stopping and picking.
Habitat Breeds in mountains on elevated tundra and steppes, mainly near water; also on sand dunes and coastal shingle on Commander Islands and in NE Siberia. Strictly coastal at other times, frequenting estuaries, tidal mudflats and beaches.
Plumage: Breeding male Variable black mask extends from ear-coverts to lores and in some races across the forehead. Crown pale brownish-chestnut, shading to chestnut on nape and hind-neck; upperparts a uniform greyish-brown. Throat white, contrasting with chestnut on breast and sides of neck, extending onto flanks; rest of underparts white. **Breeding female** Black of male almost completely replaced by brown or rufous. **Non-breeding** Lacks all traces of orange and black. White forehead and supercilium; upperparts greyish-brown. Underparts white with broad greyish-brown patches on sides of breast, which sometimes form a complete breast-band. **Juvenile** As non-breeding adult, but fresh scapulars and coverts fringed off-white or buff.
Racial variation Two distinct groups, which may be separate species: the northern, larger *'mongolus'* group comprises *mongolus* and *stegmanni*; and the southern, smaller *'atrifrons'* group comprises *pamirensis*, *schaeferi* and *atrifrons*. In breeding plumage, *mongolus* group birds are on average larger; the rear flanks usually have orange or greyish-brown markings – diagnostic when present – and their shorter bills are well con-toured, with a rather blunt, bulbous tip. They have white foreheads, with a narrow vertical dividing line and a narrow black line that borders the upper breast. Birds of the *atrifrons* group have a largely black forehead, with occasional white 'headlights' to the sides, but invariably there is a broad vertical dividing line; also lack the black border to the upper breast and are longer billed, particularly *schaeferi*. Non-breeding *atrifrons* has warmer brown upperparts than *mongolus* and lacks the flank marks that some *mongolus* have. Juvenile *mongolus* tends to have dark, greyish-brown sides

to the breast, and often a full dark breast-band; dark rear flank marks are diagnostic when present. Fresh scapular feathers and the coverts have cold off-white fringes. Juvenile *atrifrons* tend to have less distinct greyish-brown breast sides, with a warmer buff breast and clean white flanks. Fresh scapulars and coverts have golden-buff fringes.
Confusion species The Greater Sand Plover is similar to *mongolus*-type birds, with which there are overlaps in size, but has white rear flanks. In non-breeding plumage Lesser Sand Plovers are similar to Semipalmated, Ringed and Kentish Plovers (plates 11 & 13), but these all have white hindneck collars.

Greater Sand Plover

Charadrius leschenaultii   See also plate 58

Key ID features L 220–250mm. A medium-sized chunky wader, with longer legs, a longer more pointed bill and a narrower chestnut breast-band, compared to most races of Lesser Sand Plover.
Behaviour When feeding, will sometimes probe into sediment with the bill.
Habitat Breeds in desert or semi-desert areas up to 3,000m, usually within the vicinity of water and at lower altitudes than the *mongolus* races of Lesser Sand Plover. Favours coastal regions when not breeding; sandy and shell beaches, as well as estuarine mud.
Plumage: Breeding male Similar to *mongolus* Lesser Sand Plover's plumage but upperparts are generally a little paler. The tibiae are longer. **Non-breeding** Similar plumage coloration to *mongolus* Lesser Sand Plovers. **Juvenile** As non-breeding, but upperpart feathers are extensively fringed warm buff and the supercilium washed buff.
Racial variation The nominate race has a bill of intermediate length; *crassirostris* has the longest bill, legs and wings; *columbinus* is the shortest billed and is more extensively rufous on the back, and the chestnut of the breast extends onto the flanks.
Confusion species Although considerable variation exists in bill lengths, the proportions can aid separation from *mongolus* and *atrifrons* Lesser Sand Plovers; the bill lengths of Greater Sand Plovers are usually greater than the distance from the bill base to the rear of the eye. In non-breeding plumages, Caspian and Oriental Plovers (plates 15 & 16) are similar but have broader, complete breast-bands, and long wings projecting beyond the tail-tip.

Lesser Sand Plover

♂ br *pamirensis*

♀ br *atrifrons*

♂ br *mongolus*

juv *atrifrons*

non-br *mongolus*

Greater Sand Plover

♂ br *columbinus*

♀ br *columbinus*

♂ br *crassirostris*

♂ br *leschenaultii*

juv

non-br

Plate 15 CASPIAN AND MOUNTAIN PLOVERS, AND DOTTEREL

Caspian Plover
Charadrius asiaticus   See also plate 58

Key ID features L 180–200mm. A slim, slender-billed and fairly long-legged plover, with a distinctive supercilium.
Behaviour A gregarious species; post-breeding flocks often gather on banks of rivers, and by lakes and water-holes trampled by cattle.
Habitat Nests among sparse vegetation in lowland desert and desert steppe, preferably in salt-pans and on saline soil subject to seasonal flooding. On migration favours short grassland.
Plumage: Breeding male Uniform brown upperparts, including crown, nape and ear coverts. Clean white supercilium, forehead and throat. Broad chestnut breast-band, with narrow black border contrasting with white underparts. **Breeding female** Lacks chestnut and black border line on breast. **Non-breeding** Head and face pattern pale brown, breast greyish-brown. Fresh upperpart feathers are fringed buff. **Juvenile** The brown upperpart feathers are broadly fringed warm buff when fresh, creating a scaly appearance.
Confusion species Resembles closely related Oriental Plover (plate 16) which is larger; the breeding male Oriental has a broader black breast-band and a white head, and in winter has more obvious rufous fringes to fresh upperpart feathers. Non-breeding Caspian are similar to Greater and Lesser Sand Plovers (plate 14) but have finer bills, more pronounced supercilia and broader breast-bands. Also, these latter species tend to be more coastal.

Dotterel
Charadrius morinellus   See also plate 58

Key ID features L 200–220mm. Unmistakable in breeding plumage, with distinctive white supercilia meeting in V at nape. Uniquely among plovers, the female has the brighter plumage.
Behaviour May be unusually confiding, but often runs rather than flies if disturbed. Gregarious in winter.
Habitat Breeds on extensive open, flat uplands, mountain ridges and plateaux, with sparse vegetation. On migration 'trips' will frequently stopover at traditional lowland sites. In winter favours dry sandy, or stony areas on high plateaux.
Plumage: Breeding female Dark brown cap contrasts with white supercilia that meet on nape; white face sides and throat. The upperpart feathers are dark brown, fringed cinnamon. On the underparts the breast is maroon-grey bordered by narrow black and white bands that contrast with the deep-chestnut of the upper belly; an extensive black patch on the lower belly contrasts with the white vent and undertail coverts. **Breeding male** Similar to female but crown finely streaked, breast browner and less black on belly. **Non-breeding** The dark brown crown is streaked buff; the supercilium a creamy-buff; the upperpart feathers are fringed with a dull sandy-buff; the sides of neck, breast and flanks are mottled buffish-brown, with an indistinct, narrow whitish breast line. **Juvenile** Dark brown upperpart feathers are boldly fringed pale buff; the coverts are a paler grey-brown, with dark shaft streaks and subterminal bars.
Confusion species On migration may be confused with slightly larger Eurasian Golden Plover (plate 9), which shares similar habitat, while American Golden Plover (plate 10) also has a prominent supercilium. However, the nape-meeting supercilia and whitish breast-line are diagnostic, also separating Dotterel from Caspian, Oriental (plate 16) and Mountain Plovers, which have shorter supercilia and longer legs.

Mountain Plover
Charadrius montanus   See also plate 54

Key ID features L 210–235mm. A fairly plain, pale brown plover, except in the breeding season, when black lores and frontal bar contrast with white forehead and supercilia.
Behaviour Post-breeding flocks form on the nesting grounds and in winter may number several hundred.
Habitat Nests on upland short-grass prairie and winters on heavily grazed open grasslands.
Plumage: Breeding Upperpart feathers sandy-brown fringed cinnamon. Sides of neck and breast warm buff, rest of underparts white. **Non-breeding** Crown feathers are dark brown with buff fringes, creating a scaly appearance; fresh upperpart feathers broadly fringed bright cinnamon. On the underparts, buffier patches may extend across breast. **Juvenile** Crown similar to non-breeding; upperpart feathers are brown, with narrow darker subterminal bars and pale buff fringes, creating a scaly pattern.
Confusion species Similar to the Caspian Plover but ranges do not overlap. Smaller than darker plumaged American Golden Plover (plate 10).

Caspian Plover

♀ br

♂ br

non-br

juv

Dotterel

♀ br

♂ br

non-br

juv

br

Mountain Plover

non-br

juv

Plate 16 **ASIAN PLOVERS AND LAPWINGS**

Long-billed Plover

Charadrius placidus   See also plate 55

Key ID features L 190–210mm. A long-tailed plover, with a longish black bill; brown lores and ear-coverts; and yellowish-pink legs.
Behaviour Not a gregarious species and usually scattered when feeding, though may occasionally form small groups.
Habitat Nests on stony or shingle areas associated with rivers or lake shorelines. At other times inhabits similar areas, as well as coastal mudflats.
Plumage: Breeding White forehead; brown lores and ear-coverts; broad black frontal bar and brown crown divided by an indistinct narrow white line that meets the white supercilium above the eye. Underparts white, with narrow black breast-band, which broadens at the sides; a thin black line extends round the hindneck, separating the white collar from the brown upperpart feathers, which are fringed buff, when fresh. **Non-breeding** Duller than breeding plumage, lacking the contrasting black, and a buffish rear supercilium. **Juvenile** Similar to non-breeding, but lacks contrasting crown frontal bar; upperpart feathers are fringed with warm buff.
Confusion species Similar to Little Ringed Plover (plate 11) but structurally different, and the browner dark loral lines do not meet above the base of the bill.

Oriental Plover

Charadrius veredus   See also plate 58

Key ID features L 220–255mm. A medium-sized plover with long yellowish legs and a long neck. The almost-white head of a summer male is diagnostic.
Behaviour Runs rapidly, sometimes on stretched legs, but also moves stealthily.
Habitat Breeds on dry deserts and steppes. Migrants visit a variety of habitats, including grassland, airfields and lakeside dried mud, but rarely occur on the coast.
Plumage: Breeding male The rich chestnut breast-band has a black lower border. **Breeding female** Similar to non-breeding but with a more defined, darker breast-band, occasionally with some chestnut and black. **Non-breeding** Forehead and broad supercilium buffy-white; upperpart feathers brown, initially with bold rufous or buff fringes. Underparts white with breast mottled buff-brown forming an indistinct breast-band. **Juvenile** Similar to non-breeding birds but upperpart feathers are more extensively fringed a paler buff.
Confusion species Caspian Plover (plate 15) is smaller and in non-breeding and juvenile

plumages has a more distinctive breast-band. Greater and Lesser Sand Plovers (plate 14) are similar in non-breeding plumage, but are smaller, more compact, with narrower breast-bands and usually winter on coasts.

Red-wattled Lapwing

Vanellus indicus   See also plate 53

Key ID features L 320–350mm. A medium to large distinctive lapwing, with obvious red wattles, red base to the bill and yellow legs.
Behaviour A noisy species, that often calls at night and is strongly territorial. Normally seen in pairs or family groups but small flocks form out of the breeding season.
Habitat Essentially a waterside species, which nests on cultivated land, or grassland with ditches and small pools.
Plumage: Adult Forehead, crown, hindneck, throat and breast black; the sides of the neck and the rest of the underparts are white. Upperpart feathers are a uniform grey-brown, with a greenish sheen. **Juvenile** Black head and breast feathers of adult are instead largely sooty-black, tipped buff; upperparts are a warmer brown, with rufous and dark subterminal bars, with buff fringes.

Grey-headed Lapwing

Vanellus cinereus   See also plate 53

Key ID features L 340–370mm. A large heavy-looking lapwing with tiny yellow wattles; head, neck and breast are grey, bordered black; the bill is yellow with a black tip and the legs are bright yellow.
Behaviour Often feeds in shallow water. Strongly territorial, noisy and aggressive when breeding. Gregarious away from the breeding grounds and mixes with other lapwings and smaller plovers.
Habitat Nests in edges of marshland, wet grasslands and rice-paddies. Frequents similar habitats in winter, but also drier, agricultural land and short grass.
Plumage: Breeding Upperpart feathers are a uniform brown; the white of the greater coverts is usually visible and the primaries are black. The underparts, apart from the breast, are white. **Non-breeding** Head, neck and breast are brownish-grey, with a less distinct breast-band. **Juvenile** Similar to non-breeding birds but upperpart feathers have neat buff fringes and dark subterminal markings; the brownish breast-band may be poorly defined or initially absent.
Confusion species A juvenile White-tailed Lapwing (plate 8) shows some similarities but is smaller and slimmer, with well marked upperparts, a longish, all-black bill and no wattles.

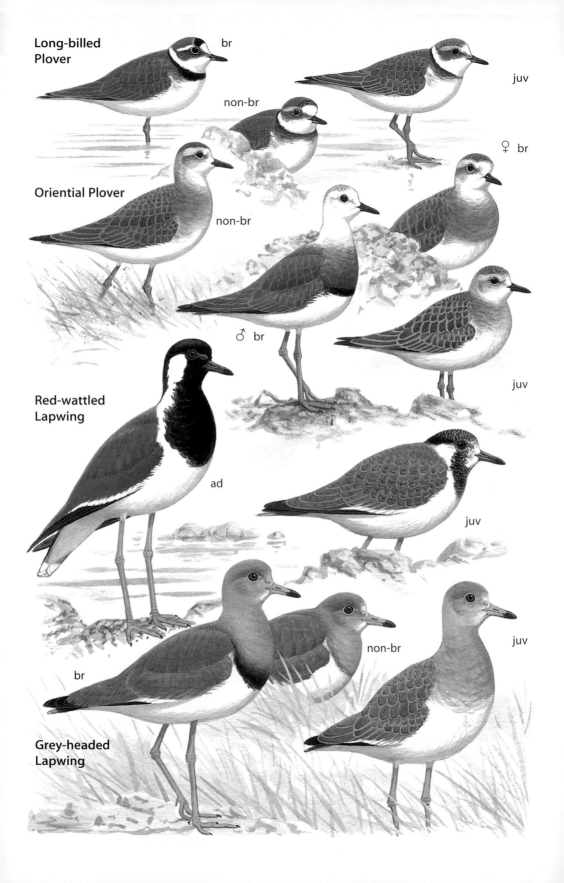

Long-billed
Plover

br

juv

non-br

Oriental Plover

♀ br

non-br

♂ br

juv

Red-wattled
Lapwing

ad

juv

br

non-br

juv

Grey-headed
Lapwing

Plate 17 GREAT SNIPE AND WOODCOCKS

Great Snipe
Gallinago media   See also plate 59

Key ID features L 270–290mm. A bulky, comparatively short-billed snipe, with prominent white tips to wing-coverts.
Behaviour Males perform extravagant courtship displays on 'leks', beginning at twilight, when they simultaneously rattle their bills, making continuous clicking noises. They also stretch into a peculiar upright stance, puff out their chests, cock and fan their tails to expose the white feathers, and leap into the air.
Habitat Mainly frequents marshy grounds with *Sphagnum*-covered tussocks and willow scrub, usually fed by numerous tiny streams. Nests in adjacent drier areas with dense herbs and willows. On migration and in winter found singly or in small numbers in marshland and on flooded fields.
Plumage: Adult Narrow loral stripe; cheek bar obscured by diffuse facial spots and streaks; wing-coverts have white tips, particularly prominent on median and greater coverts. Flanks and belly heavily barred. **Juvenile** Pale mantle and scapular Vs are narrower than on adult; white tips to dark brown greater coverts are also narrower.
Confusion species Common Snipe (plate 19) has a longer bill, extensive white belly and lacks prominent white-tipped coverts.

American Woodcock
Scolopax minor   See also plate 59

Key ID features L 265–295mm. Longish, heavy, straight bill and short legs; broad blackish bars on crown and nape and unbarred orange-buff underparts.
Behaviour Solitary and secretive. Feeds mainly at night by probing deeply. Walks slowly with constant rocking and bobbing motion of body. However, superb camouflage makes it rarely seen until flushed, but may only fly a short distance. Establishes a 'display station' on bare open ground, where the male performs a spectacular display, adopting a peculiar upright posture and uttering *peent* calls repeatedly, before rising vertically for a display flight.
Habitat Nests in young forest plantations. At other times favours moist mature deciduous woodlands, with dense understorey.
Plumage: Adult Forehead, supercilium and sides of neck greyish; mantle, scapulars and tertials blackish-brown, barred and fringed cinnamon, with grey fringes on edges of mantle feathers forming neat silver-grey V, with less clearly defined grey lines on lower scapulars. **Juvenile** Virtually identical to adult, but may show broader buff tips to wing-coverts.

Confusion species Larger Eurasian Woodcock has heavily barred underparts and lacks the grey neck of American Woodcock.

Eurasian Woodcock
Scolopax rusticola   See also plate 59

Key ID features L 330–350mm. Heavily-built with a long bill (though variable); large dark eyes, set back in the head, under a broadly barred crown; obvious white or buff tips to the wing-coverts.
Behaviour Solitary and secretive. Feeds mainly at night by probing deeply, or picking from surface. Superb camouflage makes it rarely seen until flushed.
Habitat Nests in both broad-leaved and mixed woodlands, with drier dense understorey and clearings, also in coppiced woodland. Feeds in damper, more open areas, including pasture.
Plumage: Adult Upperpart feathers create a complex, cryptic plumage; blackish or reddish-brown centres are fringed buff, grey and white; the grey fringes produce broad mantle and scapular Vs.
Juvenile Virtually identical to adult.
Confusion species The smaller American Woodcock has uniform underparts. Very similar to Amami Woodcock (see Key ID features for that species), which has a diagnostic pink bare skin patch around eye, more noticeable to rear. Wood Snipe (plate 18) has a streaked rather than barred crown and nape.

Amami Woodcock
Scolopax mira   See also plate 59

Key ID features L 340–360mm. Low sloping forehead; bare pink area around the eye; blackish markings on throat and upper breast; whitish area on lower breast merges into barred underparts; finely vermiculated wing-coverts, with indistinct white tips.
Behaviour Forages by probing in the soft earth and short vegetation by forestry tracks at night. When disturbed may often run for cover rather than fly.
Habitat Occurs in subtropical evergreen broad-leaved hill forest, preferring damp areas.
Plumage: Adult Crown and nape heavily barred dark brown, with a contrastingly narrow first bar above the eye. Narrow dark cheek bar and loral line virtually parallel. Pink eye-patch more extensive to rear of eye.
Confusion species Eurasian Woodcock (compare Key ID features). Also, Amami Woodock has a deeper based bill, and the indistinct white tips to the wing-coverts create a darker and more uniform appearance. Note also behavioural differences between the species.

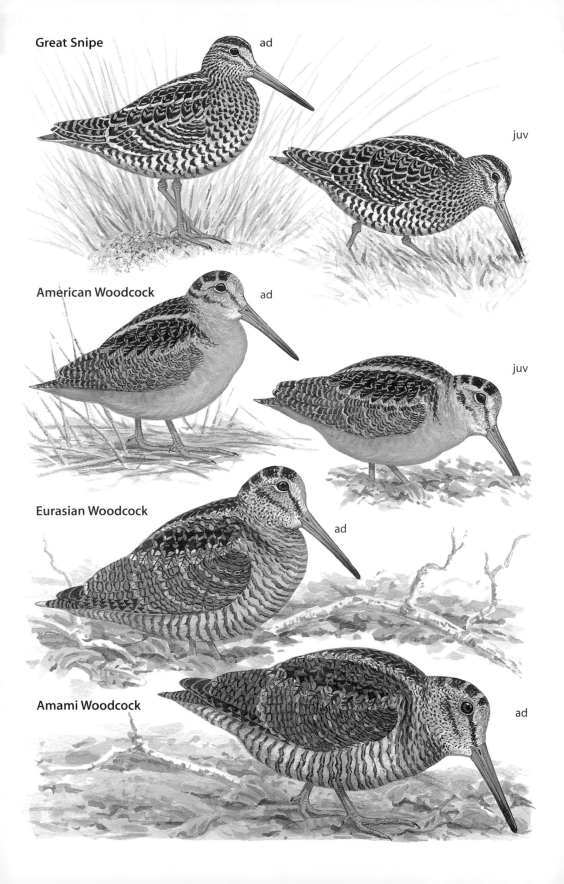

Great Snipe ad

juv

American Woodcock ad

juv

Eurasian Woodcock ad

Amami Woodcock ad

Plate 18 SWINHOE'S, LATHAM'S, WOOD AND SOLITARY SNIPES

Separating certain snipe species can be extremely challenging, as a combination of characteristics rather than any one feature need to be noted. Typical birds may be more straightforward, but it is important to remember that variation within a species can be considerable, leading to overlaps in size, structure and plumage, as between Pintail and Swinhoe's Snipes, for example. However, birds in the hand can be separated by the number and shape of the tail feathers.

Swinhoe's Snipe
Gallinago megala   See also plate 61

Key ID features L 270–290mm. Medium-length bill, thick legs often yellowish, and a fairly long tail that projects beyond tertial tips, which overlap or end level with the primary tips.
Behaviour Like Pintail Snipe, feeds by picking as well as probing.
Habitat Favours open woodland along river valleys for nesting. At other times frequents edges of wetlands, including rice paddies and freshwater streams.
Plumage: Adult Supercilium is broad at base of bill, compared with narrow loral and lateral crown stripes. Underparts white, with flank barring sometimes extending across lower breast. **Juvenile** Lower scapulars are uniformly fringed pale buff; wing-coverts are neatly fringed buffish-white. Primary projection is sometimes evident.
Confusion species Pintail Snipe (plate 19). Common Snipe (plate 19) is longer billed, has a broader loral stripe and wider dark tertial bars.

Latham's Snipe
Gallinago hardwickii   See also plate 61

Key ID features L 280–300mm. A heavy looking snipe, with a long tail that projects beyond the tertials, which overlap the primary tips.
Behaviour In some localities feeds mainly at night, taking refuge in drier, denser cover during the day.
Habitat For nesting favours drier heath or moorland, light birch or larch woodland. At other times occurs by freshwater wetlands, in rice stubble and on riverbanks.
Plumage: Adult Creamy supercilium is broader than the dark lateral crown stripes and lores in front of the eye; wing-coverts are broadly tipped whitish-buff. **Juvenile** Wing-coverts are neatly fringed buffish-white. Primary projection is sometimes evident.
Confusion species Swinhoe's Snipe, with shorter wings and tail, can appear less elongated than Latham's. See also Solitary Snipe.

Wood Snipe
Gallinago nemoricola   See also plate 61

Key ID features L 280–320mm. A bulky, more woodcock-like snipe, with a generally dark plumage, a deep bill-base and heavily barred underparts.
Behaviour Usually found singly.
Habitat Dense foliage at high altitude close to the tree-line. After breeding also found at lower altitudes in densely vegetated marshes or swamps.
Plumage: Adult Blackish upperparts, including the crown, with narrow buff median stripe; mantle and scapular feathers are blackish; the brownish-buff fringes produce typical mantle and scapular lines of variable strength; wing-coverts are barred brown and buff. **Juvenile** Similar to the adult plumage but the upper scapulars have whitish-buff fringes while the narrow pale-buff fringes to the wing-coverts produce a scaly appearance.
Confusion species Eurasian Woodcock (plate 17), which has an obvious barred crown and nape. See also Solitary Snipe.

Solitary Snipe
Gallinago solitaria   See also plate 61

Key ID features L 290–310mm. A longish tail creates an elongated appearance. The bill is long, legs bright yellow to greenish-yellow and the gingery-brown breast is unique in snipe species.
Behaviour Bobs when feeding like a Jack Snipe. Often crouches when disturbed; if flushed, usually alights again quickly.
Habitat Nests in mountain bogs and river valleys above the tree-line. Frequents similar areas outside the breeding season, often by running water.
Plumage: Adult Face and neck-sides are speckled greyish-white, with a narrow dark eye-stripe behind the eye and a dark cheek bar; upperpart feathers are reddish, barred dark brown; the edges of mantle and upper scapular feathers are edged white, forming typical snipe-like Vs. The breast is mottled, washed gingery brown; the underparts are extensively barred. **Juvenile** Virtually identical to the adult.
Racial variation The two races are almost identical; *japonica* may show richer red and less white on the upperparts than nominate.
Confusion species Wood Snipe is stockier, darker plumaged, with extensively barred underparts. Latham's Snipe lacks the gingery wash on the breast and the whiteness of the mantle and scapular Vs.

Swinhoe's Snipe

ad

juv

Latham's Snipe

ad

juv

Wood Snipe

ad

juv

Solitary Snipe

ad

Plate 19 JACK, COMMON, WILSON'S AND PINTAIL SNIPES

Jack Snipe
Lymnocryptes minimus　　　　See also plate 60

Key ID features L 170–190mm. The smallest snipe, with a relatively short bill, a large-head without a median crown-stripe and a dark mantle, with scapulars glossed purple and green.
Behaviour Often a solitary species, that does not rise until virtually trodden on. When feeding, the body frequently bobs rhythmically.
Habitat Nests in open marshes and bogs, and sometimes in drier forest clearings. At other times the Jack Snipe frequents freshwater and brackish wetlands, favouring dense vegetation.
Plumage: Adult The broad buffy-yellow supercilium is split, enclosing a dark line above the eye; the conspicuous parallel lines are formed by the golden-buff fringes between the mantle and upper scapular feathers and on the lowest tips of the upper scapulars. The underparts are white, with a brown streaked breast and fine brown streaking on the undertail-coverts. **Juvenile** Virtually identical but with less streaking on undertail-coverts.
Confusion species At a glance the dark plumage and split supercilium may suggest Broad-billed Sandpiper (plate 40).

Common Snipe
Gallinago gallinago　　　　See also plate 60

Key ID features L 250–270mm. Cryptically plumaged like all snipe, the Common Snipe has dark brown upperparts and a white belly; a very long straight bill; and a longish tail.
Behaviour Probes deeply in soft mud, sometimes in small, scattered flocks. When disturbed, sometimes freezes, or disappears rapidly into cover.
Habitat Nests in or near open fresh or brackish marshlands with tussocky vegetation. At other times frequents a variety of wetlands.
Plumage: Adult The brown loral stripe broadens towards the bill base, where it is wider than the supercilium. Two broad creamy-buff lines edge the mantle and upper-scapular feathers; the lower scapular fringes are wider on the lower edge; the dark tertial bars are wider than the pale ones. **Juvenile** Virtually identical to adult plumage but wing-coverts, uniformly fringed buffy-white with black subterminal bands, create a scaly appearance.
Racial variation The northern race *faeroeensis* is more deeply tinged rufous on the hindneck, scapulars, throat, breast and undertail-coverts.
Confusion species The longest-billed snipe but still very similar to Wilson's, Pintail, Swinhoe's and Latham's (plate 18). When wing is raised, the axillaries of Common Snipe show wider white and narrower black bars but on Wilson's they are of equal width.

Wilson's Snipe
Gallinago delicata　　　　See also plate 60

Key ID features L 250–270mm. The plumage is generally cold-toned, with the darker areas almost black; mantle and scapular stripes are whiter-buff rather than creamy-buff; white-fringed lesser and median coverts contrast with dark greater coverts.
Behaviour and Habitat Similar to Common Snipe.
Plumage: Adult The loral stripe is narrow and parallel-sided; the upperparts are very dark; the buff tertial bars are usually extremely narrow, with the feather colour becoming ghostly, as it fades towards the tertial bases. **Juvenile** Virtually identical to adult but the wing-coverts, uniformly fringed white with black subterminal bands, create a more scaly appearance.
Confusion species Common Snipe (compare Plumage descriptions). Also, the flanks of Wilson's are generally white rather than washed buff and, when the wings are raised, the blacker flank barring is typically more extensive, nearly 50/50 black-and-white, mirroring the axillaries' pattern; but note that the underwing of juvenile Common shows less white than adult.

Pintail Snipe
Gallinago stenura　　　　See also plate 60

Key ID features L 250–270mm. The normally squat, short-tailed appearance is emphasised by the tertials overlapping the primary tips and falling just short of the tail-tip. The diagnostically unique shape of the outer tail feathers is virtually impossible to see in the field. The bill is of medium-length.
Behaviour Feeds by picking as well as probing.
Habitat Nests in drier areas of damp meadows with shrubs or amongst dwarf birch. At other times found in various drier areas as well as wetlands, including muddy shorelines.
Plumage: Adult The face pattern is distinctive, with normally a narrow dark loral stripe and bulging supercilium; the lesser and median coverts appear barred; the inner and outer webs of the lower scapulars have buff fringes of equal width; the pale tertial bars are equal to or wider than the dark ones. **Juvenile** The lower webs of the lower scapulars are fringed whitish-buff, with the upper webs usually darker. The wing-coverts are neatly fringed whitish, creating a scalloped appearance.
Confusion species Common Snipe (note Pintail Snipe Key ID features and compare Plumage descriptions above) and the very similar Swinhoe's Snipe (plate 18).

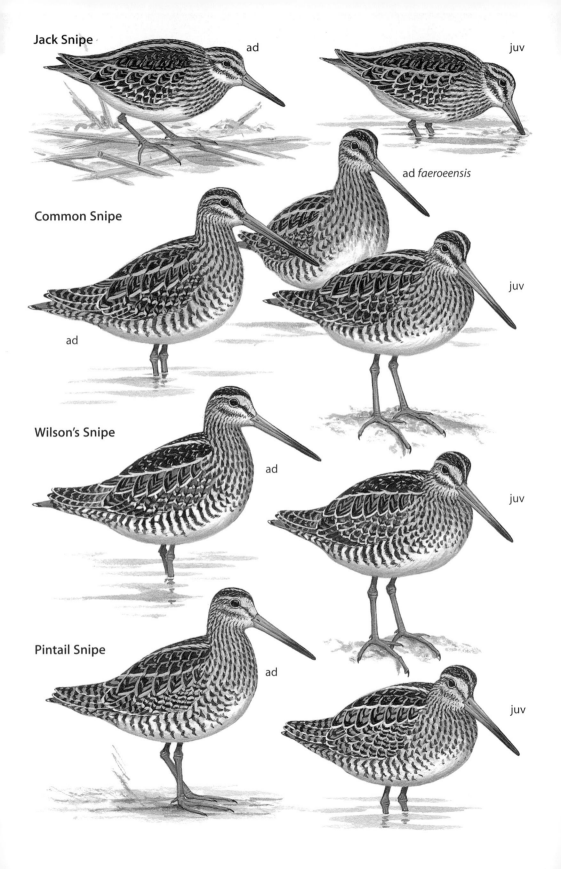

Jack Snipe ad juv

Common Snipe ad *faeroeensis*

ad

juv

Wilson's Snipe ad

juv

Pintail Snipe ad

juv

Plate 20 DOWITCHERS

A combination of characteristic features rather than any one, apart from call, needs to be noted to separate these extremely similar species, particularly in worn breeding and non-breeding plumages. Structural differences can be a useful guide. The distal third of the bill on Short-billed Dowitcher usually appears slightly drooped compared with the very straight bill of Long-billed Dowitcher.

Short-billed Dowitcher
Limnodromus griseus   See also plate 62

Key ID features L 250–290mm. A snipe-like wader, with very long bill (longest in female), comparatively short greenish legs and rich cinnamon underparts in breeding plumage. The primary projection is short, with two tips normally visible, and the tips of the folded wings align approximately with the tail-tip.

Behaviour When feeding, probes deeply, usually moving the head quite rapidly, like an animated sewing machine.

Habitat Short-billed is the dowitcher of salt water, most common on mudflats, but breeds in wet clearings in boreal forest and also occurs inland on migration.

Plumage: Breeding Crown brown, flecked cinnamon; pale supercilium; dark loral line; cheeks and neck pale cinnamon. Mantle feathers, scapulars and coverts are black centred, with cinnamon fringes. Wing-coverts will normally include a few non-breeding feathers, the latter are greyish-brown with pale fringes. The tertials are broadly barred cinnamon. Breast rich-cinnamon shading to white on belly and vent; neck and breast are spotted and flanks barred brown.
Non-breeding White supercilium contrasts with grey-brown crown; rest of upperpart feathers a paler grey-brown, fringed off-white. Underparts whitish; neck and breast pale grey, finely spotted grey-brown. Flanks faintly barred. **Juvenile** Dark crown gives a capped appearance, contrasting with grey of neck and white supercilium. Mantle feathers, scapulars and tertials dark brown, with broad, bright cinnamon fringes and internal markings. Breast is a bright peachy-buff, often spotted
Racial variation In breeding plumage the nominate eastern race *griseus*, the smallest, has a mainly white belly, heavily barred flanks and a densely spotted breast; the central race, *hendersoni*, has completely pale rufous underparts, heavily spotted on the undertail, upper flanks and sides of breast but almost unspotted in centre of breast; the western race *caurinus* is the largest; it may show the whole range of underpart patterns, often with large spots on the flanks.
Confusion species Long-billed Dowitcher, which, in breeding plumage, has all the underparts rufous and barring on the flanks extending to the

breast sides, which are more often spotted on Short-billed. In non-breeding plumage the dowitchers can be difficult to separate, but Long-billed has throat and entire breast grey and unspeckled, while Short-billed has throat and upper breast pale grey and finely speckled. A juvenile Short-billed plumage is generally more contrasting, but the tertials provide a key to identification: on Long-billed they are usually plain, with paler fringes while on Short-billed they are dark brown, with conspicuous bright buff fringes and internal markings. Another possible confusion species, Red Knot (plate 33) is similar in size and colour, in breeding plumage, but has a short bill.

Long-billed Dowitcher
Limnodromus scolopaceus   See also plate 62

Key ID features L 270–300mm. A snipe-like wader with a very long bill (longest in female), comparatively short greenish legs and rich reddish-cinnamon underparts in breeding plumage. Tertials and primary tips are equal in adults, and normally fall short of the tail-tip.

Behaviour No discernible differences from Short-billed apart from a preference for feeding more in freshwater habitats. In parts of their ranges the two species may flock together.

Habitat Nests in wooded wetlands and marshes; at other times favours freshwater localities, but not exclusively so.

Plumage: Breeding Upperpart feathers mostly black and rufous, tipped white; tertials have narrow rufous bars; some grey winter coverts are retained. Underparts entirely reddish-cinnamon, with dark brown chevrons, initially tipped white, along the flanks and onto the breast.
Non-breeding The white supercilium contrasts with the slaty-brown of upperpart feathers, which are fringed paler. Underparts whitish, neck and breast washed uniformly grey, merging into whitish belly; flanks grey with indistinct broad bars. **Juvenile** Head and underparts similar to non-breeding, except for a pinkish flush to the breast-sides and upper flanks. Mantle and scapular feathers are greyish-brown, notched and fringed rufous, with dark centres towards the tips; the tertials are plain greyish with rufous and white fringes.

Confusion species Short-billed Dowitcher and Red Knot (see Confusion Species of Short-billed above). The range overlaps with Asian Dowitcher (plate 32), which is larger with proportionately longer dark grey legs and flatter forehead, and unmarked chestnut-red underparts in breeding plumage. In silhouette both dowitchers are similar in structure and feeding behaviour to some snipe species.

Short-billed Dowitcher

br
caurinus

br
hendersoni

br *griseus*

juv

non-br

1st-w

Long-billed Dowitcher

juv

br

non-br

1st-w

Plate 21 EURASIAN GODWITS

Black-tailed Godwit
Limosa limosa   See also plate 63

Key ID features L 360–440mm. A large, tall, elegant godwit, with a long neck, long legs and very long, virtually straight bill, which has a variable orange or pinkish base.

Behaviour The feeding gait is slow and graceful, frequently in deep water. Huge feeding and roosting flocks form away from the breeding grounds.

Habitat Breeds on wet lowland grassland near freshwater wetlands and on boggy moors. On passage and in winter favours sheltered mudflats and estuaries, also flooded grassland and inland marshes.

Plumage: Breeding male The head, neck and breast have variable amounts of chestnut; the supercilium is pale in front of the eye and chestnut behind; the mantle, scapulars and tertials are blackish, scalloped chestnut-buff; some winter-type feathers are present in varying numbers; the wing-coverts are generally plainer grey, fringed off-white. The belly is whitish and the flanks are barred. **Breeding female** The plumage is highly variable, some almost resembling males, the majority distinctly duller, often with more winter-type feathers; the breast is a paler orange; the belly white with less barring; the bill is distinctly longer. **Non-breeding** Overall a plain dull grey plumage, with the wing-coverts narrowly and faintly fringed off-white. **Juvenile** The crown, neck and breast are washed orange-grey; the mantle, scapulars and some tertials are dark brown, fringed buff producing a neat scaly appearance.

Racial variation Nominate *limosa* is largest, with *islandica* intermediate in body size and *melanuroides* (not illustrated) obviously smaller. In breeding plumage shorter-billed *islandica* and *melanuroides* show more breeding-type brighter rufous mantle feathers and darker rufous-orange underparts, and numerous chevrons on the flanks. However, some long-billed female breeding *islandica* are similar to male *limosa*. Compared with *limosa* the plumage of juvenile *islandica* has richer cinnamon tones.

Confusion species The nominate race can be separated at all ages from nominate Bar-tailed Godwit by structure, appearing taller, with longer legs, the tibiae noticeably longer; and slightly longer, straighter bill. Confusion is far more likely with Hudsonian Godwit (plate 22) particularly in non-breeding plumage, when upperparts of both are plain grey. Hudsonian shares proportions and structure of Bar-tailed but a similar flight pattern to Black-tailed. Further confusion

occurs in southeast Asia, where Black-tailed *melanuroides* is smaller than Bar-tailed *baueri*. At a distance, in non-breeding plumage, may initially be confused with curlew species, but the straight rather than decurved bill should rule out further confusion.

Bar-tailed Godwit
Limosa lapponica   See also plate 62

Key ID features L 370–410mm. A shorter-legged godwit, with a long slightly upturned bill and a long primary projection.

Behaviour The gait is usually slow, with the body typically flat-backed, as it feeds in loose parties along the water's edge, or in shallow water.

Habitat Nests in the high arctic tundra and is essentially an estuarine species at other times, forming large flocks in the wintering areas. In western Europe is also common on sea passage in spring, but relatively scarce inland.

Plumage: Breeding male The head, neck and underparts almost entirely deep rufous; the mantle and scapular feathers are dark brown, irregularly notched and fringed chestnut-buff; the wing-coverts and tertials are a plainer grey, fringed whitish. **Breeding female** The chestnut-red colour is much reduced, often a pale, blotchy pinkish-buff, sometimes virtually absent. The bill is distinctly longer. **Non-breeding** Lacks all chestnut; the grey upperpart feathers are fringed white, with noticeable dark brown shaft streaks; the elongated scapulars tend to droop a little over the wing-coverts, creating a straggly appearance. **Juvenile** The upperpart feathers are dark brown, intricately notched and edged warm buff and white. The breast is washed with a warm buff and finely streaked dark brown.

Confusion species In Europe most likely to be confused at all ages with Black-tailed Godwit. Bar-tailed is dumpier and shorter-legged, with a shorter, more upturned bill; shows a steeper forehead and the supercilium behind the eye is more obvious; in breeding plumage shows all red unbarred underparts; the upperparts of non-breeding birds appear streaked, while Black-tailed are always plainer or neatly scalloped. In Alaska, Hudsonian Godwit (plate 22) closely resembles Bar-tailed structurally, but has plumage features more like a Black-tailed. Juveniles show similarities with Marbled Godwit (plate 22). At a distance on mudflats, Bar-tailed Godwits could be mistaken for Whimbrels (plate 24) until the decurved bill of the latter is seen.

Black-tailed Godwit

♂ br
islandica

♀ br

♂ br

juv

non-br

juv
islandica

Bar-tailed Godwit

♂ br

♀ br

1st-w

non-br

juv

Plate 22 **AMERICAN GODWITS**

Hudsonian Godwit
Limosa haemastica   See also plate 63

Key ID features L 370–420mm. A smallish godwit with a long, slightly upturned bill, the distal third of which is blackish and the basal two-thirds variable pinkish-red. The contrastingly long white supercilia, from the base of the bill, are finely streaked as are the white cheeks and, along with the deep maroon underparts of the breeding adult male, are diagnostic. There is a long primary projection and the wing-tips extend beyond the tail-tip.

Behaviour Feeds, often in flocks, by deep vertical probing, frequently wading into deeper water.

Habitat Breeds on arctic tundra and winters on pampas marshes and coastal mudflats.

Plumage: Breeding male Compared with the rest of the body, the head is contrastingly pale; the mantle, scapular and tertial feathers are black, irregularly notched warm buff; the wing coverts are a plainer grey, narrowly fringed off-white. The underparts are a deep maroon-red, with scattered black bars and chevrons, and whitish tips to belly, vent and undertail-covert feathers. **Breeding female** The plumage is highly variable but generally much paler; the underparts are less rufous with heavy barring; and the bill is usually longer. **Non-breeding** A generally uniform grey; the forecrown is darker, contrasting with the white supercilium; the upperpart feathers are a plain grey with narrow pale fringes. The neck and breast are also plain grey and the rest of the underparts white. **Juvenile** The face, neck and underparts have a warm buffish-brown wash; the mantle and scapular feathers are dark grey and brown, with buff notches, giving a noticeably neat scaly appearance; the wing-coverts are grey, fringed pale buff; the tertials and some coverts are deeply notched dark brown and buff.

Confusion species In many ways Hudsonian Godwit may be seen as intermediate between Black-tailed and Bar-tailed Godwits (plate 21), sharing the structure of the latter – bill length and shape, and leg length – but plumage characters of the former, with barred underparts on breeding birds, and plain grey or scaly upperparts in non-breeding and juvenile birds respectively.

Clearly, in western Europe, any 'odd looking' godwit amongst a party of Black-tails may well be worth closer inspection. Differs from breeding Bar-tailed Godwit, which has deep-rufous extending to neck and face, and from non-breeding Bar-tailed, which has upperpart plumage entirely fringed white with noticeable dark brown shaft-streaks.

Marbled Godwit
Limosa fedoa   See also plate 63

Key ID features L 420–480mm. The largest of the godwits, with a long, slightly upturned bill, the tip of which is blackish and the basal half bright pink. The overall cinnamon colour is unique in godwits and this species is unmistakable, when the bill is not hidden.

Behaviour These large godwits move slowly when feeding, probing steadily, burying their bills to the hilt.

Habitat Nests on wet grasslands, near pools on the prairies, and coastal marshland. Winters mainly on the coast in sheltered estuaries and on salt-marsh. Inland, tends to favour broad dry margins of reservoirs.

Plumage: Breeding Mantle feathers, scapulars, coverts and tertials are dark brown notched with buff; underparts are a rich buff and the breast and flanks are heavily barred brown. **Non-breeding** Little different from breeding plumage, but with unbarred underparts and only sparse barring on the flanks. **Juvenile** The coverts are plainer; a paler buff-brown, with just darker brown shaft-streaks, fringed a paler buff. The cinnamon-buff underparts lack any obvious breast streaks and are completely unbarred.

Racial variation The western race *beringiae* is smaller, with no obvious plumage differences.

Confusion species Juveniles of Hudsonian Godwit and Bar-tailed Godwit are similar, but have whitish, not buff bellies. When the bill is not visible, there is a similarity with Whimbrel (plate 24), with which it may feed, but the all buff underparts and richer brown uppers distinguish it. The colour of the plumage is more like that of Long-billed Curlew (plate 25) but that species is far larger, longer-necked, and has a decurved bill.

Hudsonian Godwit

♀ br

br to non-br

♂ br

juv

♀ non-br

Marbled Godwit

♂ br

juv

♀ non-br

Plate 23 UPLAND SANDPIPER AND LITTLE CURLEW

Upland Sandpiper
Bartramia longicauda   See also plate 64

Key ID features L 280–320mm. A unique, medium-sized, curlew-like wader, with a long thin neck; a smallish head; a fairly plain face, with a large dark eye and a shortish, thin, straight bill; this species also has an exceptionally long tail, which projects well beyond the wing-tips.
Behaviour Like a number of other waders, frequently perches on fence-posts or telegraph poles. Its manner of feeding is sometimes plover-like, alternating short runs with sudden stops; picking prey items or probing for them; sometimes forages alone but also in small groups; occasionally teeters like Spotted and Common Sandpipers, but not as actively as those species.
Habitat Nests mainly on prairie grasslands, requiring taller grasses and broad-leaved vegetation for cover. At other times occurs on a variety of short-grass habitats, like airfields and golf courses, as well as rough grasslands and even on suburban lawns; well away from water at all times.
Plumage: Adult The crown feathers are dark brown, narrowly fringed buff, but the buffish median crown-stripe is not always distinct. The upperpart feathers vary from olive to dark brown, with darker barring and narrow buffish fringes; the tertials are barred rather than notched. The neck and breast are washed buffish, with brown streaks, which form chevrons on the lower breast and flanks; the rest of the underparts are white. **Juvenile** The scapulars are mainly dark-centred; some are paler with dark subterminal lines and neat conspicuous buff fringes, which create a scalloped appearance. The buff wing-coverts have dark subterminal lines, shaft streaks, and neat pale fringes. The dark brown tertials are neatly notched with buff.
Confusion species Looks similar to Little Curlew, which has a longer, decurved bill. The Buff-breasted Sandpiper (plate 38) frequents similar habitats, but looks smaller and structurally different, with plain buff underparts.

Little Curlew
Numenius minutus   See also plate 64

Key ID features L 290–320mm. A small curlew, with a Whimbrel-like median crown-stripe and comparatively short, decurved bill.
Behaviour Feeds visually, mostly by picking. On the breeding grounds may be seen perching in trees. A highly gregarious species on its southern wintering grounds and may also form large flocks on migration.
Habitat Nests in loose colonies in grassy clearings among larch, osier and birch forests, or on open, recently burnt areas. On migration visits a variety of habitats, including inland grassy plains, bare cultivated land and freshwater margins, but occurs less frequently on the coast.
Plumage: Adult Has a distinctive buff and brown head pattern; a dark brown eye-stripe is formed by a small triangle in front of the eye and a narrow line behind, from just beneath the eye. The rest of the lores are pale. The upperpart feathers are darkish-brown, fringed and spotted pale buff; the tertials are barred. The neck and breast are washed buff, with fine brown streaks ending neatly across a creamy belly; the flanks are lightly barred. **Juvenile** In fresh plumage, can be separated from an adult bird as the brown tertial feathers have conspicuous pale buff notches.
Confusion species Similar to Upland Sandpiper and Whimbrel (plate 24), particularly the Hudsonian race, though the latter is considerably larger, with a longer bill and a complete dark loral line.

Upland
Sandpiper

♂ ad

♀ ad

juv

Little Curlew

♂ ad

♀ ad

juv

Plate 24 SMALLER CURLEWS

In all Numenius species there is little seasonal variation in plumage. However, there is considerable variation in bill length; this often determines the sex as the bill of the adult female is invariably longer. This is most obvious when observing flocks.

Slender-billed Curlew
Numenius tenuirostris   See also plate 64

Key ID features L 360–410mm. A medium-sized, slim curlew, with an evenly decurved, thin black bill, and primaries that project beyond the tail-tip.
Behaviour   Foraging behaviour is similar to Black-tailed Godwits, walking, watching and pecking, sometimes digging deeply for earth-worms, twisting the bill at a variety of angles. In winter may feed with Black-tailed Godwits and Eurasian Curlews; its actions are usually more rapid than the latter and it runs more often.
Habitat In winter frequents dry grassland, as well as brackish or fresh inland waters and estuarine mud.
Plumage: Breeding Fine dark streaking of head may create capped effect, contrasting with long, pale-buff supercilium and narrow brown lores. Ground colour of central breast is buffy, the rest of the underparts are white, with distinct dark streaks, enlarging into spots on flanks. The tail is a clean white, with four to five well-spaced narrower dark bars. **Non-breeding** Virtually identical to breeding. **Juvenile** Flanks are streaked rather than spotted.
Confusion species The bill of the highly variable Eurasian Curlew (plate 25) does not taper as much and its flank spots are never as rounded. The bill of the Whimbrel remains thick towards the tip; the pale median crown-stripe and dark lateral crown-stripes, provide a contrasting head pattern; the flanks are darker, with chevrons rather than spots.

Whimbrel
Numenius phaeopus   See also plate 65

Key ID features L 400–460mm. A medium-sized curlew species, with distinct head markings and decurved bill.
Behaviour Forms large flocks at roosts and on migration, but feeds alone or in small groups, usually more by picking than other curlews, but also probes.
Habitat Breeds on subarctic moorland and tun-dra, often close to the tree-line. When migrating, occurs widely inland on wetlands, as well as on short grassland. In winter regularly feeds on rocky shores, as well as estuaries and coastal grasslands.
Plumage: Adult A narrow pale median crown stripe is not always obvious, but a long pale super-cilium contrasts with a wider dark lateral crown stripe and dark lores; upperpart feathers are dark brown variously notched and fringed buffish and whitish. Neck and underparts are washed with buffish-white, with brown streaks on neck and breast, merging to chevrons on flanks. **Juvenile** As adult but scapulars, wing-coverts and tertials are cleanly notched buff.
Racial variation The 'Hudsonian' Whimbrel *hudsonicus* has more buffy underparts than the nominate race *phaeopus* and a more contrasting whiter supercilium; *variegatus* (not illustrated) is very similar to *phaeopus* at rest.
Confusion species Whimbrel is considerably smaller than Eurasian, Far-eastern and Long-billed Curlews (plate 25) and has a proportionately shorter bill. Most similar to Bristle-thighed Curlew.

Bristle-thighed Curlew
Numenius tahitiensis   See also plate 65

Key ID features L 400–440mm. A medium-sized curlew, with a Whimbrel-like head pattern; buffish-cinnamon wash to breast and flanks; and thickish blunt-tipped bill. Thigh bristles rarely seen in the field.
Behaviour When roosting, will perch in trees. Becomes flightless during wing-moult, which is unique among waders.
Habitat Nests on barren tundra in mountainous areas. Winters on remote, often tiny Polynesian islands.
Plumage: Adult Has a distinctive head pattern, with a creamy-buff median crown-stripe and a long supercilium, contrasting with a dark lateral stripe and lores; upperpart feathers are dark brown, with broad cinnamon-buff notches. The underparts can lack warm buff tones when worn; breast and flanks are heavily streaked brown. **Juvenile** Similar to adult but upperpart feathers show larger cinnamon-buff notches; underparts more buffish, with less streaking.
Confusion species The 'Hudsonian' Whimbrel *hudsonicus* is almost identical at a distance, but at close range adult Bristle-thighed Curlews have darker and more contrasting blackish-brown upperpart feathers, with rich cinnamon-buff notches. Adult Whimbrel upperparts appear more uniform dark brown, while those of juveniles show paler notches. Bristle-thighed Curlew also lacks the barred undertail-coverts of Whimbrel.

♂ br

♀ 'worn' br

Slender-billed Curlew

juv

non-br

♀ ad

Whimbrel

♂ ad

juv

♀ ad *hudsonicus*

♂ ad
hudsonicus

juv
hudsonicus

♀ 'worn' ad

Bristle-thighed Curlew

♂ ad

juv

Plate 25 **LARGER CURLEWS**

Eurasian Curlew
Numenius arquata   See also plate 66

Key ID features L 500–600mm. A large curlew, with a long decurved bill and plain head-pattern.

Behaviour Feeds mainly by deep probing in soft mud. Forms large flocks in the winter months.

Habitat Nests in a variety of open habitats, including boggy moorland, damp grassland and dry heathland. Winters on estuarine mudflats and saltmarsh, as well as coastal grasslands.

Plumage: Breeding The supercilium is indistinct, but there is a darkish loral spot in front of the eye; upperpart feathers are blackish-brown, with buffy notches and fringes. On the underparts the breast, neck and upper flanks are washed buffish, with bold streaks, becoming chevrons on the flanks; the rest of the underparts are white. **Non-breeding** Much as breeding plumage but duller. **Juvenile** Upperpart feathers are brightly contrasting, with dark centres broadly fringed and notched with warm buff. Underparts are more buffish, lacking the bold streaking on the breast and flanks.

Racial variation The flank markings on the nominate race *arquata* are chevron-shaped, whereas *orientalis* has streaked flanks and, on average, a longer bill.

Confusion species Small, short-billed Eurasian Curlews can be mistaken for Slender-billed Curlew (plate 24) but flank markings on adult Eurasians are generally chevron-shaped rather than rounded, and the wing-tips are about level with or short of the tail-tip, not overlapping as in Slender-billed Curlew. The Long-billed Curlew has buffy, less heavily streaked underparts, and the upperpart feathers of Far-eastern Curlew in breeding plumage are notched and fringed rich chestnut-buff.

Long-billed Curlew
Numenius americanus   See also plate 66

Key ID features L 500–650mm. A cinnamon-coloured large curlew, with a very long decurved bill, and droplet-shaped bill tip.

Behaviour Strides rapidly while feeding, reaching ahead with its long bill to probe for crabs or to pick insects from plants.

Habitat The favoured nesting grounds are open prairies, especially on gravelly soils. This species has adapted to the loss of this habitat and also nests in grain fields and pastures. On migration visits moist upland areas and shores of reservoirs, wintering in large numbers on inland grasslands of California, and also on coastal mudflats and estuaries.

Plumage: Adult The upperpart feathers are blackish-brown with cinnamon bars and fringes; the greyish-buff tertials are heavily barred. The underparts are entirely cinnamon, with fine streaks on the neck and breast, becoming indistinct chevrons on the upper flanks. **Juvenile** Very similar to adult but tertials are brighter than those of adults: cinnamon-buff with well-spaced dark bars; the wing-coverts lack bars and notches, but have broad dark shaft streaks with broad buff fringes.

Confusion species The large size, very long bill, overall cinnamon tones and the fine head streaking make this species difficult to confuse with the smaller Whimbrel and rare Bristle-thighed Curlew (plate 24). At roosts, when bills may be hidden, the Marbled Godwit (plate 22) will appear similar, but is smaller.

Far Eastern Curlew
Numenius madagascariensis   See also plate 66

Key ID features L 600–660mm. The largest curlew, with the longest bill of any wader.

Behaviour The feeding action is slow and deliberate; uses the bill to probe down burrows and also picks from the surface. Large flocks may form at high tide roosts.

Habitat Nests in open boggy terrain and on swampy shores of small lakes. Winters on coastal mudflats and estuaries, sandy beaches and also on inland wetlands.

Plumage: Breeding Has a faint supercilium, an indistinct dark loral line and obvious white eye-ring; upperpart feathers are dark brown, with rich chestnut fringes and notches. The underparts are washed brownish-buff, palest on the rear belly, with extensive streaking on the neck, breast and flanks. **Non-breeding** Similar to breeding, but the fringes and notches on the upperpart feathers are a duller, pale brown. **Juvenile** The upperpart feathers are neatly fringed and notched buff, and the underpart streaking is finer.

Confusion species Similar to the eastern *orientalis* race of Eurasian Curlew, which has whiter underparts, particularly on the lower belly, vent and undertail-coverts. The heavily streaked underparts of Far Eastern Curlew should separate this species from Long-billed Curlew in areas of range overlap.

Eurasian Curlew

♂ br

♀ non-br
orientalis

♀ non-br

juv

Long-billed Curlew

♀ ad

♂ ad

juv

Far Eastern Curlew

♀ ad

♂ ad

juv

Plate 26 **REDSHANKS**

Redshank

Tringa totanus   See also plate 70

Key ID features L 270–290mm. A medium-sized, brown-plumaged *Tringa*, with bright red legs and basal half of bill.

Behaviour Generally quite wary, and calls loudly when disturbed, often causing other wader species to fly as well. Feeds by picking and probing, and often wades into deeper water. At times feeds in dispersed flocks but large numbers gather to roost.

Habitat Nests inland on open, wet grasslands and also on coastal saltmarshes. At other times favours coastal mudflats, but may be found in a variety of wetland habitats, inland and coastal.

Plumage: Breeding The proportion of summer plumage type feathers attained varies considerably according to race. Head, neck and upperpart feathers are brownish, or cinnamon, with blackish or dark brown streaking and barring, and warm brown notches; some wing-coverts show narrow white fringes. Whitish underparts are heavily marked with brown streaks and chevrons. **Non-breeding** The upperpart feathers are a more uniform greyish-brown, with less conspicuous streaking and spotting. The underparts are whitish with fine streaks and a diffused brownish wash on the breast. **Juvenile** The upperpart feathers are a warm brown, extensively patterned with buff fringes and notches. The underparts are white, with fine streaking and a buffish wash on the breast.

Racial variation Though six races of this species are recognised, many populations are intermediate and only *totanus* and *robusta* are illustrated. The latter race has browner upperpart plumage, with proportionately more breeding-type feathers, and it is also marginally larger.

Confusion species Spotted Redshank (see below). The Ruff (plate 41) differs most obviously by its structural differences, with a longer neck, smaller head and shorter bill. Greater and Lesser Yellowlegs (plate 28) are larger and smaller respectively, with generally greyish upperparts rather than brown, and yellow rather than red legs; beware that juvenile Redshanks may show pale orange-yellow legs.

Spotted Redshank

Tringa erythropus   See also plate 67

Key ID features L 290–320mm. An elegant, medium-sized wader, with a unique black breeding plumage; a long and slender bill, with a red base to the lower mandible; and long red legs.

Behaviour Often feeds in small, dense flocks, swimming and up-ending; and like Greenshank and Marsh Sandpiper will drive shoals of fish into shallow water. Also feeds by picking and probing in mud, and sweeps its bill from side to side in water.

Habitat Breeds in swampy pine or birch forests and in more open heathland and shrub tundra. At other times occurs in a variety of freshwater or brackish wetlands and also on coastal mud.

Plumage: Breeding The head, neck and underparts are black; the undertail-coverts and a variable number of flank feathers are fringed white, more so in females. The upperpart feathers are blackish with prominent white notches and fringes. **Non-breeding** The white supercilium to above the eye contrasts with the dark loral line; the forehead, crown, hindneck, mantle and rest of the upperpart feathers are a uniform pale grey; the scapulars are fringed white, with black dots and the wing-coverts and tertials are notched black and white. The underparts are white, with a greyish wash on the breast sides. **Juvenile** The upperparts are brown, with off-white notches and spots; underparts are dull buff-grey, closely barred brown.

Confusion species The Spotted Redshank is unmistakable in breeding plumage; at other times similar to Redshank, but more elegant, longer-necked and longer-billed, while the pale grey non-breeding plumage is also distinctive, as are the barred underparts of juveniles.

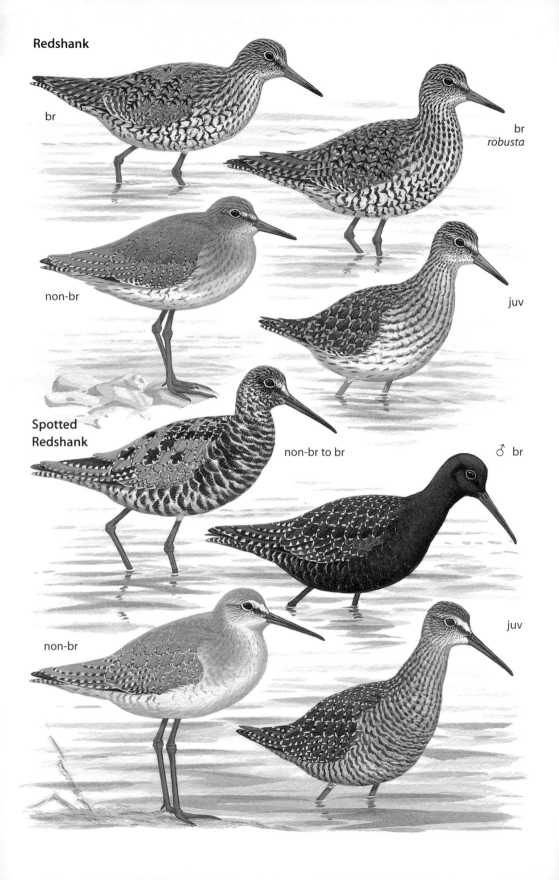

Redshank

br

br
robusta

non-br

juv

**Spotted
Redshank**

non-br to br

♂ br

non-br

juv

Plate 27 MARSH SANDPIPER, GREENSHANK AND WILLET

Marsh Sandpiper
Tringa stagnatilis   See also plate 67

Key ID features L 220–250mm. Slim, elegant and long-legged, with a needle-thin straight bill.
Behaviour Forages daintily, usually alone, picking invertebrates from surface of water. On migration and on wintering grounds, may feed communally.
Habitat Breeds in open freshwater marshland. At other times, found in fresh and brackish water habitats; only occasionally on the coast.
Plumage: Breeding Upperpart feathers greyish-cinnamon, with dark bars and pale fringes, create a richly patterned appearance. Underparts white, with dark brown breast spots, becoming chevrons on the flanks. Bill black, with the basal third greyish-green; legs dull yellowish-green.
Non-breeding Forehead and supercilium white; scapulars and coverts narrowly fringed white with narrow dark subterminal line; lesser coverts a darker grey. Underparts white, with a grey suffusion and light streaking on sides of breast.
Juvenile Crown and hindneck streaked brown; supercilium white; upperpart feathers brown, fringed buffy-white; the scapulars show dark subterminal bars; tertials are finely notched towards the tips.
Confusion species Separated from Greenshank, which has a much thicker upturned bill, by small size (see also Greenshank Key ID features). Lesser Yellowlegs (plate 28) is similar sized, thicker billed, with primary tips projecting beyond the tail-tip, and obvious yellow legs. Wilson's Phalarope (plate 42) has a different jizz, pot-bellied, with shorter, yellowish legs.

Greenshank
Tringa nebularia   See also plate 67

Key ID features L 300–340mm. Longish necked, with a slightly upcurved, thick-based bill and dull greenish-yellow legs.
Behaviour Feeding singly, picks insects off water's surface, occasionally probes for fish fry. On migration and on wintering grounds may feed communally, pursuing shoals of fish in shallow water.
Habitat Nests on open moorland and freshwater marshes, often with scattered trees. At other times found in wetland habitats, inland and coastal, where estuaries are favoured.
Plumage: Breeding Upperpart feathers are variable: blackish-centred with white fringes and notches, mixed among grey feathers with dark shaft streaks and notches. Underparts are white, strongly streaked blackish-brown on the neck and breast, with chevrons on the flanks.
Non-breeding Crown and hindneck are more finely streaked; the grey tertials are finely notched black-and-white. The underparts are white, with light greyish streaks on the breast sides. **Juvenile** The upperparts are browner-grey, with extensive buff notches and buffish-white fringes; the tertials are broadly notched.
Confusion species Marsh Sandpiper (see Confusion species for that species). Distinguished from Greater Yellowlegs (plate 28) by duller greenish legs and slightly more upturned bill; non-breeding Greenshank has almost entirely unstreaked breast. In breeding plumage Nordmann's Greenshank (plate 32) has distinct spotting on breast and chevrons on flanks, and is always shorter-legged.

Willet
Catoptrophorus semipalmatus
                   See also plate 63

Key ID features L 330–410mm. Heavier and less elegant than closely related *Tringa* species, with a heavier, dark-tipped, straight grey bill and proportionately shorter legs.
Behaviour Not as gregarious as godwits but more so than yellowlegs. Feeds by probing, more like godwits. In breeding areas often perches on fence posts.
Habitat Birds of the nominate eastern race are essentially coastal, breeding in saltmarsh vegetation. Western birds of race *inornatus* breed in freshwater marshes. In winter both races may frequent various coastal areas, including saltmarsh, mudflats, sandy beaches and rocky shorelines.
Plumage: Breeding Short, whitish supercilium, above brown lores, not extending behind eye. Narrow white eye-ring. **Non-breeding** Upperparts and wing-coverts pale grey, narrowly fringed paler grey or white, when fresh. Underparts white, washed pale grey on throat, breast sides and flanks. **Juvenile** As non-breeding adult but upperparts distinctly browner-grey, with dark subterminal bars and broad buff fringes; tertials notched with buff.
Racial variation Western race *inornatus* is larger, with longer legs and bill, often slightly upturned. In breeding plumage, breast is usually more buff, less heavily streaked, with fewer chevrons on the flanks. Juvenile has a whitish forehead and centre of breast; wing-coverts and tertials are more conspicuously patterned than on *semipalmatus*. However, there is a great deal of variability.
Confusion species Greater Yellowlegs (plate 28) and Greenshank show some plumage and structural similarities, but the Willet has shorter greyish legs and a heavier, straighter bill.

Marsh Sandpiper

non-br

br

juv

Greenshank

non-br

br

juv

Willet

br

br
inornatus

non-br

juv
inornatus

Plate 28 YELLOWLEGS AND TATTLERS

Lesser Yellowlegs
Tringa flavipes   see also plate 68

Key ID features L 230–250mm. An elegant wader with long yellow legs; bill length about equal to head; long wings project well beyond the tail-tip.
Behaviour   Usually feeds by picking from surface, during delicate, high-stepping walk; often runs through water, also feeds with a scything action. Tends to nest in loose colonies.
Habitat   Favours drier habitat than Greater Yellowlegs for nesting, usually in open woodland. On migration and in winter found in many wetland habitats, both inland and coastal.
Plumage: Breeding Underparts mostly white, with heavy streaking on breast becoming chevrons on flanks. **Non-breeding** Distinct white eye-ring and supercilium above dark lores; upperpart feathers uniform brownish-grey, with small white spots; tertials dark brown, with whitish notches; breast washed brownish-grey, with indistinct fine streaks. **Juvenile** Similar to non-breeding but upperparts are a warmer brown, with prominent white notches.
Confusion species Greater Yellowlegs (compare Key ID features). Wood Sandpiper (plate 29) is proportionately smaller – shorter legs, bill and wings – with an obvious long supercilium. Marsh Sandpiper (plate 27) has slightly longer green or yellowish-green legs and a thinner bill.

Greater Yellowlegs
Tringa melanoleuca   See also plate 68

Key ID features L 290–330mm. Tall with long neck, long yellow legs and long, slightly upturned bill about 1.5 times head length.
Behaviour   Usually feeds as it wades, picking food off the surface and from below it.
Habitat Nests in open areas, with marshy ponds and scattered trees. On migration and in winter as Lesser Yellowlegs.
Plumage: Breeding Underparts are white, with heavy blackish neck and breast streaks, which become chevrons on lower breast and flanks. **Non-breeding** Upperpart feathers initially with numerous white spots and notches; white underparts, with brown streaks on neck and breast and fine bars on flanks. **Juvenile** Warmer brown upperpart feathers profusely spotted and notched with buffy-white.
Confusion species Structurally Greenshank (plate 27) is similar but has green legs and a more obvious upturned bill.

Grey-tailed Tattler
Heteroscelus brevipes   See also plate 68

Key ID features L 240–270mm. Plain grey upperparts, tinged slightly brown; short yellow legs; primary tips fall level with tail-tip. Nasal groove is barely half bill length.
Behaviour When feeding, often alone, teeters like Common and Spotted Sandpipers, moving rapidly amongst small rock pools, picking food from rocks or crevices.
Habitat Nests along stony riverbeds. On migration and in winter found on rocky coastlines but also on mangrove-backed mudflats.
Plumage: Breeding Prominent white orbital-ring. Long white supercilia, indistinct behind eye, often meet on forehead; broad dark loral stripe. Underparts white, with fine streaks on neck and narrow chevrons on lower breast extend along flanks to edges of undertail-coverts; belly, vent and most of undertail-coverts unbarred. **Non-breeding** As breeding but lacks streaks and barring, flanks white. **Juvenile** As non-breeding but fresh scapulars, wing-coverts and tertials are notched buffy-white.
Confusion species Wandering Tattler (compare Key ID features) shows four to five primary tips beyond tertials, Grey-tailed shows three to four.

Wandering Tattler
Heteroscelus incanus   See also plate 68

Key ID features L 260–290mm. Plain slate-grey upperparts and short yellow legs. Heavily barred underparts in breeding plumage; long primary projection; primary tips project beyond tail-tip. Nasal groove extends well beyond mid-length. Juvenile and non-breeding birds have grey flanks.
Behaviour When feeding, often alone, bobs and teeters like Common and Spotted Sandpipers.
Habitat Nests by mountain streams. On migration and in winter favours rocky coastlines.
Plumage: Breeding Prominent white orbital-ring. Short white supercilium in front of eye; narrow dark loral stripe. Underparts white, with obvious neck streaks and bold chevron-like bars extending to undertail-coverts. **Non-breeding** As breeding but underparts plain slate-grey apart from whitish throat, lower belly, vent and undertail-coverts. **Juvenile** Scapulars, tertials and wing-coverts show smallish white spots. Grey of breast and flank feathers faintly tipped lighter grey.
Confusion species Surfbird (plate 31) in non-breeding plumage, but Surfbird is smaller, plumper, short-billed and has spotted underparts.

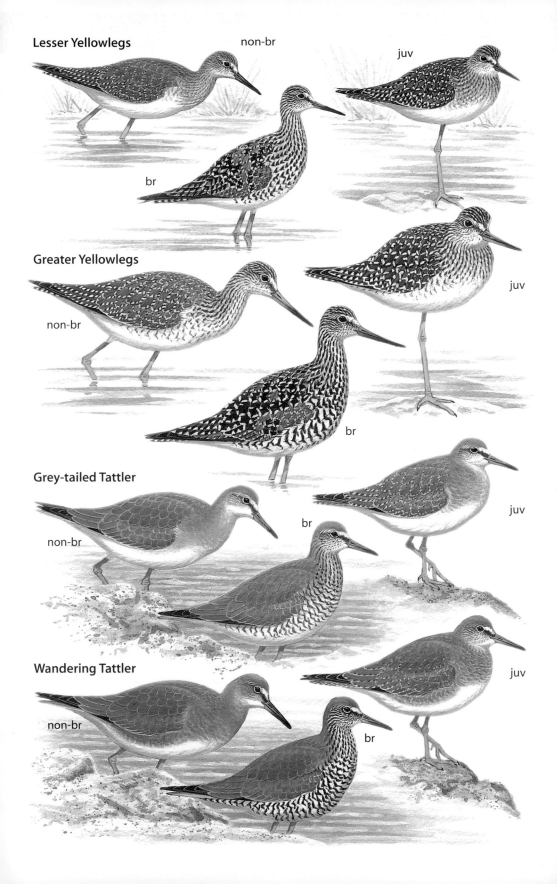

Lesser Yellowlegs

non-br

juv

br

Greater Yellowlegs

non-br

juv

br

Grey-tailed Tattler

non-br

br

juv

Wandering Tattler

non-br

br

juv

Plate 29 WOOD, SOLITARY AND GREEN SANDPIPERS

Wood Sandpiper
Tringa glareola   See also plate 69

Key ID features L 190–210mm. A slim, graceful *Tringa* with speckled brown upperparts, long white supercilium and longish, greenish legs, sometimes more yellowish. Wing and tail-tips closely align.

Behaviour All three of these *Tringa* waders have a distinct teetering gait, bobbing the head and pumping the tail end up and down. They forage visually, pecking for small prey items, and may use tree nests of other birds. Wood is a marginally more gregarious species than the other two and small migrant flocks may be seen.

Habitat Breeds in damp, open areas of coniferous forests, or in bogs and marshes with low vegetation. At other times of the year frequents freshwater habitats, including small ponds and flooded fields. Generally avoids intertidal habitats.

Plumage: Breeding Distinct long white supercilium from bill base to rear of ear coverts; thin whitish eye-ring. Upperparts dark brown, with profuse whitish notches. **Non-breeding** Upperparts paler brown, with less obvious notches. Breast washed greyish, with indistinct streaking and flanks usually unbarred. **Juvenile** Resembles non-breeding adult, but upperparts a warmer brown, with buff speckling. Breast mottled brown, flanks indistinctly marked.

Confusion species Lesser Yellowlegs (plate 28) is larger and greyer, with proportionately longer yellowish legs, a long primary projection and wing tips project well beyond tail-tip. Green and Solitary Sandpipers are darker, with less obvious speckling, shorter legs and lack the long white supercilium of Wood. Diffuse breast markings of juvenile distinct from clean-cut breast of Green Sandpiper.

Solitary Sandpiper
Tringa solitaria   See also plate 69

Key ID features L 180–210mm. A slender, dark *Tringa*; obvious white eye-ring, tear-drop shaped at rear, and fore-supercilium create a spectacled look. Long primary projection; wing-tips project well beyond tail-tip.

Behaviour Rarely seen in flocks, except on migration. Teeters (as described under Wood Sandpiper), mainly when alarmed.

Habitat Breeds in boggy, freshwater areas associated with coniferous forest. At other times of the year may be found on muddy pools in woodland, as well as inland ponds and lakes.

Plumage: Breeding White supercilium obvious in front of eye, barely visible behind. Upperparts dark brown with white spots and notches. **Non-breeding** Paler and more sooty brown than breeding; upperparts less spotted; breast streaking diffused. **Juvenile** As non-breeding adult, but upperparts browner, with more conspicuous buff spots and notches. Breast more evenly washed, with indistinct streaking, and the flanks may be more barred.

Racial variation In juvenile plumage, the nominate race *solitaria* (not illustrated) has whitish-buff notches on upperparts; *cinnamomea* tends to have warmer, almost cinnamon notching.

Confusion species The similar sized non-breeding or juvenile Spotted Sandpiper (plate 30) has plainer upperparts, whiter underparts and an incomplete eye-ring. Lesser Yellowlegs (plate 28) is larger, longer necked, with longer yellow, rather than shorter greenish, legs. Also Wood and Green Sandpipers (compare Key ID features above and below respectively).

Green Sandpiper
Tringa ochropus   See also plate 69

Key ID features L 210–240mm. Darkest species of genus; upperparts have an almost olive-brown hue and profuse small white spots. Legs greyish-green, appear dark at a distance. Short primary projection; wings project just beyond tail-tip.

Behaviour Often perches on posts or trees during breeding season. Teeters, as described under Wood Sandpiper, when alarmed and while feeding.

Habitat Breeds in damp, wooded areas, usually surrounded by bogs or marshes. Outside the breeding season, favours a wide variety of more open freshwater wetlands.

Plumage: Breeding Obvious white supercilium in front of eye, narrow white eye-ring, often broken at rear. Upperparts dark olive-brown, with bright white spots. **Non-breeding** As breeding but upperparts paler, greyish-brown, with smaller, less obvious spots. Breast greyer, with more diffuse streaking. **Juvenile** As non-breeding adult, but upperparts browner, with more conspicuous buff spots and notches. Breast more evenly washed, with indistinct streaking and upper flanks usually unbarred.

Confusion species Larger and less sleek than Solitary Sandpiper, best distinguished in flight, but note eye-ring feature. The dark upperparts and dark green legs of Green Sandpiper preclude confusion with Lesser Yellowlegs (plate 28) or *Actitis* sandpipers (plate 30) at rest.

Wood Sandpiper

juv

br

non-br

Solitary Sandpiper

juv
cinnamomea

br
solitaria

non-br
solitaria

Green Sandpiper

juv

br

non-br

Plate 30 SPOTTED, COMMON AND TEREK SANDPIPERS

Spotted Sandpiper
Actitis macularia   See also plate 70

Key ID features L 180–220mm. In breeding plumage, the obvious spotted underparts and noticeable white 'peak' between carpal joint and breast-sides are distinctive. Legs usually yellowish-orange, but variable in colour.
Behaviour Has a distinctive teetering action, habitually bobbing its head and pumping the rear part of the body up and down. To feed, *Actitis* sandpipers forage visually, pecking for small prey items, sometimes from underneath leaves.
Habitat Ubiquitous, breeding beside freshwater streams, rivers and lakes. At other times usually associated with freshwater habitats but frequents coastal areas, too, particularly on migration, when travels singly or in small parties.
Plumage: Breeding The upperparts are brown; the scapulars, tertials and wing-coverts have dark brown shaft streaks and bars, with buff tips. The bill is orange-pink with black tip. **Non-breeding** The mantle, scapulars and tertials are a plain brown; the coverts are barred buff and brown. **Juvenile** Similar to non-breeding but wing-coverts are more strongly barred dark brown and buff; some lower scapulars have narrow dark subterminal lines with buff tips; tertials are plain, apart from narrow subterminal brown bars and buff tips.
Confusion species Separated from juvenile and non-breeding Common Sandpiper by less streaked breast sides, mainly plain tertials, short tail projection beyond wing-tips, bi-coloured mainly pink bill, with black tip and usually yellowish legs.

Common Sandpiper
Actitis hypoleucos   See also plate 70

Key ID features L 190–210mm. Long tail and noticeable white 'peak' between carpal joint and breast-sides are distinctive. Legs usually greenish-grey but variable.
Behaviour Teeters constantly, as described under Spotted Sandpiper. Ground display consists of 'wing-saluting', lifting one or two wings, interspersed with chasing. On landing male holds wings up in brief double-wing salute. On migration, like Spotted, usually found singly or in small parties.
Habitat Breeds in a wide variety of habitats within vicinity of water. At other times, as with Spotted, prefers freshwater habitats but frequents coastal areas, too, particularly on migration.
Plumage: Breeding The upperparts are brown; the scapulars, tertials and wing coverts have dark brown shaft streaks and bars, with buff tips. The bill is mainly dark brown, with a dull greenish base. **Non-breeding** The mantle and scapular feathers are a warm brown, with indistinct shaft streaks and subterminal lines; the coverts are barred buff and brown; the tertials are indistinctly notched. The underparts are white with brownish, largely unstreaked patches on the breast sides. **Juvenile** Similar to non-breeding plumage but the mantle and scapular feathers have dark, narrow, dotted subterminal lines and buff fringes; the coverts are barred buff and brown; the fringes of the tertials are dotted dark brown and buff.
Confusion species Juvenile and non-breeding Spotted Sandpiper (see Confusion species for Spotted).

Terek Sandpiper
Xenus cinereus   See also plate 70

Key ID features L 220–250mm. The only short-legged smallish wader with an upturned bill.
Behaviour An extremely active species, sprinting short distances, frequently changing direction and halting abruptly. Uniquely among sandpipers and shanks, this species eats small crabs, both on migration and on wintering grounds. Occasionally feeds in shallow water using an Avocet-like scything action. Teeters frenetically, at times far more vigorously than Spotted and Common Sandpipers.
Habitat Breeds in grasslands of lowland valleys, beside lakes and large rivers. Favours estuarine mudflats on migration and in winter.
Plumage: Breeding The crown and hindneck are finely streaked; the white supercilium is most prominent between the bill and the eye; narrow dark loral line; the upperparts are a pale grey-brown, with broad shaft streaks and narrow pale fringes; the broad shaft streaks on the upper scapulars form long blackish lines. **Non-breeding** The upperparts are paler than those of breeding birds, usually lacking black lines. The breast is paler, almost without streaking. **Juvenile** The upperpart feathers are usually darker and browner than those of adults, with an indistinct dark subterminal bar and buff fringes; black upper scapular markings are often present but less well defined than in breeding plumage.
Confusion species There should be no confusion with any of the *Tringa* or *Actitis* species once the upcurved bill and distinctive gait are observed, but beware of similarly sized three-week old Avocets when observed distantly.

Spotted Sandpiper

non-br to br

juv

non-br

br

Common Sandpiper

juv

non-br

br

Terek Sandpiper

juv

br

non-br

Plate 31 **TURNSTONES AND SURFBIRD**

Ruddy Turnstone
Arenaria interpres   See also plate 71

Key ID features L 210–255mm. A medium-sized, stocky wader, with a dark mottled breast, short orange legs and a short wedge-shaped bill, which has a slightly upcurved lower mandible. This species is particularly distinctive in its breeding plumage.

Behaviour Almost unique feeding behaviour involves turning over stones and flicking seaweed sideways to find food items. Relatively tame. Walks with a rolling gait.

Habitat Nests on tundra, usually close to the sea, often on stony ground with sparse vegetation. At other times it favours rocky coasts but can also be found on sandy beaches and mudflats with patches of pebbles and seaweed.

Plumage: Breeding White head with variable amount of fine black streaks and a complex pattern of black, which extends onto the breast and along the sides of the mantle. Upperparts are mainly chestnut-orange with a second blackish patch running across the lower scapulars. Many median coverts are extra large. **Non-breeding** Lacks the chestnut of the breeding plumage; head blotchy brown; upperpart feathers dark greyish-brown with pale fringes. Breast-band is dark brownish-grey. **Juvenile** Similar to non-breeding birds but with a paler brown head and breast; the upperpart feathers are neatly fringed with orange-buff or white; this creates a scaly appearance.

Racial variation The nominate race is larger than *morinella*, with more crown streaking and paler, chestnut-orange scapulars and wing-coverts.

Confusion species Black Turnstone, but this species always has a dark chin and breast markings that end squarely.

Black Turnstone
Arenaria melanocephala   See also plate 71

Key ID features L 220–250mm. A medium-sized heavy-looking black-and-white wader, identical in shape to Ruddy, with a black chin and a white spot at the base of the bill.

Behaviour Manner of feeding is very similar to Ruddy Turnstone. Blends well among dark rocks, where it may feed and roost with Surfbirds, Rock Sandpipers, Ruddy Turnstones and Black Oystercatchers.

Habitat Rarely occurs far from the coast; nests on salt grass, in dwarf shrub meadows and by brackish pools. In non-breeding season favours rocky coastlines and barnacle-covered reefs, and can sometimes be seen foraging on adjacent sandy beaches.

Plumage: Breeding Head is black with fine white streaks; upperpart plumage is slaty-black with white fringes to the lower scapulars and coverts, including the extra large median coverts. **Non-breeding** Lacks white spot at the bill base; upperparts and breast are evenly dark with white fringes to some scapulars, coverts and tertials. **Juvenile** Lacks white spot at bill base; all of the blackish feathers are tinged brown with neat buff or buffy-white fringes to scapulars, coverts and tertials.

Confusion species Ruddy Turnstone, whose white chin, although sometimes streaked dark, is diagnostic, as are the bilobed breast markings.

Surfbird
Aphriza virgata   See also plate 71

Key ID features L 235–255mm. A medium-sized, plump, grey sandpiper, with a thick blunt-tipped bill and yellow legs.

Behaviour Often feeds with Black and Ruddy Turnstones and Rock Sandpipers. Gregarious on migration. Protects eggs from grazing Dall sheep by sitting tightly until the last minute and then flying into the face of the animal.

Habitat Breeds on high alpine tundra, among mossy vegetation. At other times favours rocky coastlines, occasionally feeds on the tideline of sandy beaches.

Plumage: Breeding Head, neck and upper breast white, heavily streaked black; the mantle and upper scapulars are blackish-brown, fringed with chestnut and white; the scapular feathers are chestnut, with broad black shaft streaks and subterminal bars. **Non-breeding** Upperpart feathers are plain slate-grey with pale fringes; the breast is grey with indistinct brownish spots, while the rest of the underparts are white, with brownish-grey chevrons on the flanks. **Juvenile** A browner-grey plumage rather than the slate-grey of non-breeding birds, with the wing-coverts showing dark subterminal bars and buffish-white fringes.

Confusion species Great Knot (plate 33) shares some similar plumages but has a longer, all dark bill. Red Knot (plate 33) in winter plumage is similar, but also has a different shaped, slightly longer bill, is a paler grey and lacks the dark breast and flank chevrons of Surfbird. A non-breeding Wandering Tattler (plate 28) is similar to a non-breeding Surfbird but is larger and has clean white underparts and a longer bill.

Ruddy Turnstone

♂ br

♀ br

♂ br
morinella

non-br

juv

Black Turnstone

♀ br

♂ br

non-br

juv

Surfbird

br

juv

non-br

Plate 32 **ASIAN SPECIALITIES**

Spoon-billed Sandpiper
Eurynorhynchus pygmeus   See also plate 72

Key ID features   L 140–160mm. A stint-like wader, with an extraordinary spatulate bill.
Behaviour   Feeds on soft wet mud or in shallow water, sweeping its bill from side to side. On migration and in winter often associates with Red-necked Stints.
Habitat   Nests close to sea coasts, on sparsely vegetated ridges near lakes and marshes. Winters on mudflats and coastal lagoons.
Plumage: Breeding   White-fringed mantle feathers may form indistinct Vs; face, neck and upper breast chestnut-red, with faint brown streaks; rest of underparts white, with a band of brownish spots across the lower breast, more obvious on sides. **Non-breeding**   Broad supercilium, forehead and underparts bright white, apart from fine streaks on breast sides and ear-coverts. **Juvenile**   Crown dark brown with rich-buff streaks; upperpart feathers dark brown, fringed warm buff and white; the latter may form indistinct Vs on edges of mantle and upper scapulars. Some juveniles lack the warm-buff tones.
Confusion species   Breeding plumaged Red-necked Stints (plate 35) look similar, but have no streaks on the chestnut breast. In non-breeding plumage looks bigger-headed and much whiter on face and underparts than stints.

Asian Dowitcher
Limnodromus semipalmatus   See also plate 62

Key ID features   L 340-360mm. A godwit-like wader, with a long, straight, usually all-black and blunt-tipped bill; the lower mandible base is pink on juveniles.
Behaviour   Often feeds in tight flocks, frequently with Bar-tailed Godwits, usually on exposed mud or belly-deep in water, when it makes rapid vertical probes.
Habitat   Nests in sparsely vegetated, mainly freshwater wetlands. In winter is strictly coastal, frequenting intertidal mudflats and lagoons.
Plumage: Breeding male   Crown brownish-chestnut; loral line brown; mantle, scapular and tertial feathers brownish-black, fringed chestnut and white. Underparts chestnut-red becoming blotchy white on belly; prominent brown chevrons on the flanks. **Breeding female**   Duller chestnut tones, with some non-breeding type feathers. **Non-breeding**   Upperpart feathers grey-brown, fringed white; flanks barred brown.

Juvenile   Long white supercilium contrasts with dark brown crown and eye-stripe; upperpart feathers dark brown, fringed warm buff. Neck, breast and flanks washed warm buff, with darker fine streaks and chevrons.
Confusion species   Resembles Bar-tailed Godwit (plate 21) but has straight all-black bill and narrow dark chevrons on flanks. Differs from Long-billed and Short-billed Dowitchers (plate 20) by larger size, and longer dark grey, rather than green or yellowish-green, legs.

Nordmann's (Spotted) Greenshank
Tringa guttifer   See also plate 67

Key ID features   L 290–320mm. The spotted underparts when breeding are diagnostic. Has a deep broad-based, almost straight, mainly all-dark bill (two-toned in juvenile); and dull brownish-yellow legs, with short tibiae. Partial toe-webbing between all three front toes is unique among *Tringa* waders.
Behaviour   Often feeds along the tideline. Prefers to stand in water when roosting.
Habitat   Breeds in sparse larch forests adjacent to marshy pools. On migration and in winter frequents coastal mudflats and lagoons.
Plumage: Breeding   Indistinct supercilium; centres of scapulars vary randomly from grey to black, deeply indented with white notches; tertials are dark-grey or blackish, with deep white notches (some plain, 'non-breeding' tertials are frequently retained by spring migrants). Underparts white, black spots spread randomly across the breast, with fine streaks and chevrons on the flanks. **Non-breeding**   Head extremely pale, with ash-grey feathering confined to the crown, nape, ear-coverts and lores. Upperpart feathers pale ash-grey, narrowly fringed white. Entire underparts white. **Juvenile**   The grey-brown crown contrasts with the broad off-white supercilium, giving a capped effect; upperpart feathers are a darker grey-brown than 'non-breeding', with buff notches and fringes, particularly evident on scapulars, greater coverts and tertials; lesser coverts darker, producing a dark carpal patch.
Confusion species   Separated from Greenshank (plate 27) at rest by the hunched appearance, produced by a heavy-breast, a pronounced ventral angle, a thicker neck held into the body and primaries that fall just short of the tail-tip. More elegant when active but always shorter legged. Viewed head-on the cross-section of the bill base is circular compared with an elliptical cross-section in Greenshank.

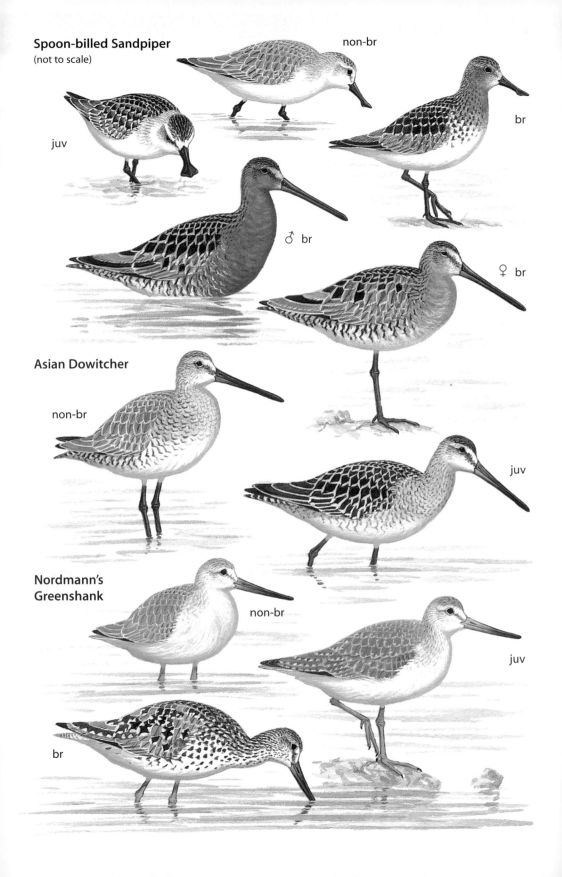

Spoon-billed Sandpiper
(not to scale)

non-br

juv

br

♂ br

♀ br

Asian Dowitcher

non-br

juv

Nordmann's Greenshank

non-br

juv

br

Plate 33 SANDERLING AND KNOTS

Sanderling
Calidris alba   See also plate 77

Key ID features L 200–210mm. "The winter tideline clockwork mouse". The only calidrid without a hind toe. Richly coloured upperparts in breeding plumage; exceptionally pale grey in winter, with short, straight, thickish black bill and short black legs.
Behaviour Extremely active, often foraging in small flocks, pausing only briefly to probe and pick for food along coastal tide-lines. Often forms large flocks, roosting with other wader species, or with their own kind.
Habitat Nests on rocky tundra with scant vegetation, often away from the coast. May occur on inland waters during migration, but favours sandy and sometimes muddy beaches.
Plumage: Breeding The head and neck are chestnut, with fine dark brown streaks; the breast is chestnut with dark crescents forming a neat pectoral band that contrasts with the white underparts. The mantle feathers, scapulars and tertials are black and rufous, with whitish fringes; the greater and median coverts are grey, fringed whitish, and the lesser coverts are blackish. **Non-breeding** Noticeably pale grey crown, hindneck and upperpart feathers, which are fringed white, with fine, dark shaft streaks. Upper lesser coverts are blackish, forming an obvious dark carpal joint. **Juvenile** The dark brown crown is finely streaked white; the whitish supercilium contrasts with the dark eye-line; the mantle and scapular feathers are blackish, with buff-white notches creating a spangled appearance; the wing-coverts are brownish-grey, with dark subterminal bars and buff-white fringes.
Confusion species Birds seen alone and out of habitat may superficially resemble several smaller calidrid species, like Red-necked and Little Stints (plate 35) or White-rumped and Baird's Sandpipers (plate 37). However, when size can be established the Sanderling is obviously larger and noticeably shorter winged than the sandpipers; close views will reveal the lack of a hind toe.

Red Knot
Calidris canutus   See also plate 74

Key ID features L 230–250mm. A bulky calidrid, with a shortish straight bill, distinctive red underparts when breeding, dull grey in winter.
Behaviour Feeds mainly by probing. Large roosting flocks pack tightly together.
Habitat Nests on moist tundra and at other times favours open mudflats.
Plumage: Breeding Chestnut-red face and underparts; heavily streaked crown; mantle feathers, scapulars and tertials are blackish-centred,

edged rufous and tipped pale grey; wing-coverts are grey, fringed paler. **Non-breeding** The upperpart feathers are pale grey, with fine dark shaft streaks and white fringes. Underparts are white, with a greyish suffusion and streaking on the breast sides; usually has indistinct chevrons on flanks. **Juvenile** The mantle feathers, scapulars and coverts have dark shaft streaks, narrow sub-terminal lines and white fringes, creating a neat, scaly appearance. The breast has a peachy-buff wash, with fine streaks, merging to chevrons on the flanks.
Racial variation In breeding plumage, the nominate is long-billed, with extensive deep chestnut underparts and chestnut scapulars; *rufa* has pale chestnut underparts and white from rear belly, with orangey-yellow scapulars; *islandica* is shorter-billed, has mid-chestnut underparts and yellowish scapulars. All these and other races show variability in colour and structure.
Confusion species Dowitchers (plate 20) in any plumage, until their long bills are seen. Curlew Sandpiper (plate 39) is similar in breeding plumage but Red Knot is larger and bulkier, with a short, straight bill. Also the larger Great Knot (compare Key ID features and Plumage descriptions).

Great Knot
Calidris tenuirostris   See also plate 74

Key ID features L 260–280mm. In breeding plumage, the black-spotted underparts are distinctive.
Behaviour Feeds mainly by probing. Often roosts in dense, mixed wader flocks.
Habitat Nests in montane tundra, favouring tidal mudflats at other times.
Plumage: Breeding The head and neck are grey, with blackish streaks; blacker on the crown; mantle feathers, coverts and tertials are blackish, with white fringes; the scapulars are rufous and black, with white fringes. Underparts are white, with bold black spots on the breast and flanks, forming an almost solid black breast. **Non-breeding** Upperparts are grey-brown, with broad dark feather shafts and pale fringes. Breast is spotted, with fine streaking extending onto flanks. **Juvenile** The upperparts are browner and darker, with whitish fringes to the mantle feathers; the scapulars and tertials have pale notches; and there are dark subterminal marks on some grey median and greater coverts. Underparts are white, with brown spots on breast extending to the flanks.
Confusion species In breeding plumage similar to Surfbird (plate 31), but the Great Knot has a longer bill and neck, and longer legs. Red Knot in non-breeding has more uniform grey upperparts.

Sanderling

non-br

br

juv

br to non-br

Red Knot

♂ br *rufa*

♂ br *canutus*

♂ br *islandica*

juv

non-br

br to non-br

Great Knot

br

non-br

juv

Plate 34 **SEMIPALMATED AND WESTERN SANDPIPERS**

Semipalmated Sandpiper
Calidris pusilla   See also plate 73

Key ID features L 130–150mm. A small calidrid, with short, straight, stubby bill, black legs and partially-webbed toes; the primary projection is short and the primary tips fall level with or just beyond the tail tip.

Behaviour Forms large flocks on migration. Feeds by picking, sometimes probing and at times in water, often with Western Sandpipers.

Habitat Nests on coastal and inland wet tundra, often near pools, lakes or rivers. In parts of Alaska nests in mixed colonies with Western. At other times frequents coastal mudflats and beaches, as well as wetlands away from the coast, particularly on migration.

Plumage: Breeding Crown is buffy-brown streaked dark brown; upperpart feathers blackish centred, fringed buff or pale chestnut; wing-coverts pale brownish-grey. Underparts white, with brown streaks on breast barely reaching flanks. **Non-breeding** Upperpart feathers fairly uniformly grey-brown, with fine dark shaft streaks and pale fringes. Underparts white, with fine diffused streaks on light grey breast sides. **Juvenile** Mantle feathers and upper scapulars blackish centred, fringed buff; mantle Vs faint or lacking; lower scapulars have grey bases, dark anchors, buff fringes and white tips; tertials and wing-coverts grey-brown, fringed buffish-white. Underparts white, breast sides initially washed buff, with fine diffused streaks on sides.

Confusion species The shorter, stubbier bill of this species can distinguish it from Western Sandpiper, which is almost identical in size and shape, but there is an overlap in bill lengths. Least Sandpiper (plate 36) is smaller, browner and has pale legs. Little Stint (plate 35) in non-breeding plumage is very similar, but the darker centres of the upperpart feathers create a more mottled rather than plain appearance. A bright juvenile Little Stint has extensive rufous fringes to the tertials and obvious white mantle and scapular lines. A non-breeding Red-necked Stint (plate 35) is also very similar. Note that identifying some stints will be virtually impossible.

Western Sandpiper
Calidris mauri   See also plate 73

Key ID features L 140–170mm. A small calidrid, with a variable medium-length bill (females longer), which is slightly decurved at the tip; the legs are black and the toes partially-webbed; the primary projection is short and the primary tips fall level with or just beyond the tail-tip.

Behaviour Runs around rapidly on mudflats, feeding by pecking; also probes more often than other short-billed stints. Feeds freely with Semipalmated Sandpipers and forms large flocks at roosts.

Habitat Nests on drier tundra with dwarf willow and other shrubs; at other times frequents coastal mudflats and beaches, but also visits inland wetlands on migration.

Plumage: Breeding Crown feathers are dark brown, fringed chestnut; ear-coverts rufous; mantle feathers blackish, narrowly fringed chestnut and buff; scapulars rufous, with black subterminal crescents, rufous fringes and white tips; wing-coverts and tertials grey-brown, with pale fringes, sometimes rufous on tertials. Underparts white, with heavy black streaks on breast and chevrons on flanks, sometimes extending to undertail-coverts. **Non-breeding** Upperpart feathers uniformly grey-brown, with fine dark shaft streaks and pale fringes; underparts white, with fine streaks on breast sides. **Juvenile** Mantle feathers blackish, fringed rufous, with white edges creating faint mantle Vs; upper scapulars blackish, fringed rufous; lower scapulars mainly grey, with dark shaft streaks and anchor-shaped subterminal margins, fringed buffy-white; wing-coverts pale grey, with buff fringes; tertials grey-brown with buff or rufous fringes. Underparts mainly white, with a faint buffy wash and fine streaks on the breast sides.

Confusion species The decurved bill tip makes Western look similar to Dunlin (plate 39) particularly in non-breeding plumage, but the small size should be apparent and the whiter underparts are diagnostic. Semipalmated Sandpiper is almost identical in non-breeding plumage, when the bill and calls are the best way to separate them. In breeding plumage the rufous-based scapulars and head markings are key features for Western and the rufous-fringed scapulars of juveniles are distinctive, though similar to those of the shorter-billed juvenile Little Stint (plate 35).

Semipalmated Sandpiper

br to non-br

br

non-br

juv

br to non-br

br

Western Sandpiper

♀ non-br

juv

Plate 35 DARK-LEGGED STINTS

There is considerable variation in the juvenile plumages of both these species, particularly in the intensity of the rufous colours. Some are very bright, while others are pale, lacking any warm tones.

Little Stint
Calidris minuta   See also plate 72

Key ID features L 120–140mm. A small, dark-legged calidrid with unwebbed toes. The summer plumage is particularly bright, with richly coloured upperparts, a buffy-orange-face and a white throat. The primary projection is short to medium.
Behaviour Feeds mainly with a rapid pecking action but sometimes probes.
Habitat Nests mainly on drier ground, often among dwarf willows, near swampy areas or coastal saltmarshes. On migration visits inland wetlands as well as coastal mudflats and lagoons.
Plumage: Breeding The split supercilium effect is usually obvious; the buffy-orange on the ear-coverts, sides of neck and breast is spotted or streaked brown; chin and throat are white. A white mantle V is prominent; the mantle feathers, scapulars, wing-coverts and tertials are blackish centred, with chestnut fringes and white tips when fresh. Underparts mainly white, with a variable amount of buffy-orange wash and fine streaks or chevrons on breast, more often confined to sides. **Non-breeding** Upperpart feather centres extensively dark, giving a less uniform effect. Underparts white, with a grey wash on the breast-sides; these are finely streaked and will occasionally form a complete breast-band. **Juvenile** Prominent whitish 'split' supercilium, accentuates darker crown; dark ear-coverts separate from eye; obvious white mantle and scapular Vs; mantle and upper scapular feathers otherwise blackish-centred, fringed chestnut; lower scapulars sharply fringed white, with solid blackish-centred tips; wing-coverts are dark brown centred with buff fringes and white tips; tertials blackish-brown, with sharply defined rufous fringes. The orange-buff wash on the underparts is usually restricted to the sides of breast, with a few dark streaks.
Confusion species Red-necked Stint is very similar. In breeding plumage compare lower scapulars, tertials and presence or absence of mantle V and split supercilium effect. For juveniles check patterns of head, scapulars, wing-coverts and tertials. Semipalmated Sandpipers (plate 34) are extremely similar in non-breeding plumage and to be 100% sure the presence or absence of webbing needs to be ascertained. Temminck's Stint (plate 36) may show a white breast-side peak.

Red-necked Stint
Calidris ruficollis   See also plate 72

Key ID features L 130–160mm. A small, dark-legged calidrid, distinctive in breeding plumage, looks attenuated with long wings and tail; has unwebbed toes and a medium to long primary projection.
Behaviour Feeds with an almost constant pecking action like a Little Stint, but sometimes probes.
Habitat Nests in drier areas of tundra at lower altitudes. Mainly coastal at other times but frequents inland wetlands on migration.
Plumage: Breeding The crown is chestnut, streaked brown; the split supercilium effect is faint or lacking; the forehead and chin are white; the extent of brick red on the head is variable; on well marked individuals the brick-red is extensive, including the throat, as well as the ear-coverts, sides of neck and upper breast; small dark arrow-heads sometimes form a complete necklace of streaks below the brick-red throat and upper-breast. Mantle and scapular feathers are rufous and black, tipped white; the mantle V is faint or lacking; wing-coverts and tertials are predominantly grey, fringed white; some are darker centred, with rufous fringes. **Non-breeding** Obvious white supercilium and dark lores; scapulars usually with narrow shaft-streaks. **Juvenile** The crown is uniformly streaked; supercilium is dull, often broken in front of the eye; dusky ear-coverts reach eye; mantle and scapular Vs faint or lacking; mantle and upper scapular feathers blackish-centred with rufous fringes; lower scapulars extensively greyish, typically with drop-shaped dark centres and white tips; wing-coverts plain and grey, with dark shaft streaks and pale buffish-white fringes; tertials grey-brown, with mainly buffish-white fringes, some more rufous. Breast-side streaking is faint grey-brown on a buffish-grey wash, which sometimes extends across the whole breast.
Confusion species Sanderling (plate 33) may seem an unlikely inclusion, but when size cannot be ascertained the breeding plumages are surprisingly similar. Note that Sanderling shows dark streaks on facial orange. Also Little Stint (compare Key ID features and Plumage descriptions). In some plumages both Semipalmated and Western Sandpipers (plate 34) are so similar that, to be entirely sure, the presence or absence of webbing between the toes needs to be seen. In parts of Asia, a stint with mud oozing out of the sides of the bill may fleetingly resemble the much rarer Spoon-billed Sandpiper.

Little Stint

br to non-br

br

non-br

juv

Red-necked Stint

br to non-br

br

non-br

juv

Plate 36 PALE-LEGGED STINTS

Temminck's Stint

Calidris temminckii   See also plate 72

Key ID features L 130-150mm. A plain stint, with a mottled grey-brown breast, a long tail that usually projects beyond the wing-tips, a short primary projection and short greenish legs.
Behaviour Often feeds alone, moving deliberately and keeping head low while picking for prey.
Habitat Nests in shrub and forest tundra, often on ground clear of vegetation. On migration favours freshwater wetlands.
Plumage: Breeding Upperparts often variegated, with a mixture of grey winter-type and summer feathers, which are blackish-centred, with pale chestnut fringes and off-white tips. Sides of neck and breast mottled buff and grey-brown, with darker streaks; rest of underparts white.
Non-breeding Upperpart feathers fairly uniform dark grey-brown, with paler fringes and some dark shaft streaks. The breast is dusky and unstreaked. **Juvenile** Upperpart feathers are a warm dull brown, with dark subterminal lines and narrow buff fringes, producing a scaly appearance.
Confusion species Pale-legged Least Sandpiper and Long-toed Stint are similar, but the juvenile upperparts of Temminck's are diagnostic, as is the more uniform greyish-brown breast in all plumages. Reminiscent of Common and Spotted Sandpipers (plate 30) in non-breeding plumage, often showing a white peak between carpal joint and breast side, but is smaller.

Least Sandpiper

Calidris minutilla   See also plate 73

Key ID features L 130-150mm. Marginally, the smallest wader in the world, with a short, slightly decurved fine-tipped bill. Short dull brownish to bright yellowish legs, often bent to produce a hunched crouching stance. No primary projection.
Behaviour Marginally more gregarious than the Long-toed Stint.
Habitat Nests on wet, well-vegetated and hummocky tundra. At other times feeds on open mud, but also attracted to fringes of inland freshwater lakes and ponds, feeding among vegetation.
Plumage: Breeding Split supercilium is usually indistinct or absent; dark lores reach the bill base, but dark crown stops short of the bill, creating a white forehead; scapulars and tertials are blackish-centred, narrowly fringed rufous and tipped grey; the tertials almost completely overlap the primary tips. **Non-breeding** Scapulars show dark brown shaft streaks, fading towards pale grey-brown fringes. Underparts are white, with a grey-brown wash across the breast streaked diffusely. **Juvenile**

Supercilia whitish, often meeting above the bill; split supercilium is faint or lacking; the solidly dark ear-coverts meet the eye, giving a subtle masked effect. Whitish mantle fringes may form clear mantle Vs; scapulars and tertials are fringed rufous and white; the grey-brown coverts are fringed buff-white. Breast washed buff, with brown streaks often forming a distinct band.
Confusion species Long-toed Stint, but a combination of subtle structural and plumage differences, particularly in relation to the head patterns, should separate the two. Temminck's Stint (see Key ID features). Least Sandpiper is generally browner in all plumages than the larger Semipalmated and Western Sandpipers (plate 34) that have dark legs. Similar in juvenile plumages to Pectoral Sandpiper (plate 38) but much smaller and shorter winged.

Long-toed Stint

Calidris subminuta   See also plate 73

Key ID features L 130–150mm. Long yellowish legs and long neck, when standing upright, are distinctive. Dark loral line connects with dark forehead at base of bill; black bill has pale base to lower mandible; central toe is always longer than the bill; and there is no primary projection.
Behaviour Feeds singly or in small mixed flocks, often by vegetation close to water's edge, or on floating weed. When alarmed, stretches neck like a miniature Ruff or Sharp-tailed Sandpiper.
Habitat Nests in boggy clearings among mosses, sedges and dwarf willows. Outside breeding season favours wetlands, but may visit mudflats.
Plumage: Breeding Prominent split supercilium; the narrow brown loral lines meet the forehead streaks at the base of the bill; the ear-coverts are rusty; the tertials and scapulars are blackish-centred, with broad rufous fringes and white tips. **Non-breeding** Has contrasting upperparts, the dark-centred feathers are fringed pale grey-brown. Underparts are white, with a grey-brown wash across the brown streaked breast.
Juvenile Supercilia whitish, broader and bulbous in front of eye, usually clearly split, but not meeting on the forehead; dark lores formed by two spots barely meeting in centre; dark grey of ear-coverts separate from eye. Whitish mantle fringes form distinct mantle Vs; obvious white fringes to dark wing-coverts; tertials fringed rufous, with white tips. Breast washed grey-buff, streaks often absent from centre.
Confusion species Least Sandpiper: in non-breeding plumages compare breast and scapular patterns; in juvenile plumages compare lores and ear-coverts; also wing-coverts and breast patterns and colour. Juveniles reminiscent of Sharp-tailed Sandpiper (plate 38), which is far larger.

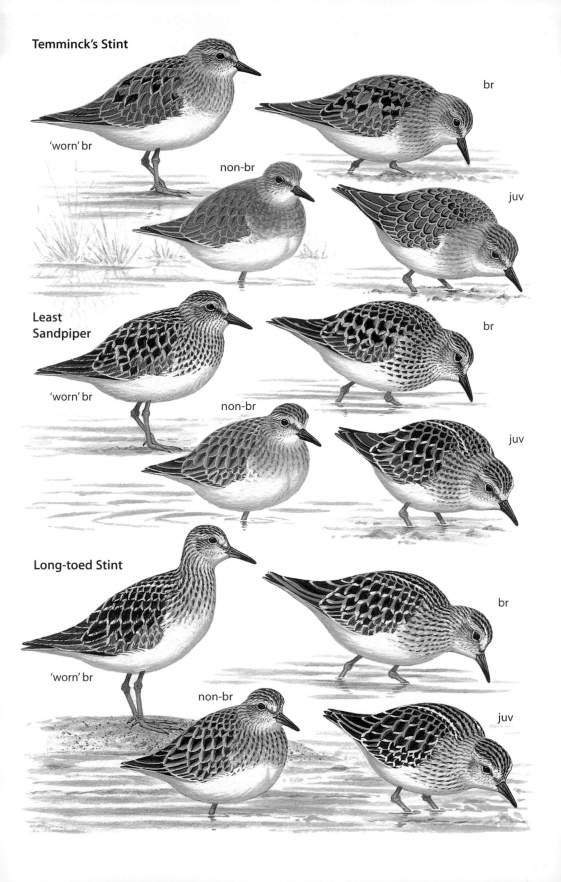

Temminck's Stint

'worn' br

non-br

br

juv

Least Sandpiper

'worn' br

non-br

br

juv

Long-toed Stint

'worn' br

non-br

br

juv

Plate 37 **WHITE-RUMPED AND BAIRD'S SANDPIPERS**

White-rumped Sandpiper
Calidris fuscicollis   See also plate 74

Key ID features L 150–180mm. A smallish calidrid, with long wings extending well beyond the tail-tip; has a distinct whitish supercilium; the pinkish-brown base to the lower mandible is diagnostic, if visible; the narrow eye-ring is usually broken in front of the eye.

Behaviour Often wades in shallow water when feeding by probing into soft mud. Unlike Baird's, male White-rumped Sandpipers leave the nesting grounds once egg-laying is complete.

Habitat Nests on wet, hummocky and well-vegetated tundra, usually near the coast. On migration favours wetter areas than Baird's, both inland and coastal, including intertidal mudflats, marshes and flooded fields.

Plumage: **Breeding** The dull chestnut cap is streaked dark brown; has a long whitish supercilium; the mantle feathers, scapulars and tertials are blackish-brown, fringed chestnut, grey and buff; the wing-coverts are grey-brown with whitish fringes. The underparts are white, with blackish streaks on the neck and breast, becoming chevrons on the flanks. **Non-breeding** Upperpart feathers are a uniform brownish-grey, with dark shaft streaks and pale fringes. Underparts are white, with a greyish wash and fine streaks on both breast and flanks. **Juvenile** A bright chestnut cap contrasts with a pale greyish hindneck; has a long white supercilium; ear-coverts often chestnut; the mantle and upper scapular feathers are blackish, brightly fringed chestnut, buff and white; the white on the edges of the mantle and upper scapular feathers forms characteristic Vs; the lower scapulars and wing-coverts are dark grey, with black subterminal marks and white fringes; the tertials are blackish, fringed chestnut-buff and tipped white. Underparts are white; the sides of the neck and breast are washed buffish-grey, with fine brown streaking.

Confusion species The breeding and juvenile plumages are much brighter than for Baird's Sandpiper. The attenuated appearance separates these two species from the smaller stints and most of the larger calidrids. The Western Sandpiper (plate 34) has a similar range of plumages but White-rumped is larger and has a relatively shorter bill with pinkish-brown base. Separation from Baird's Sandpiper follows.

Baird's Sandpiper
Calidris bairdii   See also plate 75

Key ID features L 140–170mm. A smallish calidrid, with long wings extending well beyond the tail-tip; has a fairly uniform buffish head and, with close views, a complete narrow white eye-ring should be visible; upperparts of juveniles appear scaly.

Behaviour Usually forages amongst dry vegetation, picking up prey with quick jabs of the bill. Less gregarious than other calidrids, and more often seen singly or in small groups. Both parents share incubation duties, unlike White-rumped Sandpiper.

Habitat Nests on dry, high-lying lichen tundra and on stony ridges. Primarily an inland species, frequenting lakeshores, or drier margins of wetlands, or grasslands, often far from water.

Plumage: **Breeding** The crown is buffish-brown, streaked darker; supercilium is pale buff; the mantle and scapular feathers are blackish, fringed buff; the coverts and tertials are greyish-brown, with pale fringes. Underparts are white, with foreneck and breast washed buff and finely streaked brown. **Non-breeding** Upperpart feathers are a dull grey-brown, with dark shaft streaks and pale fringes. The underparts are white, with a buffish wash on the breast, which is finely streaked brown. **Juvenile** The supercilium is less distinct than in breeding plumage; upperpart feathers are brown, with darker subterminal marks and white or buff fringes, which produce a neat, warm, scaly appearance. The neck and breast are washed buff and distinctly streaked brown, creating an obvious pectoral band.

Confusion species The bill of the White-rumped Sandpiper is very slightly decurved throughout its length, with the tip slightly swollen and the base of the lower mandible tinged pinkish-brown, which is noticeably different from the straight, all-black bill with finer tip of Baird's. The mantle Vs of White-rumped are absent from Baird's Sandpiper, as are the streaks on the flanks. A juvenile Baird's, with its pectoral band of heavy streaking on buff, shows some resemblance to juvenile Pectoral Sandpipers (plate 38) but for the dark legs and scaly upperparts. Juvenile Semipalmated Sandpipers (plate 34) have similar upperparts but lack the long wings.

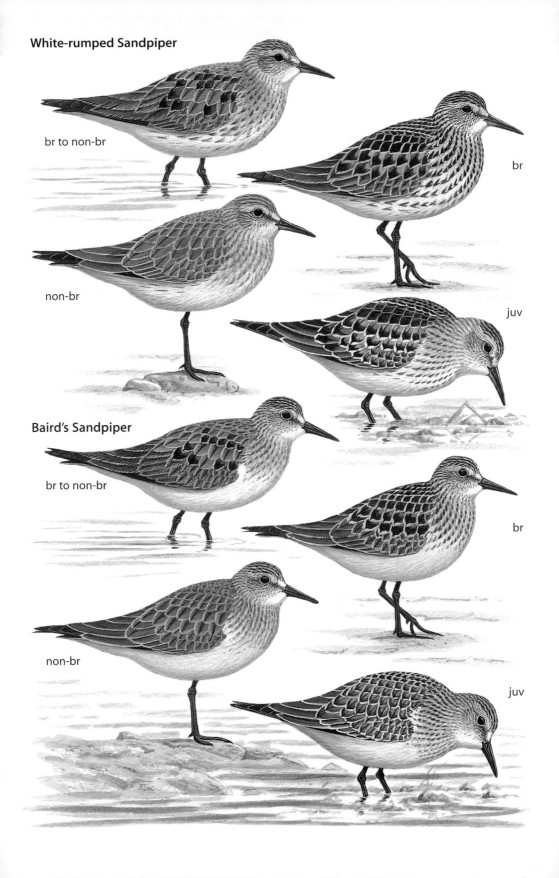

White-rumped Sandpiper

br to non-br

non-br

br

juv

Baird's Sandpiper

br to non-br

br

non-br

juv

Plate 38 PECTORAL, SHARP-TAILED AND BUFF-BREASTED SANDPIPERS

Pectoral Sandpiper
Calidris melanotos　　　　　See also plate 75

Key ID features L 190–230mm. The heavily streaked breast contrasts abruptly with a white belly; bill is shortish and slightly decurved; legs are usually yellowish.

Behaviour Feeds in fresh and salt marshes but often in drier vegetation, walking steadily as it picks and makes shallow probes. Males, which are larger, have a remarkable display, inflating a sac under the breast feathers to show off the heavily streaked chest.

Habitat Nests in drier well-vegetated areas close to wet tundra. At other times frequents wet grass-lands and freshwater margins, but also occurs on the coast.

Plumage: Breeding The dull chestnut crown is streaked dark brown; upperpart feathers are black-ish-brown, fringed variably with chestnut, brown and buffish-white; the white on some outer man-tle and upper scapulars form Vs. Neck and breast washed buff, with dark streaks forming a pectoral band; on the displaying male the breast can look almost blackish, mottled white; rest of the under-parts are white, with a few streaks on the flanks. **Non-breeding** As breeding but plainer and duller, lacking chestnut tones. **Juvenile** Similar to breeding but supercilium more distinct and often split; upperpart feathers more brightly fringed chestnut, buff and white; the white forming more distinct Vs.

Confusion species The essential differences sep-arating Sharp-tailed Sandpiper concern the head patterns and underparts. The female Ruff (plate 41) can look similar, but lacks breast streaks.

Sharp-tailed Sandpiper
Calidris acuminata　　　　　See also plate 75

Key ID features L 170–210mm. Capped app-earance is distinctive; adult underparts are heavily marked with spots and chevrons; bill shortish, slightly decurved; legs usually greenish-grey.

Behaviour Feeds as Pectoral Sandpiper, above, often amongst vegetation.

Habitat Nests in damp tundra, with drier shrub-covered hummocks. At other times, favours coastal habitats more than Pectoral, but also frequents wet grasslands.

Plumage: Breeding Crown rich chestnut, with dark streaks, contrasting with white, streaked supercilium; dark lores and chestnut ear-coverts; upperpart feathers blackish-brown, fringed dull chestnut and buffish-white; the white on some outer mantle and upper scapulars form ill-defined

Vs. Underparts are white, with a buffish wash to the sides of the neck and breast; bold spots become chevrons on the lower breast and flanks; undertail-coverts streaked brown. **Non-breeding** Similar to breeding but cap duller; ear-coverts and upperparts duller and greyer. Neck and breast washed greyish with fine streaking usually restricted to sides of breast. **Juvenile** Cap bright rufous, contrasting with long white super-cilium, and with fine streaks; dull chestnut lores and orange-buff ear-coverts; upperpart feathers blackish-brown brightly fringed chestnut and white, forming variable white Vs on mantle and scapulars. Breast and sides of neck washed orange-buff, finely streaked below the throat, more prominent at the sides of the breast.

Confusion species Juvenile Pectoral Sandpipers have streaked breasts and lack the more obvious capped effect of Sharp-tailed. Long-toed Stint (plate 36) is similar in juvenile and non-breeding plumages but much smaller.

Buff-breasted Sandpiper
Tryngites subruficollis　　　　　See also plate 75

Key ID features L 180–200mm. A short-billed sandpiper, with yellow legs and an obvious dark eye surrounded by a distinctive buff colour, which extends to the underparts.

Behaviour Foraging movements are dainty, as they bob their heads and lift their feet, while picking for insects. On 'leks' the males perform spectacular 'wing-flashing' displays.

Habitat Nests on drier ridges in moist grassy tundra. On migration favours short-grass plains, airfields and golf courses, occasionally visits high-tide lines on beaches.

Plumage: Breeding The crown and sides of the breast are buff with dark spots; upperpart feathers are blackish-brown, with buff fringes. The under-part buff feathers have pale fringes creating a mottled appearance. **Non-breeding** Virtually identical to breeding but with broader, warmer buff fringes to the upperpart feathers. **Juvenile** Upperpart feathers have white fringes, black shafts and subterminal bars, giving a more scaly appearance. The buff underparts are paler and less extensive; the lower belly and undertail-coverts are white.

Confusion species Upland Sandpiper (plate 23) is larger and longer-necked. Pectoral Sandpiper has a streaked breast. Neither has buff under-parts. The juvenile Ruff (plate 41) is similar but has a totally different jizz – smaller head, with a longer bill and neck; also buff restricted to breast.

Pectoral Sandpiper

♂ br

juv

♀ br

non-br

Sharp-tailed Sandpiper

juv

br

non-br

juv

Buff-breasted Sandpiper

br

br to non-br

Plate 39 **DUNLIN AND CURLEW SANDPIPER**

Dunlin
Calidris alpina   See also plate 76

Key ID features L 160–220mm. A small calidrid with a medium length, slightly decurved black bill and black legs; has a distinctive black belly patch when breeding. The primary projection is short and the folded primary tips align closely with the tail-tip.

Behaviour Feeds by rapidly picking and probing in soft mud, commonly wading in shallow water.

Habitat Breeds in a wide variety of habitats from wet coastal grasslands to upland moorland and high-arctic tundra. At other times favours muddy estuaries but also occurs on inland wetlands.

Plumage: Breeding Finely streaked chestnut and brown crown; whitish supercilium; dusky lores; streaked cheeks and ear coverts; the mantle feathers and scapulars are rufous, with black centres and subterminal markings, fringed whitish or grey; the wing-coverts and tertials are grey-brown, with paler fringes. The neck and breast are white, with blackish streaks; the belly is black, with the flanks, vent and undertail-coverts white. **Non-breeding** The upperpart feathers are a pale grey-brown, with whitish fringes. Neck and breast are also pale grey-brown, with fine streaks; rest of the underparts are white. **Juvenile** Mantle feathers, scapulars and tertials are dark brown-centred, with mainly buff or rufous fringes; whitish mantle edges may form Vs; the wing-coverts are grey-brown, fringed warm buff. Neck and upper breast feathers buffy-brown with dark streaks; belly and flanks black spotted; undertail-coverts white.

Racial variation The nominate race *alpina* and *sakhalina* (not illustrated) are intermediate in size; in breeding plumage the former has rusty-red upperpart fringes; *pacifica* and *hudsonia* (not illustrated), the largest and longest billed, also have the richest red upperparts; the breast streaks on the former tend to stop short of the black belly and on the latter they meet; *arctica* and *schinzii* are the smallest and shortest billed; the latter has orange-red fringes, and the former pale buffy-orange fringes; in winter plumage *hudsonia* has darker grey upperparts and striped flanks.

Confusion species Rock Sandpiper (plate 40) in summer plumage has a smaller black patch that does not reach the legs. The grey-brown non-breeding plumage and black legs can cause confusion with several calidrid species: Curlew Sandpiper is more elegant and longer-legged, with a cleaner white supercilium, a longer, more evenly decurved bill, a longer primary projection, with primaries projecting beyond tail-tip; Broad-billed Sandpiper (plate 40) is smaller and shorter-legged, with a distinctive double supercilium, and broader white fringes produce paler upperparts, with dark centred scapulars, when breeding; both White-rumped and Baird's Sandpipers (plate 37) have shorter, straight bills and longer primaries that project well beyond the tail-tip; and Western Sandpiper (plate 34) is smaller and usually shorter-billed.

Curlew Sandpiper
Calidris ferruginea   See also plate 74

Key ID features L 180–230mm. An elegant calidrid, with a longish neck, long gently decurved bill and medium-length black legs; the chestnut-red breeding plumage is most distinctive.

Behaviour A gregarious species, mixing with other waders while roosting and feeding; it often wades into deeper water, separating it from the likes of Dunlin.

Habitat Breeds in high-arctic coastal tundra. At other times frequents inland and coastal wetlands, including intertidal mudflats.

Plumage: Breeding Dark-streaked chestnut crown; mantle feathers and scapulars dark brown and chestnut, with pale grey fringes; wing-coverts may be a mix of winter and summer feathers, the former grey-brown, fringed whitish, the latter as the scapulars; the dark brown tertials are fringed rufous and white. Face, neck and underparts are a rich chestnut-red, with narrow white fringes in fresh plumage; undertail-coverts white. **Non-breeding** Long white supercilium contrasts with dark eye-line and lores; grey-streaked crown; upperpart feathers grey-brown with dark shaft streaks, evenly fringed whitish. Underparts are white, with the sides of the breast suffused grey and lightly streaked grey-brown. **Juvenile** The upperpart feathers are a warm grey-brown, with dark subterminal bars and neat buff fringes, creating a scaly appearance. Underparts are white, with neck and breast washed peachy-buff and finely streaked.

Confusion species Dunlin (see Confusion species for Dunlin above). The chestnut-red breeding plumage is similar to that of Red Knot (plate 33) but that species has bulky rather than elegant proportions, with paler, shorter legs and a short bill.

Dunlin

♂ br *pacifica*

♂ br *arctica*

♂ br *schinzii*

juv to 1st-w

♂ br *alpina*

♀ br *alpina*

non-br

juv

Curlew Sandpiper

'fresh' br

br

non-br to br

non-br

juv

Plate 40 BROAD-BILLED, ROCK AND PURPLE SANDPIPERS

Broad-billed Sandpiper
Limicola falcinellus   See also Plate 76

Key ID features L 160–180mm. Stint-like, with a long bill having a decurved tip. Generally dark above, in worn summer and juvenile plumages, with prominent mantle V and distinct split supercilium.

Behaviour Feeds by probing vertically with its long bill, usually more slowly than other calidrids.

Habitat Breeds in montane and lowland wet bogs. At other times favours coastal wetlands, occurring at inland wetlands on migration.

Plumage: Breeding Mantle feathers, scapulars and tertials blackish-brown, fringed white and rufous; white edges to the mantle and upper scapulars form characteristic Vs. **Non-breeding** Split supercilium less obvious; upperpart feathers generally pale grey, with dark shaft streaks, fringed white; lesser coverts darker. **Juvenile** Similar to breeding but upperpart feathers fringed brighter rufous, with white fringes to lower scapulars. Underparts white, with fine streaking on buff breast rarely extending to flanks.

Racial variation In breeding plumage *sibirica* (not illustrated) shows more rufous fringes to upperparts, a cinnamon wash to the breast, and less obvious split supercilium. Juvenile *sibirica* shows broader buff fringes.

Confusion species In worn breeding plumage the dark upperparts are superficially similar to Jack Snipe (plate 19). This dark coloration usually differentiates similar-sized calidrids. Similar in winter to other calidrids but the unique bill-shape separates it from larger Dunlin (plate 39) and smaller stints.

Rock Sandpiper
Calidris ptilocnemis   See also plate 76

Key ID features L 200–230mm. A cryptically plumaged, rock-loving, dumpy wader, with short slightly decurved bill, yellowish at base, and short dull yellow legs.

Behaviour Forages among rocks and captures prey by picking. Commonly roosts with Black Turnstones and Surfbirds. The nominate race habitually probes on the sandy Pribilof beaches.

Habitat Breeds on upland tundra. Away from its breeding grounds frequents rocky coasts.

Plumage: Breeding Mantle and scapular feathers fringed a deep, rich chestnut and buff. Upper breast washed buffish and variably streaked; lower breast has large brownish-black spots, fusing to form blackish patch. **Non-breeding** Very similar to Purple Sandpiper, though nominate race is paler. **Juvenile** Underparts white; foreneck and breast with buffish wash and fine brown streaking; flanks with few streaks.

Racial variation In breeding plumage, the nominate race is the largest and palest, with broad, buff fringes to the mantle feathers and scapulars. Rufous fringes are broad on *tschuktschorum*, narrow on *couesi*. Black lower-breast patch and ear patch are both comparatively obscure on *couesi*. In non-breeding plumage *couesi* is darker, with more boldly marked underparts and in juvenile plumage has brighter rufous upperparts and crown, as well as more boldly marked underparts.

Confusion species Purple Sandpiper: these two species are often considered conspecific. However, nominate race *ptilocnemis* is distinctly larger and paler. Breeding Dunlin (plate 39) is similar, with the black patch on the belly rather than on the lower breast.

Purple Sandpiper
Calidris maritima   See also plate 76

Key ID features L 200–220mm. A cryptically plumaged, dumpy wader, with short dull yellow-orange legs and a usually yellowish-orange basal third to the slightly decurved bill.

Behaviour Usually confiding. Feeds rapidly by picking for invertebrates exposed as waves recede.

Habitat Nests among lichen-covered tundra, both coastal and mountain. In winter quarters often frequents groynes and breakwaters, as well as rocky coastlines.

Plumage: Breeding Crown is dull chestnut, streaked dark brown; nape greyer; mantle feathers and scapulars blackish-brown, with chestnut and whitish fringes. Coverts and tertials duller, fringed whitish. Underparts white, with dark brown streaks and spots on throat, neck and breast, extending onto flanks. **Non-breeding** Head, neck and upperparts dark slate-grey, with faint purplish sheen to mantle and scapulars; coverts fringed greyish-white. Breast slate-grey, flanks blotchy grey-brown. **Juvenile** Similar to breeding, but mantle feathers and scapulars are smaller and neater, fringed chestnut, buff and white. Underparts white; foreneck and breast with brownish-grey wash and finer streaking extending onto flanks.

Confusion species Very similar to Rock Sandpiper in non-breeding and juvenile plumages, with some races almost indistinguishable.

Broad-billed Sandpiper

'worn' br

'fresh' br

juv

non-br

Rock Sandpiper

br couesi

br tschuktschorum

br ptilocnemis

non-br couesi

juv couesi

non-br ptilocnemis

juv ptilocnemis

br

Purple Sandpiper

juv

non-br

Plate 41 **STILT SANDPIPER AND RUFF**

Stilt Sandpiper
Calidris himantopus   See also plate 74

Key ID features   L 180–230mm. A tallish
calidrid, with long greenish legs and slightly
droopy bill. Unmistakable in breeding plumage,
with the heavily barred underparts.
Behaviour   Often wades into deep water and
feeds, dowitcher-like, probing vertically with a
rapid stitching action – unique for a calidrid.
Habitat   Nests in open, dry tundra, north of the
tree-line. At other times favours inland waters and
coastal pools.
Plumage: Breeding   The brown and rufous
crown contrasts with the long white supercilium;
the ear-coverts are also rufous; the mantle and
scapular feathers are blackish, edged white; the
brown tertials are narrowly fringed whitish; the
wing-coverts are a variable mixture of blackish,
white and rufous-fringed summer feathers
and grey-brown, pale-fringed winter plumage
feathers. The neck and upper breast are whitish,
heavily streaked brown; the rest of the underparts
are heavily barred dark brown.   **Non-breeding**
The white supercilium contrasts with the grey
crown and dark eye-stripe; upperpart feathers are
grey, with narrow pale fringes. Underparts are
white, with fine grey streaks. **Juvenile** The brown
crown is streaked buffish-white; upperpart feathers
are darker towards the tips, with pale fringes; some
upper scapulars and tertials are fringed rufous;
white mantle lines are often conspicuous. The
neck and breast are washed buff, with fine streaks
extending onto flanks.
Confusion species   In non-breeding plumage,
distinguished from long-billed Dunlins (plate 39)
by behaviour, posture and long pale legs. The scaly
juvenile upperparts are similar to several calidrids
like White-rumped and Western Sandpipers (plates
37 & 34), which are comparatively short-legged,
and the long pale legs will also separate this species
from Curlew Sandpiper (plate 39).

Ruff
Philomachus pugnax   See also plate 75

Key ID features   L male 260–320mm, female
200–250mm. A variable-sized wader, with a
distinctive jizz of a smallish head on a long neck
and rather deep-bellied and hump-backed body;
the pale lores are also distinctive.
Behaviour   Feeds mainly by picking and may
wade quite deeply and submerge its head. Males
perform communal displays at a 'lek', where they
greet approaching females with a wing-fluttering
ceremony.
Habitat   Nests in low, freshwater marsh and wet
grasslands. Frequents a variety of habitats at other
times, including ploughed fields, rice-paddies and
coastal pools.
Plumage: Breeding male   Ear tufts and ruff are
highly variable in colour and markings; the upperparts are also highly variable. The underparts
are white, but often with extensive chestnut
or black on the breast and flanks.   **Breeding
female**   Considerable variation occurs; at one
extreme individuals are black crowned, with
many black-centred upperpart feathers fringed
whitish, and at the other a light cinnamon-brown
crown and cinnamon upperpart feathers, with
black subterminal bars and pale fringes. The
breast and flanks are fairly prominently mottled
blackish-brown.   **Non-breeding**   Head is grey
streaked greyish-brown, often with a white forehead. Occasionally males show extensive white
feathers on head and neck, some individuals being
totally white, including the neck. Upperpart
feathers are greyish-brown with dark centres
and white or buff fringes. Underparts whitish,
with greyish mottling on breast and flanks.
Juvenile   The upperpart feathers are blackish-
brown, neatly fringed chestnut-buff and white.
Head, neck and breast feathers are washed with
variable buff tones; the rest of the underparts
are white.
Confusion species   In non-breeding plumage
Ruff resemble Redshanks (plate 26) in bare-part
colours and superficially in plumage and shape,
until they fly. Redshanks are longer-billed,
browner and lack the dark feather centres on
the upperparts. Buff-breasted Sandpiper (plate 38)
has similar-looking scaly upperparts, with more
extensive buff underparts and a different jizz:
more round-headed and short-necked. Although
the Pectoral Sandpiper (plate 38) may look rather
long-necked at times, its breast is streaked, creating
a pectoral band.

Stilt Sandpiper

non-br

br

br to non-br

juv

Ruff

♂ ♂ br at lek

♀ br

♂ br to non-br

♀ juv

♂ non-br

♂ juv

Plate 42 **PHALAROPES**

Two of the three phalaropes could be referred to as seabirds, as they spend over half their lives at sea, often well out of sight of land. All three species are unusual in being sexually dimorphic; the females are the more colourful and take the lead in courtship, while the males take responsibility for all of the parental duties.

Red-necked Phalarope
Phalaropus lobatus   See also plate 77

Key ID features L 180–190mm. A small-headed, long-necked, dainty wader with a needle-thin bill; this species spends much of its time swimming.
Behaviour Feeds while swimming by spinning in circles and picking insects it disturbs from the water's surface. Can be exceptionally tame.
Habitat Nests by freshwater lakes and pools with marshy margins. On migration occurs in a wide variety of usually freshwater, wetland habitats. Winters in large flocks at sea.
Plumage: Breeding female Dark grey head and face, with a small white spot above the eye; the chestnut sides and front of the neck contrast with the white throat and surrounding grey. Upperparts dark grey, with buff edges to mantle and scapular feathers forming bold stripes. **Breeding male** Plumage subdued, with patchy white supercilium joining pale chestnut neck-patch. **Non-breeding** Grey and white, with black patch mainly behind the eye; white fringes to edges of mantle and upper scapular feathers form distinct stripes on the back; rest of upperpart feathers are also fringed white. **Juvenile** Dark brown eye-patch; crown and hindneck streaked dark brown; upperpart feathers dark brown, with warm buff fringes, which form stripes on mantle.
Confusion species Grey Phalarope is bulkier, non-breeding birds have plain pale grey mantles; and shorter, thicker and broader black bills, with a small area of pinkish-yellow at the base. Wilson's Phalarope is larger and longer-legged, with a longer thin bill and lacks the dark ear-coverts in its non-breeding and juvenile plumages.

Grey (Red) Phalarope
Phalaropus fulicarius   See also plate 77

Key ID features L 200–220mm. A more bulky phalarope species, with a most distinctive chestnut breeding plumage and a shortish thick blunt-tipped bill.
Behaviour The most pelagic of the phalaropes. Winter gales sometimes force this species inland onto reservoirs or lakes.
Habitat Nests near the coast on marshy tundra

with small pools and boggy meadows; spends the winter at sea.
Plumage: Breeding female The uniform black crown contrasts with the white sides of head; the upperpart feathers are blackish-brown, with rich buffy-white stripes formed by the broad fringes to the mantle and scapular feathers. **Breeding male** Variable but generally duller, lacking contrast, with a brown and buff streaked crown. **Non-breeding** Dark eye-patch, variable amount of blackish-grey on crown and nape; upperparts almost uniform pale grey. **Juvenile** Rich dark brown upperparts, broadly fringed warm buff. Underparts white, with peachy sides to breast, initially.
Confusion species Red-necked Phalarope in non-breeding plumage has distinct white lines along edges of mantle and scapulars. The thick bill distinguishes Grey from Wilson's.

Wilson's Phalarope
Phalaropus tricolor   See also plate 77

Key ID features L 220–240mm. The largest phalarope, elegant, with a long thin black bill and long black legs when breeding. Legs are yellow in non-breeding birds.
Behaviour Like the other phalaropes, forages while swimming, but also while wading in shallow water or along the shore. May gather in large numbers during migration. Often most confiding.
Habitat Breeds around small freshwater marshes on grassy plains. On migration, found on a wide variety of freshwater lakes, ponds and small pools, showing a preference for saline waters, but rarely seen on the coast.
Plumage: Breeding female A narrow black band on the lores broadens behind the eye and becomes maroon on the neck, spreading onto breast sides and along the edge of the mantle, with another stripe across the lower scapulars; mantle and upper scapulars pale slate-grey. **Breeding male** Similar to female but variable, usually duller, with browns rather than greys and a dark grey crown. **Non-breeding** Crown, hindneck and upperparts pale grey; long white supercilium and grey stripe behind eye extend down the neck. **Juvenile** Dark brown upperpart feathers, with pale buff or white fringes of variable width create a scalloped effect.
Confusion species In non-breeding plumage similar to Lesser Yellowlegs (plate 28) but lacks spots on the upperparts and also to Marsh Sandpiper (plate 27), which has long greenish legs. In the same plumage, is also similar to the other phalaropes, but is larger, longer-billed, has long yellow legs and lacks the bold black eye-patch.

♂ br

Red-necked Phalarope

juv

non-br

♀ br

1st-w

Grey Phalarope

♂ br

♀ br

1st-w

juv

non-br

♂ br

Wilson's Phalarope

1st-w

♀ br

non-br

juv

Plate 43 **NORTH AMERICAN RARITIES**

Collared Plover
Charadrius collaris   See also plate 56

Key ID features L 140–150mm. A very small delicate plover, with relatively long pinkish–yellow legs and dark grey–brown upperparts; lacks a white hind-collar and has a slender dark bill.
Behaviour Outside the breeding season usually seen well scattered, or in pairs, but may form loose flocks. Feeds, like many plovers, by picking in between short sprints. When disturbed will often run rather than fly. Performs a ground display when the male fluffs his breast feathers and chases the female.
Habitat Nests on sandy beaches. At other times may be found in a variety of wetland habitats, including sandy beaches, estuarine mud and banks of rivers.
Plumage: Adult Broad black frontal-bar and black lores, surround a white forehead; short, white rear supercilium; pale chestnut wash on crown, hind-neck and ear-coverts. Underparts white, with narrow black breast-band. **Juvenile** Lacks black of adults; initially, has an incomplete breast-band, with just small patches at sides of breast. Upperpart feathers are neatly fringed warm buff.
Confusion species Similar to 'Snowy Plover' (plate 13) in proportions, slightly smaller and easily distinguished by paler legs and darker grey-brown upperparts; adults also have complete breast-bands. Shares some features of Semipalmated Plover (plate 11), which is larger with a white neck-collar, never shows chestnut on the crown, and has a shorter, thicker bill, with an orange base in breeding plumage.

Northern Jacana
Jacana spinosa   See also plate 46

Key ID features L 170–230mm. One of just two New World jacanas, with a three-lobed yellow frontal shield and blue at bill-base, exceptionally long toes and nails, and dark, richly coloured adult plumage.
Behaviour Highly developed polyandry and sex-role reversal, with females laying eggs for up to four males. Frequently walks on large water-lily leaves when foraging.
Habitat Freshwater marshes and ponds with floating vegetation.
Plumage: Adult Head, neck and breast black, glossed bottle-green; rest of upperparts chestnut-brown; rest of underparts chestnut-maroon.

Juvenile Dark brownish cap and nape; distinctive long whitish supercilium; blackish eye-line extends to join blackish hind-neck; upperparts dull brown, glossed green. Underparts off-white, with buffy wash on breast.
Confusion species The extralimital Wattled Jacana of Central and South America has a red frontal shield. Distant juvenile Northern Jacana may appear plover-like.

Eskimo Curlew
Numenius borealis   See also plate 64

Key ID features L 290–340mm. A medium-sized curlew, with indistinct pale crown-stripe and cinnamon-buff underparts; folded wing-tips project well beyond tail-tip.
Habitat Formerly favoured prairies and short-grass habitats on migration.
Plumage: Adult Dark brown head-stripes and buffy supercilium. **Juvenile** Scapulars and tertials narrowly fringed buff. Underparts often more buffish than adults.
Confusion species Little Curlew (plate 23), the most similar species, is shorter-winged.

Double-striped Thick-knee
Burhinus bistriatus   See also plate 49

Key ID features L 430–480mm. A large, big-eyed, long-legged thick-knee; with a striking long white supercilium, bordered by a black lateral crown-stripe.
Behaviour A crepuscular or nocturnal species that rests inconspicuously by day. Most often seen along dirt roads at night.
Habitat Favours open grassland, also agricultural land.
Plumage: Adult Upperpart feathers dark brown, broadly fringed warm cinnamon, creating a streaked appearance. Throat white; sides of neck and upper-breast buff, finely streaked brown, merging to grey-brown on lower breast to form a neat band contrasting with the white underparts. **Juvenile** Similar to adult plumage but the cinnamon fringed mantle feathers create a scaly appearance and the rest of the upperparts have broader, brighter fringes while the head, neck and breast are washed with a warmer buff.
Confusion species The only other New World *Burhinus* species is the Peruvian Thick-knee *B. superciliaris* (outside the region), which is smaller and paler, but their ranges are most unlikely to overlap.

Collared Plover
(not to scale)

ad

1st-w

juv

**Northern
Jacana**

ad

juv

**Eskimo
Curlew**

ad

juv

**Double-striped
Thick-knee**
(not to scale)

ad

juv

Plate 44 ORIENTAL VAGRANTS

Great Thick-knee
Esacus recurvirostris   See also plate 53

Key ID features L 490–540mm. A huge thick-knee, quite unmistakable with its massive yellow-based black bill and long yellow legs.
Behaviour Mainly active after dusk, but sometimes feeds by day, prising up stones with its upturned bill.
Habitat Nests close to water, usually along rivers on shingle banks or stony islets. Less frequently seen on coasts and tidal estuaries, favouring mud to sand.
Plumage: Adult White of forehead extends across lores and cheeks onto throat; white supercilium and narrow ring around eye is surrounded by blackish-brown mask; short blackish-brown malar stripe; crown, mantle and scapulars uniform pale grey-brown, with indistinct shaft streaks; some lesser coverts blackish, forming conspicuous dark bar, narrowly bordered below with white. **Juvenile** Very similar to adult but upperpart feathers, including the crown, are sandy-brown, narrowly fringed buff when fresh.
Confusion species The closely related Beach Thick-knee *E. magnirostris* of SE Asia and Australia (outside the region) has a dark crown and forehead.

Little Pratincole
Glareola lactea   See also plate 51

Key ID features L 165–185mm. Small size, pale sandy-grey plumage and contrasting long black primaries are diagnostic.
Behaviour A gregarious species, nesting in colonies. Broken-wing displays are used to distract predators. May chase insects, plover-like, across sandy ground.
Habitat Nests on riverine sandbanks. At other times often occurs in estuaries or coastal lagoons.
Plumage: Breeding Crown is brownish-grey, darkest on forehead fading towards hindneck;

upperparts uniform sandy-grey; black primaries project well beyond white-tipped tail. Black bill shows red at base; lores black; throat and breast washed buff; rest of underparts white. **Non-breeding** Duller than breeding, with pale lores and white throat bordered with fine streaks. **Juvenile** Crown spotted buff; throat encircled with fine brown spots. Scapulars and tertials show brown subterminal bars and buff fringes; less pronounced on wing-coverts.
Confusion species Small size and pale plumage separates it immediately from other pratincole species within the region.

Pheasant-tailed Jacana
Hydrophasianus chirurgus   See also plate 46

Key ID features L 390–580mm. A highly distinctive large jacana, with white wings, face and foreneck, and golden hindneck.
Behaviour Swims readily, often feeding at the same time. When not breeding forms flocks at favoured localities.
Habitat Nests on large freshwater lakes and ponds with floating vegetation.
Plumage: Breeding A narrow black line extends down the sides of the neck from the nape to the upper breast; hindneck bright golden-yellow; body feathering is dark chocolate-brown; with a purplish gloss on the scapulars. Long tail. **Non-breeding** Crown and narrow line down hindneck brown; golden-yellow reduced to pale yellowish lines; a blackish-brown necklace extends from lores, down neck to join on upper breast. Upperparts greenish-brown; tail much shorter. **Juvenile** Crown rufous; sides of neck pale buff; brownish indistinct necklace. Brown upperpart feathers extensively fringed warm buff.
Confusion species Juveniles show some similarities to the extralimital Bronze-winged Jacana *Metopidius indicus*, which occurs in India and SE Asia; it lacks the brownish necklace.

Great Thick-knee

juv

ad

non-br

Little Pratincole
(not to scale)

juv

br

non-br

Pheasant-tailed Jacana

br

non-br

juv

Plate 45 AFRICAN VAGRANTS

Kittlitz's Plover
Charadrius pecuarius   See also plate 57

Key ID features L 120–140mm. A small and relatively long-legged plover, with a conspicuous black line down side of neck of breeding adult and buffy underparts, lacking breast bands.
Behaviour Usually occurs in pairs but more gregarious when not breeding. Feeds in typical plover fashion, running, stopping and picking, also uses 'foot-trembling' to attract prey.
Habitat Nests in sandy areas, usually near water; also inhabits a variety of dry ground, with very short grass, often away from water, as well as edges of lakes, rivers and tidal mudflats.
Plumage: Breeding White forehead and black frontal-bar narrowly bordered behind by white line; black lores and ear coverts, and line down side of neck meets a half-collar at base of hindneck; white of supercilia extends to form hindneck collar above black. Upperpart feathers are sooty-brown fringed buffy; lesser coverts blackish-brown. Underparts white, with variable pinky-buff wash on breast and flanks. **Non-breeding** Dull, with black of breeding plumage absent or replaced by brown; supercilia and hind-collar with buffy wash; blackish-brown lesser-covert panel evident. Underparts variable, some with brownish sides to the breast. **Juvenile** Like a non-breeding adult, with upperpart feathers broadly fringed pale buffy-brown.
Confusion species In juvenile plumage with breast patches may resemble Lesser Sand Plover (plate 14), but Kittlitz's Plover has proportionately longer legs, blackish-brown lesser coverts and obvious buffy collar.

Three-banded Plover
Charadrius tricollaris   See also plate 57

Key ID features L 180mm. A distinctive small long-tailed plover, with conspicuous white 'headband', red eye-ring and two black breast-bands separated by a band of white.
Behaviour When feeding, darts forward in short spurts with head down, stopping to peck ground. Also 'foot-trembles' to attract prey; bobs when alarmed.
Habitat Usually nests on shingle. Throughout the year frequents margins of rivers, muddy pools and lakes; more rarely on coastal lagoons and estuaries.
Plumage: Adult White of forehead flows into long white supercilia which meet on hindneck; face pale grey; upperpart feathers uniform grey-brown. **Juvenile** Head pattern is similar to adult's, but forehead initially brownish; dark brown upperpart feathers show narrow buff fringes, subtle notches and narrow dark subterminal lines. Unusually for a *Charadrius* species, some greater coverts and the tertials are narrowly fringed buff, with brown and buff notches.
Confusion species The closely related Forbes's Plover *C. forbesi* (outside the region), which occurs in West Africa. However, the ranges of the two species are largely separate.

Black-headed Lapwing (Plover)
Vanellus tectus   See also plate 53

Key ID features L 250mm. A medium-sized plover, with a distinct crest, black–and-white head pattern, small red wattle and brown upperparts.
Behaviour Fairly inactive during the day, seeking shade from trees; more active at dawn and dusk and most active at night.
Habitat Found in semi-arid regions; open desert with annual grass; bushed grassland, or bare areas in thorn scrub. Also partial to vicinity of human habitation, nesting in gardens and near buildings.
Plumage: Adult Head and neck mainly black, with a purple sheen; white on nape extends to eye; white forehead, chin and throat; broad black neckband extends narrowly down the breast; sides of the breast washed pinkish-brown; rest of underparts white. Upperpart feathers uniform mid-brown; greater coverts tipped white. **Juvenile** Pattern as adult, with small red wattle and black of head replaced by brown, with buff tips; all sandy-brown upperpart feathers are fringed buff, with dark subterminal lines; tertials irregularly barred buff.
Confusion species Red-wattled Lapwing (plate 16) is the only similar species but lacks a crest and the black and white head pattern is totally different, lacking the white hindneck and white throat of this species. Their ranges do not overlap but the Black-headed Lapwing has occurred as a vagrant in the Middle East.

Kittlitz's Plover

non-br

br

juv

non-br variant

Three-banded Plover

juv

ad

ad

Black-headed Lapwing
(not to scale)

juv

THE CONCEPT FOR THIS BOOK was to produce plates of species that might be confused, particularly when in flight, irrespective of family. For example, the three phalaropes are grouped with the Sanderling (though there was a case for putting Wilson's Phalarope with other white-rumped species). Where possible, we have endeavoured to group similar looking species together, regardless of family, except some of the more exotic ones, of course. Hence, the first flight plate (46) includes Northern and Pheasant-tailed Jacanas, Ibisbill and the Painted Snipe; the unique Crab Plover seemed to fit reasonably well with the black-and-white oystercatchers. The system of cross-referencing by plate numbers should make it straightforward to check all the illustrative and written information available.

All the 'in flight' illustrations are of adults: when there is seasonal variation, the upperwing depicts a non-breeding plumage and the underwing breeding plumage (with the exception of Pheasant-tailed Jacana). Some species have distinct races, and illustrations of these are included when the ID features can be seen in flight; otherwise illustrations show the nominate race.

Explanation of the species accounts

The cross-reference in each species header enables the 'at rest' plates to be quickly checked. This is essentially a field guide concentrating on identification. Therefore, not all of the sections described below appear for every species, but they occur whenever there is relevant identification text to be included. Selected other information, particularly regarding display behaviour, is occasionally mentioned.

Key ID features – essentially those aspects that can usually confirm the identification in flight. For comparison, the wing length (W) is always included first. This is the measurement from the carpal joint to the tip of the longest primary.

Behaviour – usually confined to display flights that may differentiate one species, or one family, from another.

Flight action – only included when the manner of flight may provide a useful guide towards identification.

Voice   included here, as calls are often made in flight, though not exclusively so. The most usual contact calls are always described and occasionally alarm calls, when different, together with typical display songs.

Distribution and status – the maps show the breeding and wintering areas clearly, so any comments in this section refer to areas where the species has appeared as a vagrant; the ranges of any distinct races within the region are also mentioned. Status comments are only included for species with declining populations that are listed as Critically Endangered, Endangered or Vulnerable (see page 203).

Racial variation – only commented on when noticeably distinct features are visible in flight.

Confusion species – mentions those species that may cause identification difficulties. The flight characteristics that are usually diagnostic will have been mentioned in other parts of the text, to which reference may be made, or they may be repeated here for emphasis.

Key to the distribution maps

resident   non-breeding visitor   breeding visitor

Plate 46   **PAINTED SNIPE, JACANAS AND IBISBILL**

Painted Snipe

ad ♂

ad ♀

ad

ad

Northern Jacana

Painted Snipe
Rostratula benghalensis   See also plate 1

Key ID features W 125–150mm. Has broad rounded wings like a woodcock, with noticeable white stripes on either side of the mantle, that form a V towards the rump.
Behaviour The female performs a display flight, uttering single notes during a low, woodcock-like roding flight.
Flight action When disturbed flies direct but only for short distances, often with legs dangling.
Voice Usually silent outside the breeding season but when disturbed will occasionally utter an explosive *kek* or a guttural croak. During her display flight the female utters an almost continuous soft hooting, likened to the sound of blowing across the top of an empty bottle.
Distribution   Irregular spring and summer visitor to Israel.
Racial variation None within the region, but the Australian race *australis* is larger, distinctly longer winged, with shorter bill and tarsus.

Northern Jacana
Jacana spinosa   See also plate 43

Key ID features W 113-141mm. The distinctive greenish-yellow flight feathers, contrast with the chestnut mantle and wing coverts; while the long toes on the long trailing legs are unique to jacanas.
Flight action Distinctive, with long trailing legs and rapid fluttering interspersed with glides.

Voice Noisy, with a variety of rasping, clacking notes, including a squawking *scraa-scraa-scraa*.
Distribution Bred previously in southern Texas, now a vagrant to western Texas and southern Arizona.
Confusion species Wattled Jacana *J. jacana* of Central and South America is virtually identical in flight, unless the two-lobed red frontal shield can be seen – the Northern Jacana has a three-lobed yellow frontal shield.

Pheasant-tailed Jacana
Hydrophasianus chirurgus   See also plate 44

Key ID features W 190-244mm. Unique among jacana species in being migratory and also in having a non-breeding plumage. This species is unmistakable with its largely white wings at all seasons.
Behaviour Sometimes mobs raptors, lapwing-like, high in the air.
Flight action Capable of strong flight, as befits a migrant species.
Voice Breeding season calls include a far carrying *me-e-ou* or *me-onp*. A peculiar nasal *tewn* call is heard among wintering flocks.
Distribution Vagrant to Japan.

Ibisbill
Ibidorhyncha struthersii   See also plate 1

Key ID features W 230-247mm. Unmistakable with its pale grey upperparts, white inner primary

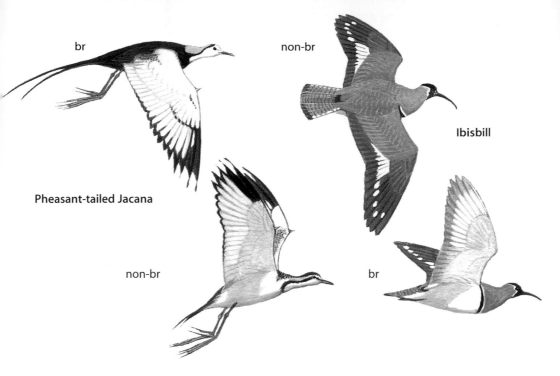

br

non-br

Ibisbill

Pheasant-tailed Jacana

non-br

br

patch, grey rump with a black crescent, and finely barred tail with a subterminal black bar.

Behaviour The Ibisbill shows some affinity to ibises, not only in its decurved bill and rounded wings, but also by its manner of flight, when it holds its head outstretched and higher than the body.

Flight action Flies with shallow, flicking wing-beats.

Voice Generally silent outside the breeding season. The call made during courtship display is similar to that of Eurasian Oystercatcher, but is louder, more melodious and consists of up to 40 penetrating notes. Another call, more usually occurring during territorial and antagonistic behaviour, consists of three to four loud, piping *kleep* notes, the first two close together and the third and fourth after short pauses.

Distribution There is some altitudinal movement in the winter months.

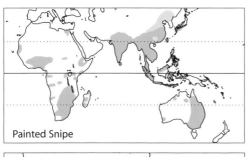

Painted Snipe

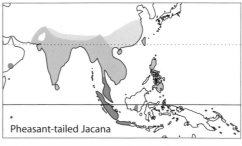

Pheasant-tailed Jacana

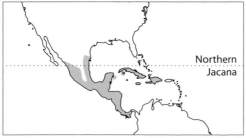

Northern Jacana

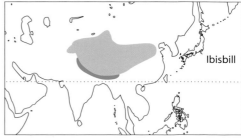

Ibisbill

Plate 47 CRAB PLOVER AND OYSTERCATCHERS

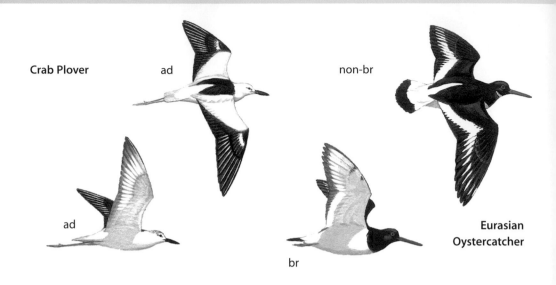

Crab Plover   ad   non-br

ad   Eurasian
                                                     Oystercatcher

br

Crab Plover
Dromas ardeola   See also plate 1

Key ID features W 200-226mm. The massive
bill is diagnostic. The white head, neck and V on
lower back contrast with the black saddle. The
largely black flight feathers also contrast with the
white innerwing. Toes and legs project well
beyond tail-tip.
Behaviour May often be seen flying in large
flocks low over water.
Flight action Wings are held quite stiffly and
wing-beats are generally slower than most other
waders.
Voice On the breeding grounds a constant
chattering *tchuck tchuck* can be heard, often well
into the night. At other times, flocks maintain a
restless chattering, occasionally interspersed with
far carrying *ha how* or *crow ow ow* notes and a more
musical *prooit*. Alarm calls consist of a sharp, loud,
repeated *kiep*.
Distribution Vagrants have occurred on the
Mediterranean coasts of Israel and Turkey.

Eurasian Oystercatcher
Haematopus ostralegus   See also plate 2

Key ID features W 235-284mm. Black upperparts, with broad white wingbar and white of
rump extending in a V onto back. Long straight,
bright orange-red bill. Underwing virtually all
white.
Behaviour During the display flight a lone bird,
typically the male, flies buoyantly with slow, stiff,
deep butterfly-like flaps, very different from

normal flight.
Flight action Strong and direct, with shallow
wing-beats; groups often fly in untidy lines.
Voice Calls are based around a strident, piping
kleep, with variations in both frequency and rapid-
ity. In aerial display there is also a more melodic,
steady metronomic *tee-teeoo*.
Distribution The nominate race occurs in western Europe and western Russia, *longipes* in Siberia
and *osculans* from Kamchatka to north China.
Vagrant to Japan, Commander Islands, Greenland
and Newfoundland.
Racial variation The wingbar on the race
osculans is marginally shorter; it lacks white on
the shafts of the outer two to three primaries and
shows no white on the outer webs of the outer
five.

American Oystercatcher
Haematopus palliatus   See also plate 2

Key ID features W 232-275mm. Dark brown
upperparts, with white rump and broad white
wingbar across secondaries onto bases of inner-
primaries. Underwing shows contrast between
white coverts and brown flight feathers. Long
orange-red bill.
Voice Similar to other oystercatchers, loud,
piping *kleep* and *kip kip*.
Distribution The nominate race occurs along
the Atlantic and Gulf coasts and *frazari* on the
Pacific coast of the Baja Peninsula and Mexico.
Vagrant inland to Ontario and Idaho.
Racial variation Nominate *palliatus* shows some
white on the inner primaries; this is absent in

ad
frazari

**American
Oystercatcher**

ad

ad

ad

**Black
Oystercatcher**

ad

ad

frazari, which also has dark markings on the uppertail-coverts, so usually has less than half the tail white.

Black Oystercatcher
Haematopus bachmani   See also plate 2

Key ID features W 254–266mm. Though wings, mantle and tail are dark brown, appears all black and, with a long orange-red bill, is unmistakable. The wings are relatively broad and more rounded than in other oystercatchers.

Behaviour As with other oystercatchers, the pairing and display flights can be spectacular, often involving small groups making accelerated and multiple piping calls.
Flight action Heavy and direct, with bowed wings, usually low over the water.
Voice The flight calls are loud, piping whistles *wheep wheep*.
Distribution Vagrant to Idaho.
Confusion species Upperparts are uniformly dark brown compared with the bold white rump and wingbars of the American Oystercatcher.

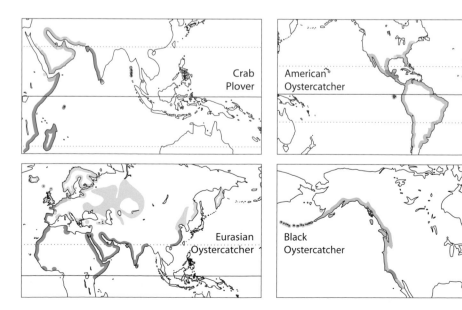

Crab
Plover

American
Oystercatcher

Eurasian
Oystercatcher

Black
Oystercatcher

Plate 48   AVOCETS AND STILTS

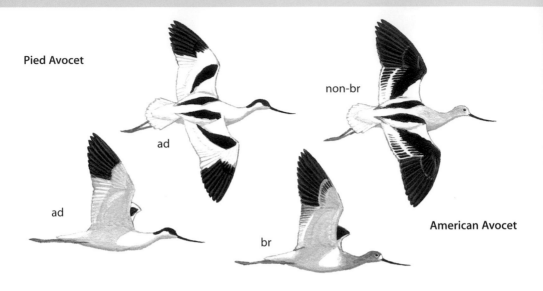

Pied Avocet

non-br

ad

ad

br

American Avocet

Pied Avocet
Recurvirostra avosetta   See also plate 4

Key ID features W 206-240mm. The black and white upperwing pattern is quite distinctive and the black crown, nape and hindneck unique amongst avocet species.
Behaviour Noisy and aggressive on the breeding grounds, frequently giving chase.
Flight action Flies on stiff, straight wings, often in dense flocks and low over water.
Voice The usual call is a clear, liquid, disyllabic *kluit*. When alarmed it becomes shorter, more stilt-like and is repeated rapidly.
Distribution Vagrant to Japan.
Confusion species The black crown and hindneck immediately separate this species from the American Avocet, and their current ranges do not overlap.

American Avocet
Recurvirostra americana   See also Plate 4

Key ID features W 213-242mm. Broader-winged and shows less white than Pied Avocet. Black scapular stripes and largely black wings, apart from white on some innerwing and greater coverts, and inner secondaries.
Behaviour Aggressive at their sometimes large breeding colonies, often dive-bombing visitors at high speed.
Flight action More powerful than stilts, rapid, with fast wing-beats.
Voice Usual call note is an almost disyllabic *wheet*, but shorter and repeated rapidly when agitated. They are noisy on their breeding grounds

but almost silent on migration.
Distribution Has been recorded on Caribbean Islands. Vagrant to Greenland.
Confusion species Unlikely to be confused with any other wader, even at a distance, when the lack of black on the head and neck quickly eliminates Black-necked Stilt.

Black-winged Stilt
Himantopus himantopus   See also plate 3

Key ID features W 206-255mm. Unmistakable with black wings, white rump extending in V onto back, greyish tail, long, thin bill and exceptionally long legs and toes that project far beyond tail-tip. Juvenile shows white trailing edge to inner primaries and secondaries. Underwing virtually all black, apart from white inner lesser and median underwing-coverts.
Behaviour Aggressive behaviour may involve a short head-and-neck-down flight, when the aggressor takes off with neck extended, head drooped and legs dangling, then hovers, wings in a V over the opponent. Aerial displays include a 'butterfly-flight', which involves hovering up to ten metres from the ground, flying another ten metres or more and hovering again. Also a theatrical, high-leaping display concludes with a parachute-like descent on widespread wings.
Flight action Free and rapid, with shallow, flicking wing-beats and glides.
Voice Particularly noisy on the breeding grounds, but often at other times too. Various calls are usually based around a resonant *kek*. Also a high-pitched *kikikikiki*.
Distribution Vagrant to Aleutians.

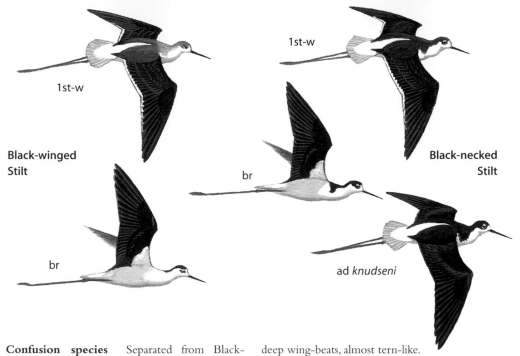

1st-w

1st-w

Black-winged
Stilt

br

Black-necked
Stilt

br

ad *knudseni*

Confusion species Separated from Black-necked Stilt by lack of black on sides of neck. The all-black wings eliminate any possible confusion with similarly sized Pied Avocet.

Black-necked Stilt
Himantopus mexicanus　　　　See also plate 3

Key ID features W 206-255mm. As Black-winged Stilt but black of crown, which extends onto hindneck, sides of neck and upper mantle, is diagnostic and obvious in profile view.
Behaviour Similar to Black-winged.
Flight action As Black-winged; at times with deep wing-beats, almost tern-like.
Voice Particularly noisy on the breeding grounds, but often at other times, too, making a resonant, persistent *kek kek kek kek*.
Distribution Vagrant across southern Canada. The race *knudseni* is a rare, endangered resident of Hawaii.
Racial variation The Hawaiian race *knudseni* has more extensive black extending onto the breast sides. The bill and legs are even longer than those of the nominate race.
Confusion species All-black wings eliminate any possible confusion with similar, slightly larger, American Avocet.

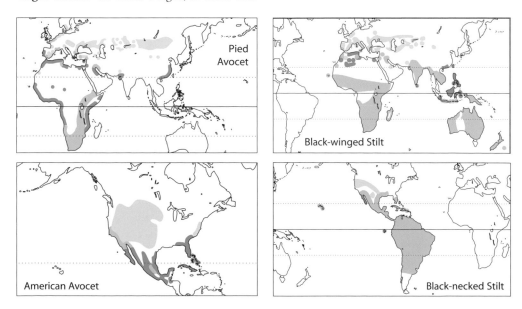

Pied Avocet

Black-winged Stilt

American Avocet

Black-necked Stilt

Plate 49 **THICK-KNEES**

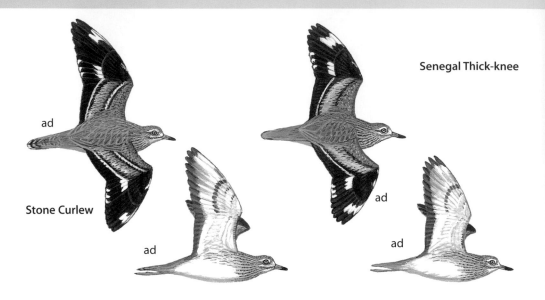

Senegal Thick-knee

ad

Stone Curlew

ad

ad

ad

Stone Curlew
Burhinus oedicnemus   See also plate 5

Key ID features W 224–255mm. A large wader, with sandy-brown upperparts, wing coverts and long graduated tail; the flight feathers are mainly black, with small patches of white in the primaries; has a distinctive pale mid-wing panel bordered by narrow black and white wingbars, formed by white, black and grey innerwing-coverts. The underwing is largely white, with a black trailing edge and a black bar across the primaries only, formed by the black tips to the greater primary-coverts.
Flight action Flies with stiff wing-beats and wings bowed, like other thick-knees.
Voice Generally silent by day, becoming vocal at dusk during the breeding season. The *cur-lee* call is often far carrying, emphasis is on the second syllable which is higher.
Distribution Three races are found within the region. The nominate *oedicnemus* occurs across Europe east to the Caspian Sea; *saharae* in North Africa, on the Mediterranean Islands, in S Greece, SW Turkey and N Arabia; and *harterti* is found south and east of the Caspian Sea.
Confusion species Where the ranges overlap there can be confusion between these three Old World *Burhinus* species, but the different upperwings are diagnostic. Note carefully the colours and pattern of the innerwing panel.

Senegal Thick-knee
Burhinus senegalensis   See also plate 5

Key ID features W 203–222mm. Similar to Stone Curlew but mid-wing panel pale grey, with single white wingbar across greater coverts; white patches on primaries are more extensive.
Voice Wailing calls are similar to Stone Curlew but less strident. Display song, given in flight as well as from the ground, is *pi pi pi-pi-pi-pi-pi-pi-pii-pii-pii pi pi* reaching a crescendo just before the last two notes.
Distribution Within the region, occurs in the Nile valley.
Confusion species Stone Curlew and Spotted Thick-knee (see respective Key ID features).

Spotted Thick-knee
Burhinus capensis   See also plate 5

Key ID features W 236–273mm. Distinctive uniform spotted brown upperparts and wing coverts, contrast with the black flight feathers; there are small white flashes on the outer primaries and on the base and tips of the inner primaries; the graduated tail is finely barred. The underwing is white, with a broad black trailing edge and an obvious narrow, central black bar formed by the black tips to the greater primary-coverts and greater coverts.
Voice Has a harsh, growling *chrrr* anxiety note, piping alarm notes and a *keh-keeh* when threatened. The rhythm of the whistled display song is similar to that of *senegalensis ti-ti-ti-tee-tee-tee ti ti ti.*
Distribution The race *dodsoni* occurs in southern parts of the Arabian peninsula.
Confusion species Distinguished from Stone Curlew and Senegal Thick-knee by the distinctive pattern of the upperparts, including a barred tail.

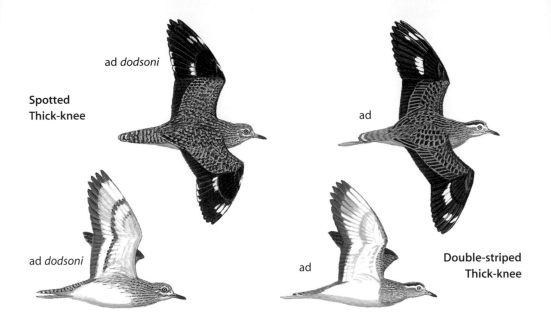

Spotted Thick-knee

ad *dodsoni*

ad *dodsoni*

ad

ad

Double-striped Thick-knee

Lacks a pale wing-panel, and the full black under-wing bar is also diagnostic.

Double-striped Thick-knee
Burhinus bistriatus See also plate 43

Key ID features W 236–273mm. Shows bold white flashes across the bases of the outer and inner primaries; has relatively long wings and a graduated tail, with an off-white subterminal bar and dark tip; and the long legs project beyond the tail-tip.

Voice Strident, chattering calls, rising then fading away, are most often heard at night.

Distribution Vagrant to southern Texas.

Confusion species The only other New World *Burhinus* species is the Peruvian Thick-knee *B. superciliaris* (outside the region), which is smaller and shows a distinct grey wing-panel, but their ranges are most unlikely to overlap.

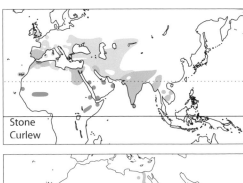

Stone Curlew

Spotted Thick-knee

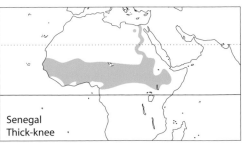

Senegal Thick-knee

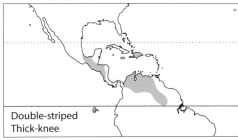

Double-striped Thick-knee

Plate 50 COURSERS AND EGYPTIAN PLOVER

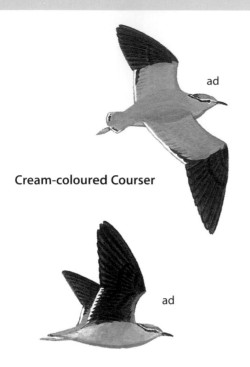

Cream-coloured Courser

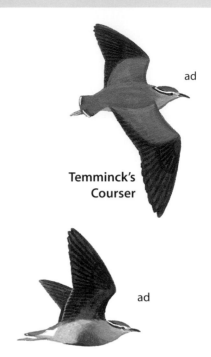

Temminck's Courser

Cream-coloured Courser

Cursorius cursor   See also plate 6

Key ID features W 153–172mm. The upperwing pattern of black primaries contrasting with the sandy mantle and forewing is distinctive. There is a similarly marked contrast between the black underwing and the sandy–cream body. An obvious white-trailing edge is visible on both the upperwing and the underwing.

Behaviour Circular or gliding flights are used in display.

Flight action The long-winged, leisurely, flicking wing-beats are pratincole-like.

Voice The usual call is a short *quit* or *quit-quit*. During the display flight a *quit-quit-whow* is uttered.

Distribution The nominate race *cursor* breeds in North Africa across to the Arabian Peninsula and winters south to Saudi Arabia, Somalia and northern Kenya; *bogolubovi* breeds from southeast Turkey through northern Iran to Turkmenistan and winters south to northwest India. Vagrant to Mediterranean countries and farther north in Europe. Bred in southern Spain in 2001.

Confusion species A glimpse of the underwing only might suggest Black-winged Pratincole (plate 51). Similar to Temminck's Courser, which has generally darker upperparts and black extending across the secondaries.

Temminck's Courser

Cursorius temminckii   See also plate 6

Key ID features W 117–131mm. The contrast of sandy-brown innerwing-coverts and back with black primaries and secondaries is distinctive. The underwing is dark, with a variable width, but usually conspicuous white trailing edge to the secondaries.

Flight action The wing-beats are rapid, jerky and flickering.

Voice Normally quiet, but the contact note is a high, metallic, twittering *err-err-err*, somewhat reminiscent of the creaking sound of a rusty hinge.

Distribution Occurs in Mauritania, on the fringes of the Western Palaearctic.

Confusion species Cream-coloured Courser, which has much paler upperparts, with the black restricted to the primaries.

ad

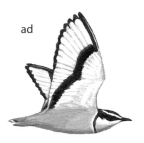

ad

Egyptian Plover

Egyptian Plover
Pluvianus aegyptius   See also plate 6

Key ID features   W 127-144mm. The unique
pattern of black, white and grey is unmistakable.
The underwing is essentially white with a
contrasting black bar across the flight feathers.
Flight action   Fast and low with a flicking
series of wing-beats.
Voice   A series of rapid, harsh notes, usually
uttered in flight: *cherk-cherk-cherk-cherk*. A single,
rising *wuip* whistle is given as a mild alarm call.
Distribution   Used to frequent the Nile valley.
However, the only relatively recent Western
Palearctic record concerns an individual in Libya
in August 1969.

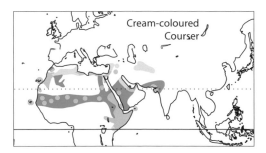

Cream-coloured Courser

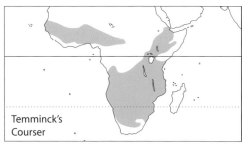

Temminck's Courser

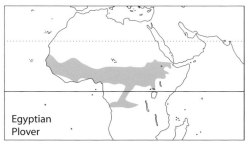

Egyptian Plover

Plate 51 **PRATINCOLES**

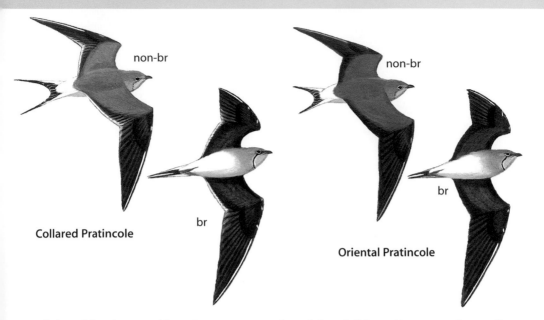

All three of these larger tern-like waders appear very similar in flight and all have white rumps and uppertail-coverts and usually show a white shaft on the outer primary. The subtle variations between their plumages means that particularly good views are essential, ideally as the bird flies away from the sun, against a dark background. In these conditions it should be possible to confirm the presence or absence of a white trailing edge to the secondaries, but beware variation caused by moult and wear. Similarly, the colour of the axillaries can be difficult to ascertain. As with other groups of similar waders, to be confident of a specific identification, it is important to note a number of characteristics.

Collared Pratincole

Glareola pratincola See also plate 7

Key ID features W 171-203mm. The mantle and wing-coverts are paler than the flight feathers; there is a narrow white trailing edge to the secondaries; the inner secondaries are distinctly darker than the outer ones; and the underwing-coverts and axillaries are chestnut.
Behaviour Feeds by flying after swarming insects, often at dawn and dusk.
Flight action Most graceful and tern-like.
Voice A harsh, tern-like *kik* or *kirrik*, often a more rolling *keerr-ik-ik*. Pratincoles are particularly noisy in their breeding colonies.
Distribution Vagrant to Barbados and northern Europe.
Confusion species Compare respective Key ID features for Oriental and Black-winged Pratincoles.

Oriental Pratincole

Glareola maldivarum See also plate 7

Key ID features W 170-200mm. The dark flight-feathers, which contrast only slightly with the dark brown upperparts, and the lack of a white or buffish trailing edge to the secondaries are both

characteristics which are indicative of this species. But note also the chestnut underwing-coverts and axillaries, and the short tail-streamers.
Behaviour Feeding behaviour as described for Collared Pratincole.
Flight action Most graceful and tern-like.
Voice Similar to Collared, with a sharp *kyik*, or *chik-cheik* and a mellow *ch-wheet*.
Distribution Vagrant to Israel, England, Sweden and Aleutian Islands.
Confusion species Collared and Black-winged Pratincoles (see their Key ID features).

Black-winged Pratincole

Glareola nordmanni See also plate 7

Key ID features W 180-216mm. The mantle and wing-coverts show little contrast with the flight feathers; and the secondaries lack a white trailing edge. The underwing and axillaries are uniformly black.
Behaviour Forms large post-breeding flocks. Feeding behaviour as for Collared Pratincole.
Flight action Most graceful and tern-like.
Voice Lower pitched and slower than Collared: *pwik-pwik-ik*, *chree-it* or single *kirip*, and distinguishable from Collared with experience.
Distribution Vagrant through Europe to Britain,

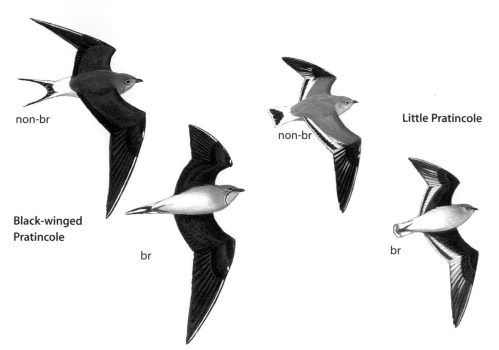

non-br

Little Pratincole

non-br

Black-winged
Pratincole

br

br

Norway and Iceland.

Confusion species This species looks slightly broader winged than Collared Pratincole. Compare Key ID features for other differences and also to separate Oriental Pratincole. Possible momentary confusion with Cream-coloured Courser (plate 50), if only seen from below.

Little Pratincole
Glareola lactea   See also Plate 44

Key ID features W 146-163mm. A tiny, pale grey, swallow-like pratincole, with the black outer-wing contrasting with a broad white panel across the secondaries and an almost square-ended tail. The pattern of the underparts is a most distinctive black-and-white.

Behaviour Feeds mostly by hawking insects in flight.

Flight action Quick, angular and swallow-like.

Voice In flight gives a high-pitched *prrip* or *tiririt*. Also makes a short *tuc-tuc-tuc* when nesting.

Distribution Vagrant to the Arabian Gulf and Oman.

Confusion species Difficult to confuse with any other species within the region.

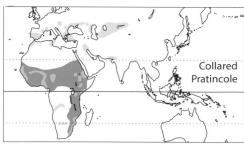

Collared Pratincole

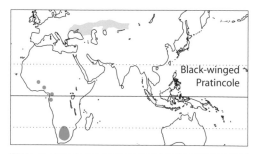

Black-winged Pratincole

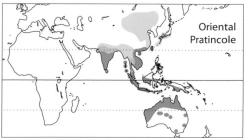

Oriental Pratincole

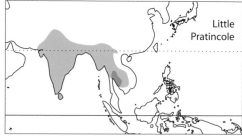

Little Pratincole

Plate 52 **LAPWINGS**

Sociable Lapwing

non-br

non-br

Northern
Lapwing

br

br

Northern Lapwing
Vanellus vanellus   See also plate 8

Key ID features W 215-237mm. Unmistakable, with broad, rounded wings and distinct black-and-white underparts.
Behaviour The spectacular display flight of the male includes a butterfly flight close to the ground, rolling from side to side and zigzagging, ascending high, then dropping, with agile twists and turns performed at great speed.
Flight action Free deep flapping flight; wing-beats remarkably rapid on take-off.
Voice Call is usually a plaintive, disyllabic *peewi*. The display song, usually given in flight, involves three units strung together: *hrre-willoch-o-weep, weep-weep* and *cheew-o-weep*.
Distribution Eurasian migrant or partial migrant. Vagrant to east coast of N America, inland to Ohio.

Sociable Lapwing (Plover)
Vanellus gregarius   See also plate 8

Key ID features W 194-221mm. Distinctive fairly broad wings, with contrasting black primaries and unmarked white secondaries, grey-brown mantle and wing coverts. Tail white, with black subterminal band.
Behaviour No flight display known but, traditionally, males gather in spring to perform terrestrial displays.
Flight action Steady, slow wing-beats, but noticeably faster when compared with that of the Northern Lapwing.

Voice Generally noisy when breeding, uttering a tri-syllabic *krek*, recalling Grey Partridge *Perdix perdix* but softer. Alarm note is a short, harsh *rrer*, repeated rapidly to sound more rattle-like.
Distribution and status VULNERABLE, following a decline of 90% since 1990. Now very scarce throughout range. Vagrant to western Europe.
Confusion species Similar upperwing colour pattern to White-tailed and Spur-winged Lapwings but the extent of black differs, as does the tail pattern. The White-tailed Lapwing has a pure white tail, beyond which the long yellow projecting legs are diagnostic. The Spur-winged Lapwing shows less white on the wing, a white rump and nearly all black tail. The outer tail feathers of Sociable Lapwing are entirely white.

White-tailed Lapwing (Plover)
Vanellus leucurus   See also plate 8

Key ID features W 168-187mm. Bold upper-wing pattern of white secondaries, extended by broad white tips to greater coverts and most primary-coverts, contrasts with black-edged pale grey-brown wing-coverts and grey-brown mantle, and black primaries and tips to outer secondaries.
Flight action Similar to other *Vanellus* species, with impression of more power than Northern Lapwing.
Voice Calls not dissimilar to Northern Lapwing. Breeding birds make a rapid, squeaking *pet-oo-wit,* the middle syllable starting lower but rising in pitch. At other times a subdued, less plaintive *pi-wick* call may be heard.
Distribution Scarce vagrant to Europe.

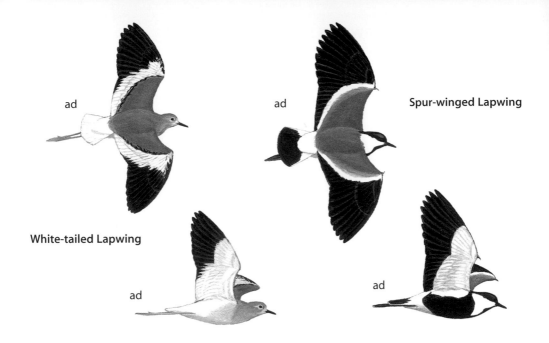

ad

ad

Spur-winged Lapwing

White-tailed Lapwing

ad

ad

Confusion species The all-white tail and long projecting yellow legs separate this species from Sociable and Spur-winged Lapwings.

Spur-winged Lapwing (Plover)

Vanellus spinosus   See also plate 8

Key ID features W 190–220mm. Broad wings show prominent white bands from carpals to inner secondaries, which contrast with the largely grey-brown wing-coverts and mantle, and the black primaries and outer secondaries. Nearly all-black tail contrasts with white rump.

Behaviour Less gregarious than other *Vanellus* species, more often seen in pairs or singly than in flocks.

Voice Alarm and mobbing call is a loud, metallic *pitt* or *zik*, repeated incessantly in ones and twos. The territorial call or song is a loud *did-he-do-it* or a tinkering *ti-ter-el ti-ti-ter-el ti-ti-ter-el*.

Distribution Scarce vagrant to Europe.

Confusion species Separated from the White-tailed and Sociable Lapwings by the distinctive underwing pattern of black rather than white secondaries (see Confusion species for Sociable Lapwing for upperwing differences between these species).

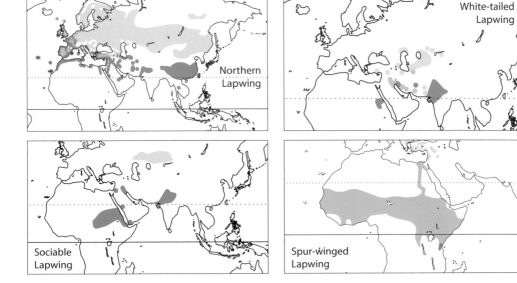

Northern Lapwing

White-tailed Lapwing

Sociable Lapwing

Spur-winged Lapwing

Plate 53 **SOUTHERN LAPWINGS AND GREAT THICK-KNEE**

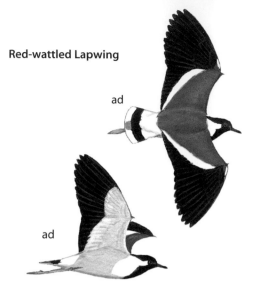

Red-wattled Lapwing

ad

ad

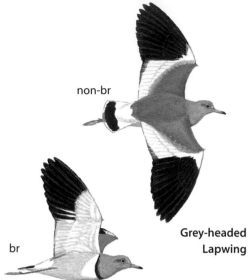

non-br

br

Grey-headed
Lapwing

Red-wattled Lapwing
Vanellus indicus   See also plate 16

Key ID features W 208-247mm. A white diagonal wing-panel divides the brown back and wing-coverts from the black primaries and secondaries, and the white tail has a black subterminal bar. The extensively white underparts contrast with the black of the primaries, secondaries and breast.
Behaviour Performs rapid, tumbling dives, during the display flight.
Voice A rhythmic, strident *did-did-he-do-it*.
Distribution Two races are present on the fringes of the region: the nominate *indicus* occurs in Nepal and *aigneri* between Iraq and West Pakistan. Vagrant to Israel and Syria.
Racial variation There are no apparent distinguishing features, only clinal variations.
Confusion species Yellow-wattled Lapwing *V. malabaricus* (outside of the region), which occurs in India, shows a similar upperwing pattern, with less white on the tail; its underwing has more extensive white across primary bases. The Spur-winged Lapwing (plate 52) also has a similar upperwing pattern, but has a paler grey-brown rather than brown mantle and innerwing coverts and the tail has a broader terminal bar.

Grey-headed Lapwing
Vanellus cinereus   See also plate 16

Key ID features W 231-257mm. Another *Vanellus* lapwing with a distinctive upperwing pattern of black primaries, white secondaries and outer wing-coverts, brown inner-wing coverts and back; white tail has a black subterminal band. Underwing is all white apart from black primaries, contrasting with black-bordered grey breast.
Voice The contact call is a plaintive *chee-it*, and when agitated utters a rasping *cha-ha-eet*.
Distribution Strongly migratory species. Vagrant northward to Transbaikalia and Vladivostoc and westward to Kashmir.
Confusion species White-tailed Lapwing (plate 52) has a similar upperwing pattern but lacks the black tail-bar and has longer legs, which project well beyond the tail-tip.

Black-headed Lapwing (Plover)
Vanellus tectus   See also plate 45

Key ID features W 180-201mm. The distinctive black of the head, tail-bar, primaries and secondaries, contrasts above with the white primary-coverts and bases of flight feathers, and the brown of the mantle and innerwing-coverts. The underparts are extensively white, contrasting with the black flight feathers. The toes just project beyond the tail-tip.
Behaviour Has a habit of wagging its tail on alighting after a short flight.
Voice Flight call is a piercing *kir-kir-kir*.
Distribution One was shot at Wadi Araba, on the Jordan-Israel frontier in 1869. In April 1995 another was seen in the same area.
Confusion species Red-wattled Lapwing has some similarities (see Key ID features for that species) but Black-headed is smaller and paler,

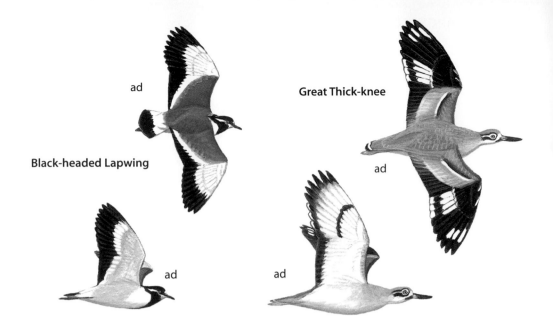

Great Thick-knee

ad

Black-headed Lapwing

ad

ad

ad

with more extensive white upperparts, including primary-coverts. However, their ranges are unlikely to overlap.

Great Thick-knee
Esacus recurvirostris See also plate 44

Key ID features W 257–271mm. The upper-wing pattern is rather bustard-like, with fingered black-and-white primaries; there is a distinctive pale grey panel across the median and greater coverts; the blackish flight feathers contrast with the white flashes on the outer primaries and a broad white patch across the bases of the inner primaries, which are white-tipped with a black subterminal band.

Flight action Strong and powerful.

Voice The territorial call, given mainly at night, is a series of wailing whistles, with a rising inflection *kree-kree-kree kre-kre-kre-kre*. When alarmed gives a loud, harsh *see-eek*.

Confusion species None within the region, but its range overlaps with the Beach Thick-knee *E. magnirostris* in SE Asia and Australia, which has an even heavier, thicker bill and an extensive area of white and pale grey on the upperwing.

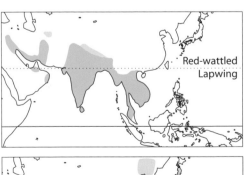

Red-wattled Lapwing

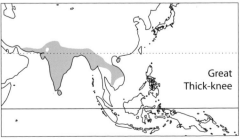

Black-headed Lapwing

Grey-headed Lapwing

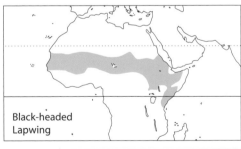

Great Thick-knee

Plate 54 **LARGE PLOVERS**

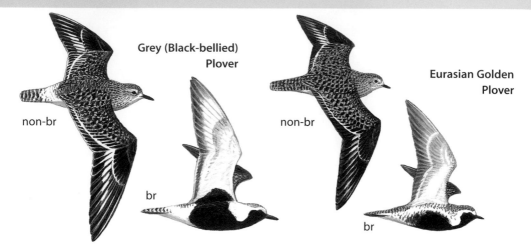

Grey (Black-bellied) Plover

Eurasian Golden Plover

non-br

non-br

br

br

Grey (Black-bellied) Plover
Pluvialis squatarola   See also plate 9

Key ID features W 178–215mm. Black axillaries contrasting with white underwing are diagnostic. From above shows a white rump and uppertail-coverts; and white wingbars, particularly on the inner primaries.

Behaviour The Grey and three Golden Plover species have subtle differences in their display flights; they all include a 'butterfly' flight, which for *squatarola* and *apricaria* is strikingly level, the wing-beats are shallow, rarely extending below the horizontal.

Flight action Often flies in irregular lines, rather than dense flocks, with powerful wing-beats, not as rapid as Eurasian Golden Plover.

Voice A far-carrying, plaintive *pee-uu-ee* with the second syllable lower in pitch.

Distribution Virtually cosmopolitan.

Confusion species Separated from the three Golden Plovers by Key ID features above. Possible confusion with non-breeding similarly sized species like Red and Great Knots (plate 74), or even Bar-tailed Godwit (plate 62) in distant flight, but black axillaries eliminate other species.

Eurasian Golden Plover
Pluvialis apricaria   See also plate 9

Key ID features W 170–203mm. White axillaries and underwing-coverts; uniform brown upperparts, with thin white wingbar, more conspicuous on bases of inner primaries.

Behaviour For display flight behaviour see Grey Plover.

Flight action Fast and direct, with rapid beats.

Voice A penetrating, whistling *luu-ee*.

Distribution Vagrant in spring to Newfoundland,

southern Greenland and Spitzbergen, one in winter in southern Alaska.

Confusion species Separated from American and Pacific Golden Plovers by the white axillaries and underwing-coverts.

American Golden Plover
Pluvialis dominica   See also plate 10

Key ID features W 169–193mm. Grey axillaries and underwing-coverts; uniform grey-brown upperparts, with thin, pale wingbar.

Behaviour In the 'butterfly' display flight, the wing-beats are deep, but less so than in Pacific.

Voice Fairly high-pitched, disyllabic *klee-u*, the second note shorter and lower, distinguishable from Pacific Golden.

Distribution Regular autumn vagrant to western Europe.

Confusion species Separated from Eurasian Golden Plover by grey axillaries and underwing-coverts and from Pacific by showing little or no toe projection.

Pacific Golden Plover
Pluvialis fulva   See also plate 10

Key ID features W 152–173mm. Grey axillaries and underwing-coverts; uniform brown upperparts, with thin, pale, inconspicuous wingbar; toes just visible beyond tail-tip.

Behaviour The 'butterfly' display flight is most exaggerated with this species, the wings seem to almost meet above the back and below the belly.

Voice Distinguishable from American and Eurasian Golden Plovers. A rapid *chu-wi* similar to Spotted Redshank, with the second note higher and accented; also a plaintive *ki-wee* not unlike Northern Lapwing.

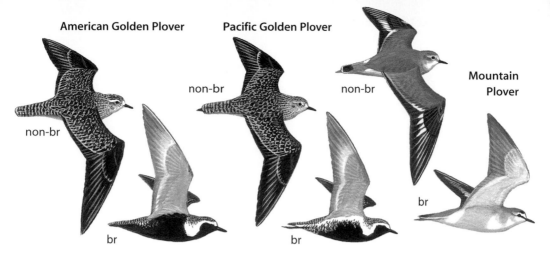

American Golden Plover

Pacific Golden Plover

non-br

non-br

non-br

Mountain Plover

non-br

br

br

br

Distribution Vagrant to Europe, west to Britain.
Confusion species With longer legs the toes just project beyond tail-tip, separating this species from American and Eurasian Golden Plovers.

Mountain Plover
Charadrius montanus   See also plate 15

Key ID features W 144–159mm. Long-winged, with white flash on base of inner primaries; dark subterminal band and narrow white fringes to tail.
Behaviour Performs 'butterfly' and 'falling leaf' display flights.
Flight action Usually low and rapid, with down-curved wings.
Voice Usual flight note is a low *krrrk*, but also makes various penetrating whistles.
Distribution and status VULNERABLE following changes in agricultural practices leading to loss of preferred grazing habitst. Vagrant to both coasts of North America.

Confusion species Though similar to Caspian and Oriental Plovers (plate 58), their ranges do not overlap. Possible confusion with American Golden Plover but Mountain is paler and has distinct upperwing white flashes and white under-wing-coverts; the tail pattern is also distinctive. Lacks the obvious white wingbars of Killdeer (plate 56) and Semipalmated Plovers (plate 55).

American Golden Plover

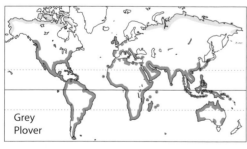

Grey Plover

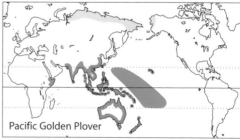

Pacific Golden Plover

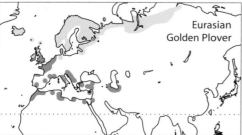

Eurasian Golden Plover

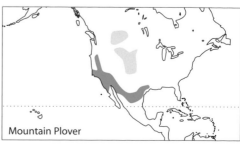

Mountain Plover

Plate 55 **RINGED PLOVERS**

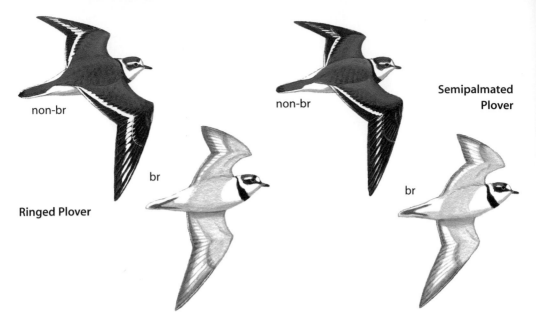

non-br

br

Ringed Plover

Semipalmated Plover

non-br

br

Ringed Plover
Charadrius hiaticula   See also plate 11

Key ID features W 120–144mm. The bold white wingbar extends onto the outer primaries.
Behaviour Displays include a slow-flapping territorial flight. Away from their breeding areas, small flocks may be seen flying to communal roosts.
Flight action Rapid, often low, with loosely clipped wing-beats and a glide before alighting.
Voice A fluty, rising *too-eep* whistle. When alarmed, makes a low *tooweep* and a loud *telee-telee*. The song, given in display flight, is a repeated *teeleea* or *leea*.
Distribution The nominate race *hiaticula* breeds from northeast Canada to western Europe; *tundrae* from northern Scandinavia to northeast Siberia. Vagrant to Alaska.
Confusion species Little Ringed Plover lacks a distinct wingbar. Semipalmated Plover: see Key ID features for difference from that species. Long-billed Plover has a narrow, indistinct white wingbar across the greater coverts only. Sand Plovers appear similar in flight but lack white neck-collars.

Semipalmated Plover
Charadrius semipalmatus   See also plate 11

Key ID features W 113–131mm. The distinct white wingbar is narrow and less obvious on the primaries.
Behaviour When displaying, a slow-motion nighthawk-like flight is accompanied by constant song.
Flight action Compared with Ringed, less free and fluid, more like Little Ringed or even small calidrids.
Voice A distinctive, rising *che-weet* quite reminiscent of Spotted Redshank; also a piping alarm note *chip-chip* similar to Little Ringed Plover. The song, given in display flight, is a repeated, slightly harsh *kerr-ree*.
Distribution Vagrant to Europe.
Confusion species Similar to larger and longer-billed Wilson's Plover (plate 56). Compare Key ID features for difference from Ringed Plover. Piping Plover (plate 56) is paler and has white uppertail-coverts contrasting with black subterminal tail-bar.

Little Ringed Plover
Charadrius dubius   See also plate 11

Key ID features W 105–117mm. The upperparts are a uniform brown, with an indistinct wingbar.
Behaviour Display of male includes a 'butterfly' flight.
Flight action Fast, often gaining height rapidly when disturbed.
Voice A far-carrying, descending *pee-oo*. Song is a repeated, rusty-sounding *cree-ah cree-ah*.
Distribution The only race that occurs within the region is *curonicus*, which is strongly migratory, and breeds in north Africa and across Eurasia from Britain to Japan. Vagrant to Alaska.

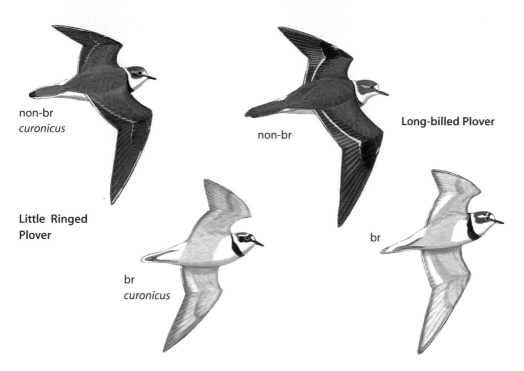

non-br
curonicus

non-br

Long-billed Plover

Little Ringed Plover

br
curonicus

br

Confusion species Like the larger Long-billed Plover, which has a weak wingbar, and a similarly longish, graduated tail. The lack of a distinct white wingbar separates this species from other 'ringed' plovers.

Long-billed Plover
Charadrius placidus   See also plate 16

Key ID features W 135-154mm. Brown upperparts, with white collar and narrow white wingbar; dark brown primary-coverts; pale outer secondaries and inner primaries form a weak wing-panel; and longish graduated brown tail.

Behaviour During aerial display flights holds its wings high.

Voice A penetrating, rising *peewee* and, when breeding, a musical *toodulu*.

Distribution Resident in part of the range.

Confusion species The smaller Little Ringed Plover, which has uniform upperparts with an indistinct wingbar and lacks the pale wing-panel.

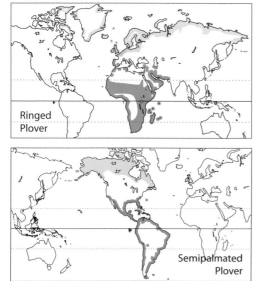

Ringed Plover

Semipalmated Plover

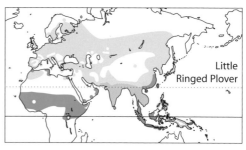

Little Ringed Plover

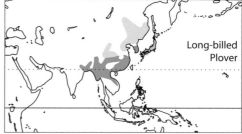

Long-billed Plover

Plate 56   KILLDEER, AND WILSON'S, COLLARED AND PIPING PLOVERS

Killdeer
Charadrius vociferus   See also plate 12

Key ID features   W 147–175mm. A most distinctive plover, with its bold white wingbars and long, grey, graduated white-edged tail, which has a broad, dark subterminal patch and buff and white tips; rump and lower back rusty orange.

Behaviour   During its display, the male, sometimes accompanied by the female, performs a 'butterfly' flight, circling overhead with slowly beating wings.

Flight action   The normal flight is leisurely and graceful.

Voice   The typical, penetrating *kill-deer kill-deer* notes are usually given in display. Alarm calls include a musical *tir-eeee* and a harder *dee*.

Distribution   Vagrant to Hawaii and western Europe, where it is usually recorded between November and April.

Confusion species   None, the orange of the rump and lower back is unique among waders.

Wilson's Plover
Charadrius wilsonia   See also plate 12

Key ID features   W 111–128mm. The large bill is usually noticeable, along with the short white wingbar; the white sides to the base of the tail, which has a dark subterminal bar, with white edges.

Voice   The call note is a high, whistled *whit* and the alarm note a lower, sharp *quit* or *quit-it*.

Distribution   There are two races within North America: *wilsonia* occurs along the Atlantic and Gulf coasts and *beldingi* along the Pacific coast.

Confusion species   Similar to Semipalmated Plover (plate 55), but Wilson's has a much larger bill, a shorter wingbar and a different tail pattern. Compare also Piping and 'Snowy' Plovers (plate 57 – Kentish Plover), both of which have paler upperparts, as well as Collared Plover, which lacks a white hind-collar and has a thin black and longish bill for a plover.

Collared Plover
Charadrius collaris   See also plate 43

Key ID features   W 94–110mm. A small plover, with a narrow white wingbar that extends onto the inner primaries; the white sides to the tail contrast with the dark centre; this species lacks the white-collar of similar plovers.

Voice   A sharp, metallic *chit* or *pit*.

Distribution   Vagrant to southern Texas.

Confusion species   Similar to 'Snowy' Plover (plate 57 – Kentish Plover), which has pale sandy-brown upperparts, a more obvious wingbar and a distinctive white neck-collar. The Semipalmated Plover (plate 55) is larger and darker above, with a more prominent wingbar and an obvious white neck-collar.

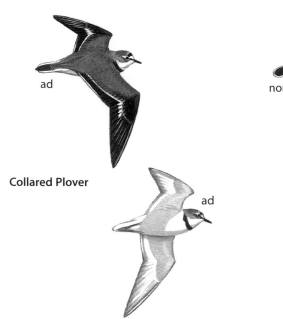

ad

Collared Plover

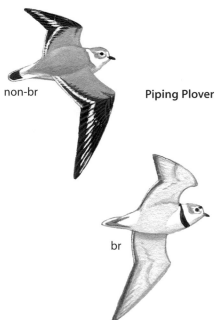

non-br

Piping Plover

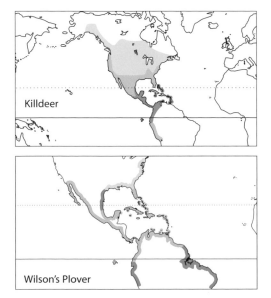

ad

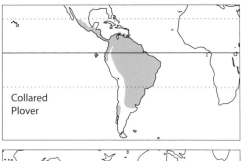

br

Piping Plover
Charadrius melodus See also plate 13

Key ID features W 114–127mm. The long prominent white wingbar contrasts with the pale grey upperparts and wing-coverts, and the blackish secondaries, primaries and primary-coverts; the white uppertail-coverts contrast with a dark subterminal tail-bar, which is edged and tipped white.
Voice A piping, but plaintive, descending *peep-u*,

from which its name is derived.
Distribution and status VULNERABLE due to habitat loss and human disturbance on beaches. Vagrant to California, Oregon and Washington.
Confusion species Piping Plover looks very pale in flight; note how the uppertail-coverts differ from 'Snowy' (plate 57 – Kentish Plover), which are dark-centred with prominent white edges, and Semipalmated (plate 55), which are also dark-centred and similar in colour to the back.

Killdeer

Collared Plover

Wilson's Plover

Piping Plover

Plate 57   KENTISH, KITTLITZ'S AND THREE-BANDED PLOVERS

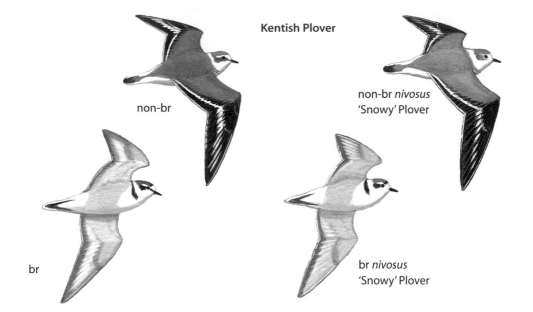

Kentish Plover

non-br

non-br *nivosus*
'Snowy' Plover

br

br *nivosus*
'Snowy' Plover

Kentish (Snowy) Plover
Charadrius alexandrinus   See also plate 13

Key ID features   W 102-123mm. The light grey-brown back and innerwing coverts contrast with the bold white wingbar, and the blackish primaries and primary-coverts. The prominent white sides to the tail are particularly distinctive as the bird alights.
Behaviour   Often runs as it alights. Performs a 'butterfly' display flight.
Flight action   Quick, with fluttery wing-beats.
Voice   The usual flight call is a sharp but quiet, sometimes repeated *pit* and the alarm calls are a hard *prrr* and a plaintive *too-eet*. The territorial call of the *nivosus* male is a whistled *pree-eet*, the second half higher and louder. The display song is a rhythmic repetition of a rattled *tjekke*.
Distribution   Three races occur within the region: the nominate *alexandrinus* from Eurasia east to Korea; *dealbatus* from east China and Japan; and *nivosus* of North America, also known as the 'Snowy' Plover.
Racial variation   In flight there is very little variation between the races, but *nivosus* has paler, more sandy–brown upperparts.
Confusion species   Piping Plover (plate 56), which is paler and has a different tail pattern. Sanderling (plate 77), in non-breeding plumage, has a similar bold white wingbar but lacks the white collar and dark breast sides, and the

tail pattern also differs. Smaller than the similar looking Lesser Sand Plover (plate 58), which also lacks a white neck-collar.

Kittlitz's Plover
Charadrius pecuarius   See also plate 45

Key ID features   W 98-112mm. The white sides to the tail and the narrow white wingbar are distinctive; the paler median coverts contrast with the dark leading edge of the wing, and with the dark primary-coverts and flight feathers. Also, most unusually for a small plover, the toes project well beyond the tail-tip.
Voice   The usual note is a gentle *towhit*; also gives a *prrrt* alarm note and a trilling *trit-tritritritrit* flight call.
Distribution   Annual to Israel; vagrant to Morocco, Spain, France and Cyprus.
Confusion species   The combination of projecting toes and the upperwing pattern make this species unmistakable within the region.

Three-banded Plover
Charadrius tricollaris   See also plate 45

Key ID features   W 106-117mm. A most distinctive small plover species, with uniformly dark brown upperparts, an indistinct white wing-bar and white trailing edge, broader on the inner secondaries; a longish tail, with white sides and the

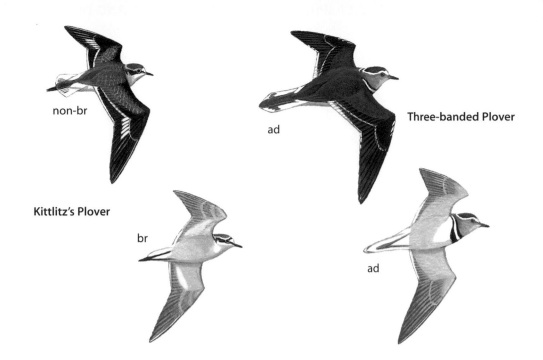

non-br

Kittlitz's Plover

br

ad

Three-banded Plover

ad

tip mostly unbarred.
Behaviour Usually only flies short distances and upon alighting bobs its tail.
Flight action Erratic flight with jerky wing-beats.
Voice Usual flight call is a high–pitched *tiuu-t-tiuu-t*; when alarmed utters a loud *wick-wick*; and when chasing another bird makes a rattling *kee-kee-kirra-kirra*.
Distribution One in Egypt in March 1993 is the only record within the region.
Confusion species The almost unique long-tailed proportions and upperparts, as described above, make this species unmistakable in flight.

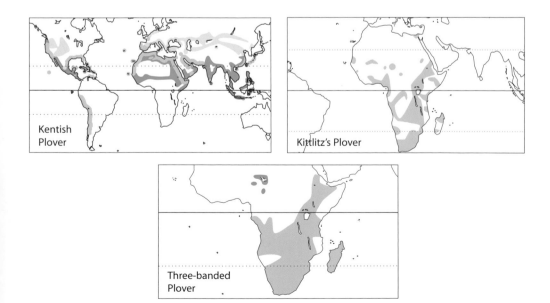

Kentish Plover

Kittlitz's Plover

Three-banded Plover

Plate 58   SAND PLOVERS, CASPIAN AND ORIENTAL PLOVERS AND DOTTEREL

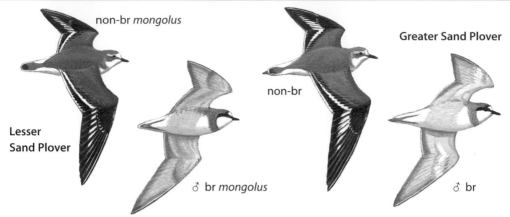

non-br *mongolus*

Greater Sand Plover

non-br

Lesser
Sand Plover

♂ br *mongolus*

♂ br

Lesser Sand Plover
Charadrius mongolus   See also plate 14

Key ID features W 118–145mm. The white wingbar is narrow across the innerwing and wider, usually with parallel edges, on the inner primaries.

Voice Call, distinguishable from Greater Sand Plover's, a short hard *chitik*, reminiscent of the Ruddy Turnstone (plate 71). Has a unique short grating song when displaying, *trit-it-it-it-turkhweeoo*.

Distribution Nominate race *mongolus* breeds inland E Siberia, winters Taiwan to Australia; *stegmanni* breeds NE Siberia and Commander Islands, winters Taiwan to E Australia; *atrifrons* breeds in Himalayas and S Tibet, winters India to Sumatra; *pamirensis* breeds central S Siberia, winters W India to E and S Africa; *schaeferi* breeds E Tibet, winters Thailand to Greater Sundas. Vagrant to Europe, Canada and USA.

Racial variation Compared to *atrifrons*, upper-tail of *mongolus* is darker, forming a broad band clearly contrasting with paler uppertail-coverts and upperparts, and shows less white on tail-sides.

Confusion species Greater Sand Plover shows more white on the tip and sides of the tail (see also its Key ID features). Caspian Plover, like Greater Sand Plover, has toes that project beyond the tail-tip. Other coastal plovers like Ringed and Semipalmated (plate 55), Wilson's Plover (plate 56) and Kentish Plover (plate 57) have obvious white neck collars.

Greater Sand Plover
Charadrius leschenaultii   See also plate 14

Key ID features W 132–153mm. The white wingbar, less prominent across the innerwing, bulges on the inner primaries; tail has a dark sub-terminal bar and toes project beyond the tail-tip.

Voice Call is a soft, trilling *trrri*.

Distribution The nominate race *leschenaultii* breeds in western China and Mongolia, winters in Australasia; *crassirostris* breeds between the Caspian Sea and Lake Balkash, winters in east and south-east Africa; *columbinus* breeds in Turkey and Jordan east to the Caspian Sea, winters Red Sea and southeast Mediterranean. Vagrant to California and western Europe.

Confusion species Lesser Sand Plover (compare Key ID features). Caspian Plover has less white on the wing and favours grassland rather than coasts, as does Mountain Plover (plate 54), but their ranges are most unlikely to overlap.

Caspian Plover
Charadrius asiaticus   See also plate 15

Key ID features W 140–157mm. Long-winged; narrow white wingbar on tips of greater coverts, broadens on bases of inner primaries to form a distinct white flash; upperparts otherwise a uniform brown, with darker flight feathers; toes project a little beyond tail-tip.

Behaviour Gregarious, often occurs in dense flying flocks.

Voice Flight call a loud, sharp *tyup*, or a soft, sharp *kit* usually repeated a few times. Loud trisyllabic calls are given in display.

Distribution Vagrant across Europe, including Britain.

Confusion species Oriental Plover lacks any primary flashes on upperwing and has darker grey-brown rather than the paler greyish under-wing-coverts of Caspian.

Oriental Plover
Charadrius veredus   See also plate 16

Key ID features W 156-178mm. Long-winged, with almost uniform brown upperparts and indistinct wingbar; the uniformly dark grey-brown underwing contrasts with the white belly;

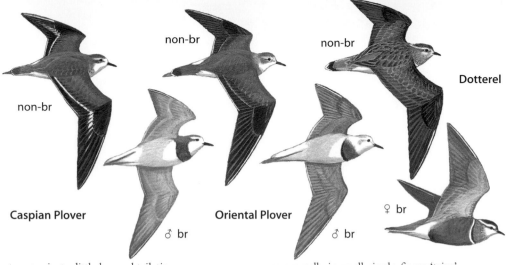

non-br

non-br

non-br

Dotterel

Caspian Plover

♂ br

Oriental Plover

♂ br

♀ br

toes project a little beyond tail-tip.

Flight action Fast, powerful, with erratic turns.

Voice A sharp *chip-chip-chip*, also a short, piping *klink*.

Distribution Vagrant to Finland.

Confusion species Caspian Plover is smaller, has an obvious white patch on the base of the inner primaries, a narrow white wingbar and pale greyish rather than dark grey-brown underwing-coverts.

Dotterel
Charadrius morinellus   See also plate 15

Key ID features W 143 - 163mm. Plain grey-brown upperparts, wings and base of tail; tail has a blackish subterminal bar and white tip. White supercilia meet on the nape.

Behaviour On migration, visits traditional sites; occasionally forms larger flocks of 20-80, but more usually in small, single-figure 'trips'.

Voice Not very vocal, particularly in winter. Usual flight note is a soft, but penetrating *pweet-pweet-pweet*.

Distribution Regular in Japan in autumn; scarce but regular in NW Alaska in summer; vagrant to Washington and California, Iceland and Spitzbergen.

Confusion species Uniform upperparts are similar to Golden Plover species (plate 54) and Buff-breasted Sandpiper (plate 75) but note tail pattern.

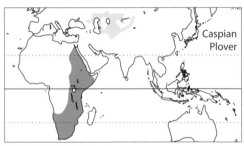

Caspian Plover

Lesser Sand Plover

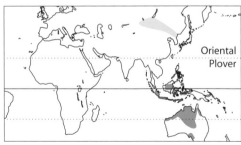

Oriental Plover

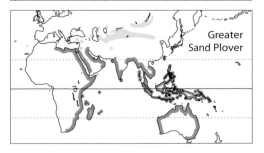

Greater Sand Plover

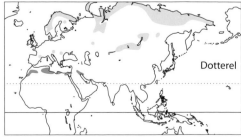

Dotterel

Plate 59 WOODCOCKS AND GREAT SNIPE

American
Woodcock

ad

ad

Eurasian
Woodcock

ad

ad

American Woodcock

Scolopax minor   See also plate 17

Key ID features W 128–146mm. Longish bill; rounded wings; reddish-brown upperparts, with silvery-grey mantle Vs; uniform orange-buff underparts, including underwing-coverts, are diagnostic.

Behaviour Performs spectacular displays at dawn and dusk. From a display ground the male rises vertically on 'twittering' wings, sings as he circles, then returns in a rapid spiral. The twittering sound, made by the movement of air over the outer primaries, begins steadily as the bird rises, comes in well-spaced bursts as the bird circles and during the downward spiral becomes a series of louder, more varied *tewp tilp tiptooptip* chirps.

Flight action Relatively slow and erratic on quick fluttering wing-beats.

Voice Virtually silent except when displaying, when a loud buzzing *peent* call, reminiscent of Common Nighthawk but less harsh, is uttered from the ground.

Distribution Vagrant west to Montana, Colorado, California and Mexico.

Confusion species Smaller than Eurasian Woodcock, with distinctive orange-buff underparts that lack barring.

Eurasian Woodcock

Scolopax rusticola   See also plate 17

Key ID features W 182–218mm. Barrel-shaped body; long bill; broad rounded wings; reddish-brown upperparts and heavily barred underparts are distinctive.

Behaviour Display flights, known as 'roding', take place at dawn and dusk. The wing-beats are slower than normal, giving the flight an owl-like quality; bill often held almost perpendicular to body.

Flight action When flushed, bursts out of cover with noisy wing-beats and twists away through trees.

Voice Invariably silent when flushed, though may make a snipe-like *schaap*, when disturbed from feeding grounds at night. Roding song composed of two parts: a guttural *quorr-quorr-quo-ro* followed by a high-pitched *pietz*.

Distribution Vagrant to northeastern North America and Alabama, Greenland, Iceland and Kuwait.

Confusion species Larger than American Woodcock with heavily barred underparts. Similar to Amami Woodcock (see Confusion species for Amami).

Amami Woodcock

Scolopax mira   See also plate 17

Key ID features W 198–215mm A broad-winged woodcock, with dark rufous-brown upperparts and a fairly uniform, shortish tail.

Behaviour Known to fly only very short distances when disturbed.

Voice Occasionally makes a snipe-like *jheet* note.

Distribution and status VULNERABLE due to limited range.

Confusion species Eurasian Woodcock, which winters on islands where Amami is resident, is extremely similar and separation in flight is difficult but, with good views, the longer tail of Eurasian shows a dark subterminal band and broad, silvery grey tips; white tips to the wing-coverts of Eurasian create a less uniform dark appearance compared with Amami.

Amami
Woodcock

ad

ad

ad

Great Snipe

ad

Great Snipe
Gallinago media   See also plate 17

Key ID features W 139–155mm. A bulky snipe, with chequered lesser coverts; dark central wing-panel bordered by white wingbars; heavily barred underparts and diagnostic white outer-tail feathers.

Behaviour Very different from Common Snipe when flushed; flies low and often drops down again within a short distance.

Flight action Invariably flies silently after disturbance with heavy, straight and level flight.

Voice Exceptionally silent on migration and in winter but a low, guttural croaking *heert* may occasionally be uttered by a bird when flushed. During the ground display produces a twittering *bipp-bipp-bippbippbipp* call.

Distribution Vagrant to Spitzbergen.

Confusion species Common Snipe, when flushed, invariably zigzags away, often high, with rapid wing-beats and frequent calls. When plumage is seen well the dark secondaries of Common Snipe, with a white trailing edge, will be obvious, but Great Snipe has dark greater coverts and greater primary-coverts sandwiched by white wingbars formed by the white tips. The white outer tail feathers of Great Snipe (particularly of adult, but also of juvenile) are most easily seen as the bird lands with tail spread.

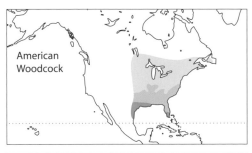

American
Woodcock

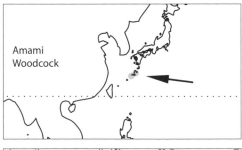

Amami
Woodcock

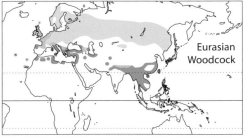

Eurasian
Woodcock

Great
Snipe

Plate 60 **COMMON, WILSON'S, PINTAIL AND JACK SNIPES**

ad

ad

ad

ad

Common
Snipe

Wilson's Snipe

Common Snipe
Gallinago gallinago   See also plate 19

Key ID features W 123–144mm. Long bill, with broad white trailing edge to wing; white under-wing-coverts.
Behaviour Display flights involve 'drumming', a winnowing sound produced by the vibration of the outer-tail feathers as the bird dives, with spread tail, flapping its wings.
Flight action When flushed, flies with a rapid zig-zagging trajectory often climbing quite high.
Voice Call, usually given when flushed, is a rasping, almost disyllabic *ska-ip*. The display song, often given from a post, is a repeated *chip-er-chip-er-chip-er-chip*.
Distribution The nominate race occurs throughout most of the Palearctic; *faeroeensis* in Iceland, Faeroes, Orkney and Shetland, a majority of which migrate to Ireland for the winter. Nominate race *gallinago* is a vagrant to Labrador and regular on the Aleutians.
Confusion species Jack Snipe is significantly smaller and drops down quickly once flushed. The larger Great Snipe (plate 59) has distinctive white outer tail feathers. Pintail Snipe looks shorter-billed, lacks the bold white trailing edge to sec-ondaries and has a pale upperwing-panel, which contrasts with the rest of the duller brown wing (see also Key ID features for Pintail). Swinhoe's Snipe (plate 61) is more like Pintail Snipe. Latham's Snipe (plate 61) also lacks a bold white trailing edge to secondaries.

Wilson's Snipe
Gallinago delicata   See also plate 19

Key ID features W 123–144mm. Narrow white trailing edge to secondaries; underwing dark, extensively barred.
Flight action Tends to tower when disturbed.
Voice Call and song similar to Common Snipe, but the winnowing sound is higher, less full-toned.
Distribution Vagrant to Britain.
Confusion species The lack of reddish tones and the Key ID features help to separate it from Common Snipe. The winnowing display involves pairs of narrow outer tail feathers compared with single, broader feathers of Common Snipe.

Pintail Snipe
Gallinago stenura   See also plate 19

Key ID features W 125–143mm. Medium length bill; pale buff-fringed median and lesser coverts form distinct pale panel; pale trailing edge to wing barely visible; toes project well beyond tail-tip.
Behaviour Escape flight usually less towering than Common. Has a similar ascending display flight to Swinhoe's and when reaching a plateau delivers repeated calls as it circles. During a steep plunging descent, in a wide arc, a buzzing whistle is given, blended with and then replaced by a humming sound from the fanned outer-tail feath-ers. The wings are three-quarters closed and motionless during the rapid descent.
Flight action Slow, heavier, often low with few zigzags, when flushed.
Voice Call when flushed similar in form to Common Snipe but less harsh, a nasal *tchak* resembling a duck's quack. Display song involves repeated *zhzhik* calls that become a continuous buzzing whistle *zhzhik-zhzhik-zhik-zhik-zhzhii-*

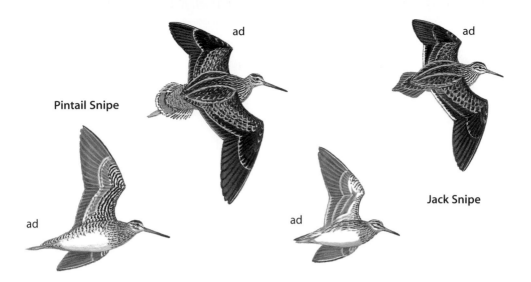

Pintail Snipe

ad

ad

Jack Snipe

ad

ad

zhzhii-shchshchiiishchshchiiii.
Distribution Vagrant to Aleutians, Israel and Italy.
Confusion species Common Snipe (see Confusion species for Common). Swinhoe's Snipe (plate 61).

Jack Snipe
Lymnocryptes minimus   See also plate 19

Key ID features W 105–121mm. Small; comparatively short bill; wedge-shaped tail; bold creamy mantle stripes; dark brown flight feathers, with narrow white trailing edge; all make this a distinctive species.

Behaviour Display flights, most often in early morning and early evening, involve switchback movements, with steep climbs and dives, wings half-folded and decurved below the body, giving 'cantering horse' calls throughout.
Flight action Rather slow and reluctant when flushed.
Voice Invariably silent when flushed but may utter a short low *gech*. During display, one song sounds like a 'cantering horse' *ogogogIK-ogogog-IK-ogogogIK-ogogogIK*, also a rapid knocking and various high-pitched whistles.
Distribution Vagrant to North America.
Confusion species Its small size eliminates any confusion with other snipe species.

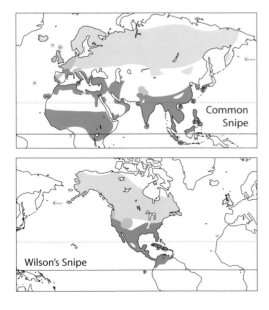

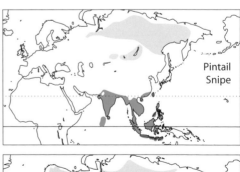

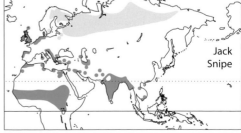

Plate 61   **SWINHOE'S, SOLITARY, LATHAM'S AND WOOD SNIPES**

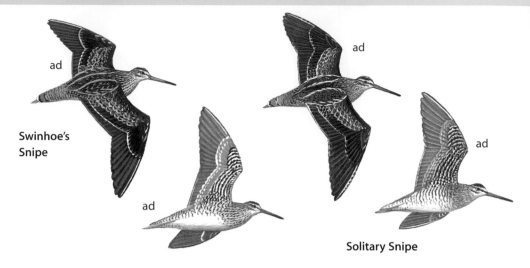

Swinhoe's Snipe

Solitary Snipe

Note that variations within each species lead to overlaps in size, structure and plumage, and a combination of typical characteristics is essential for correct identification.

Swinhoe's Snipe

Gallinago megala   See also plate 18

Key ID features   W 137–151mm. Heavy-looking; creamy-buff fringes to median and lower-lesser coverts form distinct pale wing-panel; which contrasts with the dark brown primaries and paler brown secondaries; lacks pale trailing edge to secondaries. Underwing-coverts evenly barred.

Behaviour   Display flight involves ascent in stages, with rapid wing-beats on the climb then long glides; followed by a similar alternating pattern in wide horizontal circles, giving a series of calls; then a steep arc-like descent with tail-feathers spread, the outer ones vibrating to produce a low humming sound. The descent is rapid on half-closed wings, with periodic bursts of shallow wing-beats.

Flight action   When flushed usually flies only a short way, making fluttering, more pigeon-like wing-beats.

Voice   Rarely calls when flushed, except when repeatedly disturbed and, when compared with Common Snipe's harsh *ska-ip*, utters a less harsh, higher-pitched *tcheeek*, sounding longer than Pintail's. Display song in flight a repeated *striki-strik-kr-kr*, may also be given from a post or from the ground.

Distribution   Vagrant to northern Caucasus and Urals.

Confusion species   Calls and displays can separate Swinhoe's Snipe from Pintail Snipe, the toes of which project further beyond the tail-tip, but their plumages are very similar, see plates 19 and 60.

Solitary Snipe

Gallinago solitaria   See also plate 18

Key ID features   W 157–174mm. A heavy-looking snipe, with long bill, wings and tail; pale wing-panel across median-coverts; narrow wing-bar and inconspicuous white trailing edge to secondaries; closely barred underwing appears dull brown.

Flight action   Relatively slow and heavy.

Voice   Flight call similar to Common Snipe but a less harsh *shreep* or a shorter, hoarse *jep*.

Distribution   Validity of two races is uncertain; nominate throughout most of range; *japonica* winters in Japan; some winter south to Korea

Confusion species   Wood Snipe has broader, more rounded wings and heavily barred underparts (compare Key ID features).

Latham's Snipe

Gallinago hardwickii   See also plate 18

Key ID features   W 157–168mm. A heavy-looking snipe, with long wings and tail; fairly obvious pale wing-panel across median-coverts, contrasts with dark lesser and greater coverts; dull greyish trailing edge to secondaries; underwing closely barred appears dull brown.

Behaviour   Particularly visible during dramatic courtship display, with chases accompanied by harsh calls and steep zigzag dives, which include 'drumming'. Can also be heard displaying at night. Display calls made from poles and tree tops.

Flight action   When flushed flies heavily, with few zigzags and drops back quickly into cover.

Voice   A short, rasping *krek*. Regular *zrack* calls are

ad

ad

Wood Snipe

ad

ad

Latham's Snipe

given between drumming plunges during display flights. The flight call is a distinctive *zubi-yak zubi-yak* and the display call a *je-jee je-jee je-jee*. Display-flight vocalisations consist of two parts: a *tsupiyaku-tsupiyaku-tsupiyaku* followed by *gwo-gwo-gwo-gwo-gwo-gwo*, then a drumming sequence.

Distribution Strongly migratory.

Confusion species Common Snipe (plate 60) has conspicuous white trailing edge to the secondaries, as opposed to grey.

Wood Snipe

Gallinago nemoricola   See also plate 18

Key ID features W 142–156mm. Heavy and woodcock-like bird, with a deep bill-base; broad rounded wings; very dark upperparts and heavily barred underpart feathers; paler median and greater covert panel; narrow greyish trailing edge to the wing and virtual absence of white in the tail.

Behaviour When flushed rarely flies far.

Flight action Reminiscent of woodcock, slow and wavering.

Voice When flushed from cover may give a low croaking *chok-chok*.

Distribution and status VULNERABLE. A little-known species.

Confusion species Solitary Snipe occurs at similar altitude but favours wetter areas; note the bright chestnut on the tail and white belly of that species (compare Key ID features).

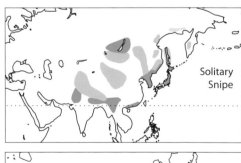

Swinhoe's Snipe

Solitary Snipe

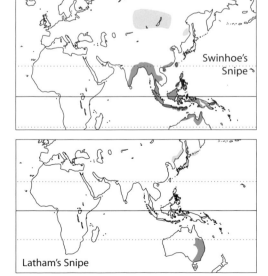

Latham's Snipe

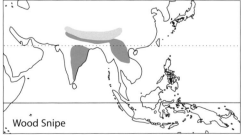

Wood Snipe

Plate 62 **BAR-TAILED GODWIT AND DOWITCHERS**

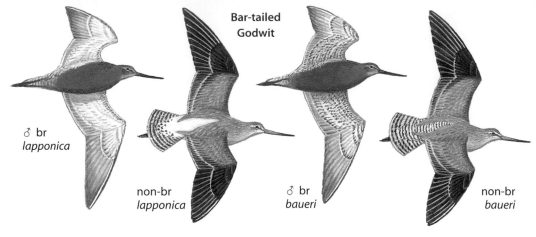

Bar-tailed
Godwit

♂ br
lapponica

non-br
lapponica

♂ br
baueri

non-br
baueri

Bar-tailed Godwit
Limosa lapponica   See also plate 21

Key ID features W 190–231mm. White rump and V up back, plain brown wings and mantle, darker primary-coverts and barred tail; long, slightly upturned bill.

Behaviour Often makes remarkable aerial manoeuvres, twisting, gliding and turning, with sudden downward swoops and gushing of wings during display flights.

Flight action Birds in migrant flocks usually hold heads in close to deep chest, giving short-necked appearance.

Voice Usually rather quiet. Birds in migrating flocks occasionally utter a harsh but subdued *kirruk*.

Distribution Nominate *lapponica* breeds Lapland east to Taymyr, winters from North Sea to W South Africa, *baueri* breeds NE Russia to Alaska, winters China to New Zealand. Vagrant to Pacific and Atlantic coasts of N America.

Racial variation The nominate *lapponica* has the lower back and rump white, contrasting with the barred tail; *baueri* is larger (W 199–256mm) and the lower back is barred brown and the rump and tail are whitish, heavily barred with brown; the underwing is heavily barred, unlike mainly white of *lapponica*. The difference is similar to that between the Eurasian and Hudsonian races of Whimbrel.

Confusion species Similar to Whimbrel at a distance, but straight or slightly upturned bill is diagnostic. Larger than both Short-billed and Long-billed Dowitchers, which have a more pronounced white trailing edge to the secondaries and white confined to the back. The eastern race *baueri* is very similar to Asiatic Dowitcher from above, but the white underwing of the latter is diagnostic.

Short-billed Dowitcher
Limnodromus griseus   See also plate 20

Key ID features W 135–156mm. In flight, almost inseparable from Long-billed other than by call. Back and upper rump white; lower rump, uppertail-coverts and tail white, with dark brown bars; white trailing edge to secondaries; and long snipe-like bill.

Behaviour Male sings during a hovering display flight.

Flight action More plump looking than Bar-tailed Godwit. Often flies with periods of long, fast glides, otherwise strong and swift, and often in lines, rather than flocks.

Voice Typically, a fast and low, trisyllabic *tu-tu-tu*, faster than Greenshank, or Lesser Yellowlegs, a rhythm more like the rattle of the Ruddy Turnstone (plate 71). The song is a broken trill concluding with a buzzy *dowitcher*.

Distribution Nominate *griseus* breeds in eastern Canada and winters in the Gulf States, Caribbean and W Atlantic coasts south to Brazil; *hendersoni* breeds in central Canada and winters on the coasts of Central America; *caurinus* breeds in southern Alaska, winters along the E Pacific coast south to Peru. A scarce vagrant to the Western Palearctic.

Confusion species Bar-tailed Godwit, but Short-billed Dowitcher is smaller, lacks white rump and has white trailing edges to the second-aries. Long-billed Dowitcher has light bars on the tail that are never wider than the black ones and are usually narrower; on Short-billed the light bars are usually wider, but not always, partly dependent on the race. Possible confusion with Spotted Redshank (plate 67) when that species flies with its legs retracted, though it lacks the white trailing edge to secondaries of Short-billed Dowitcher.

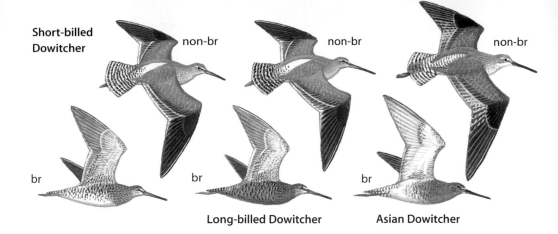

Short-billed Dowitcher

non-br

non-br

non-br

br

br

br

Long-billed Dowitcher

Asian Dowitcher

Asian Dowitcher

Limnodromus semipalmatus See also plate 32

Key ID features W 174-188mm. A pale panel across the inner primaries and outer secondaries is distinctive; the back, rump and uppertail-coverts are white, heavily barred brown; and the white tail is similarly barred brown. The underwing is virtually pure white and toes project beyond tail-tip.
Behaviour Often flies in tight flocks.
Flight action Powerful and often aerobatic.
Voice Contact calls include a soft moaning *kiaow*, strangely reminiscent of a distant human voice, and a quiet *chowp* or *chep-chep*. A soft *kewik-kewik-kewik-ku* is uttered on the breeding grounds.
Distribution Occurs on passage in Japan, eastern China and Hong Kong.
Confusion species Similar to the eastern race *baueri* of Bar-tailed Godwit from above, but the dowitcher's white underwing is diagnostic. Long-billed and Short-billed Dowitchers show white

backs and broad white trailing edges to the secondaries and barred rather than white underwings.

Long-billed Dowitcher

Limnodromus scolopaceus See also Plate 20

Key ID features W 140-159mm. Virtually identical to Short-billed Dowitcher.
Voice Call-note is a high, often repetitive, thin *keek*. Song is similar to Short-billed but with subtle differences.
Distribution Vagrant along the W Pacific coast to Japan, Hong Kong and India, also to western Europe, most frequently in Britain and Ireland, where autumn juveniles are regular.
Confusion species Short-billed Dowitcher and Bar-tailed Godwit (see Confusion species for both). Range overlaps with Asian Dowitcher, which has less white on the back and rump, lacks the clear white trailing edge to the secondaries and is nearly all white on the underwing.

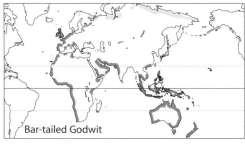

Bar-tailed Godwit

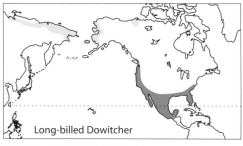

Long-billed Dowitcher

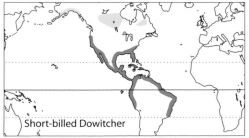

Short-billed Dowitcher

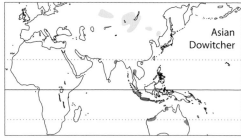

Asian Dowitcher

Plate 63   **WILLET AND GODWITS**

br
inornatus

Willet

br *semipalmatus*

non-br

non-br
inornatus

non-br
semipalmatus

br

**Hudsonian
Godwit**

Willet
Catoptrophorus semipalmatus   See also plate 27

Key ID features   W 186-222mm. The broad white wingbar contrasts with the black distal half of the primaries and primary-coverts, and grey mantle and innerwing-coverts; toes visible beyond tail-tip.

Behaviour   Display flight is *Tringa*-like, with stiffly-held down-curved wings.

Voice   Noisy alarm calls include a ringing *kyaah-yah*, a more intense *kip-kip-kip* and a raucous, rolled *krrri-lii-liit*. During the song flight utters a musical onomatopoeic *pill-will-willet*.

Distribution   Western race *inornatus* is strongly migratory; breeds on the prairies of SW Canada and NW USA, migrates S to winter along the Pacific coast, the Atlantic and Gulf coasts, in the Caribbean and coastal South America. The nominate, eastern race *semipalmatus* is more sedentary, and breeds along the Atlantic and Gulf coasts of the USA and in the Caribbean. Vagrant to the Western Palearctic; with single birds to the Azores, Finland and Norway between 1979 and 1992.

Racial variation   Breeding plumage of *inornatus* usually has unbarred or finely barred central tail feathers and usually less barring on flanks.

Confusion species   At a glance the dark underwing-coverts and axillaries are similar to those of Hudsonian Godwit, while the upperwing is similar to that of Black-tailed Godwit, but proportions and bill lengths should rapidly dispel any confusion between these species and Willet, which has more rounded wings.

Hudsonian Godwit
Limosa haemastica   See also plate 22

Key ID features   W 200-229mm. Conspicuous, narrow white wing bars; largely black tail with narrow white band across uppertail-coverts; black axillaries and underwing-coverts; toes project well beyond tail-tip.

Flight action   Swift and powerful, as required for a long-distance migrant.

Voice   Often silent on migration but the usual flight call is a rising *kweh-weh*, similar to Marbled Godwit, but higher pitched.

Distribution   Rare vagrant to western Europe. Rare on Pacific coast south of Oregon.

Confusion species   Black-tailed Godwit has white not black underwing-coverts.

Marbled Godwit
Limosa fedoa   See also plate 22

Key ID features   W 205–255mm. Almost uniform cinnamon-buff plumage is unique among godwits. Distinct long, almost straight bill; toes project well beyond tail-tip.

Behaviour   Like other godwits, performs an impressive ceremonial display, which includes a range of ascending and tumbling flights.

Voice   Flight call rather harsh, two-syllabled *cor-ack*, not unlike that of Bar-tailed Godwit.

Distribution   Nominate *fedoa* breeds on the northern Great Plains of N America, winters southern California to Chile; *beringiae* breeds in Alaska, winters US Pacific coast probably S to central California.

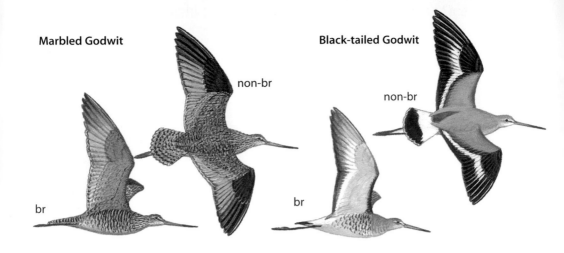

Marbled Godwit

non-br

br

Black-tailed Godwit

non-br

br

Confusion species Long-billed Curlew (plate 66) is similarly coloured but larger with distinct decurved bill. Bar-tailed Godwit, particularly the eastern race *baueri*, is similarly proportioned, with toes that only just project beyond tail-tip, could be mistaken for a faded Marbled Godwit.

Black-tailed Godwit
Limosa limosa　　　　　　See also plate 21

Key ID features W 201–240mm. Prominent white wingbar, black tail and white rump; underwing white, with black edges; toes and lower tarsi extend beyond tail-tip.

Behaviour Males perform impressive ceremonial display flights in breeding season, including a vertical nose-dive with corkscrews and wind noises.

Voice Calls infrequently, a quiet, short *tuk* or *kik*. When breeding has a rhythmic *wick-a-wick-a-wick-a* call and a *wee-eeh* like Northern Lapwing.

Distribution Nominate *limosa* breeds in western Eurasia, winters in Mediterranean, east to India; *islandica* breeds in Iceland, N Norway and Shetland, winters in Ireland, Britain and western Europe; disjunct populations of *melanuroides* breed in Siberia and China, winter in Thailand and further south. Rare spring migrant in Alaska. Vagrant to US east coast.

Confusion species Separated from Bar-tailed Godwit (plate 62) not only by upperpart pattern, but by longer neck and bill, and greater leg projection, which give this species a more attenuated appearance. Separated from Hudsonian Godwit by the distinctive white rather than blackish underwing.

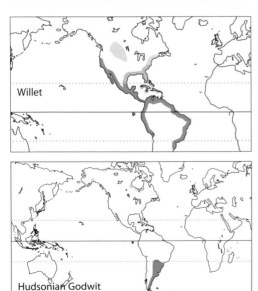

Willet

Hudsonian Godwit

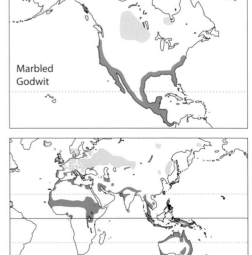

Marbled Godwit

Black-tailed Godwit

Plate 64   SMALLER CURLEWS AND UPLAND SANDPIPER

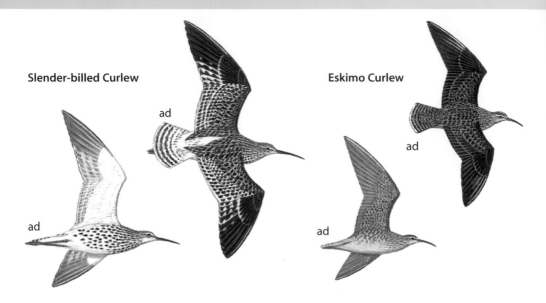

Slender-billed Curlew

ad

Eskimo Curlew

ad

ad

ad

Slender-billed Curlew
Numenius tenuirostris   See also plate 24

Key ID features W 243–259. Upperwing shows a noticeable contrast between the almost black outer primaries and dark primary covert patch, and the rest of the sandy-grey wing; the underwing appears all white, though the pale grey primaries, with dark tips and faintly barred pale secondaries do provide some contrast with the unmarked white coverts. The white tail has four to five distinct broad dark bars.

Voice Generally silent, but a similar call to the *cour-lee* of Eurasian Curlew is higher pitched and shorter. A probable alarm call is a short and distinctly high-pitched *kwee*, sometimes repeated twice and usually uttered during take-off and landing. A less often heard third call is a rapid *ti-ti-ti-ti-ti-ti-ti* which rises progressively in pitch.

Distribution and status CRITICALLY ENDANGERED. Breeding and wintering grounds now unknown; small numbers wintered in Morocco until mid-1990s. Migrants have been very occasionally seen in the Mediterranean basin. Vagrant to the Atlantic coast of western Europe and to Britain; single old records from Ontario and Japan.

Confusion species Eurasian Curlew, a species that shows considerable degree of variation in overall size and in bill length, particularly between sexes. Even the Key ID features detailed above are consistent with Eurasian Curlew (plate 66) subspecies *orientalis* and occasionally with *arquata*. Whimbrel (plate 65) never shows a sharp upperwing contrast and the underwing is less white.

Eskimo Curlew
Numenius borealis   See also plate 43

Key ID features W 187–226mm Uniformly dark brown upperparts; relatively long and pointed wings; rich cinnamon underwing-coverts and axillaries; toes do not project beyond tail-tip.

Voice Soft, repeated, melodious whistles.

Distribution and status Considered CRITICALLY ENDANGERED, though now probably extinct. No fully documented records since 1963.

Confusion species Most like Little Curlew, which is slightly smaller but which has longer legs and so its toes project just beyond tail-tip.

Little Curlew
Numenius minutus   See also plate 23

Key ID features W 176–193. Upperparts appear uniform buffy-brown; underwing-coverts are buff, barred brown; toes project just beyond tail-tip.

Behaviour During the male's display flight, a whistling sound emanates from the wings and tail as he dives spectacularly from a great height.

Voice A soft, rising *te-te-te* whistle, also a *tchew-tchew-tchew* similar to Greenshank but lower and harsher. Song includes rising *corr-corr-corr* followed by a more level-pitched *quee-quee-quee*.

Distribution Vagrant to Alaska, Washington and California, Britain, Norway and Sweden.

Confusion species Until the bill and underwing-coverts (compared in parentheses) are seen clearly, could be confused with Upland Sandpiper (dark, strongly barred brown), Pacific Golden Plover (plate 54, uniformly grey), and even

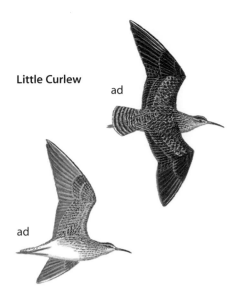

Little Curlew

ad

ad

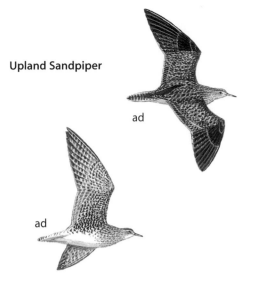

Upland Sandpiper

ad

ad

Buff-breasted Sandpiper (plate 75, white) or Whimbrel (plate 65, white, buff, or barred brown, depending on race).

Upland Sandpiper
Bartramia longicauda   See also plate 23

Key ID features W 156–191. Entirely brown from above, with long graduated tail.
Behaviour Display flights are lengthy, often taking place high in the air; on landing the bird holds its wings aloft.
Flight action On the breeding grounds often flies with stiff bowed wings, reminiscent of

Common and Spotted Sandpipers.
Voice One flight call is a Whimbrel-like *quip-ip-ip-ip*, another a liquid *pulip*. The song is a trilling, ascending and descending *whrrreeeee-wheeeeyuuuu-uuu*, like a 'wolf-whistle'.
Distribution Vagrant to California, Iceland and Western Europe.
Confusion species Upperparts similar to Little Curlew and Pacific Golden Plover (plate 54) but their ranges are unlikely to overlap; Buff-breasted Sandpiper (plate 75) lacks the long neck and tail, is smaller and has white underwings; the similar American and Eurasian Golden Plovers also lack the long neck and tail.

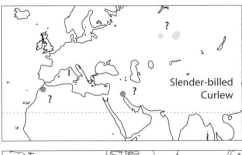

Slender-billed Curlew

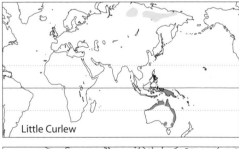

Little Curlew

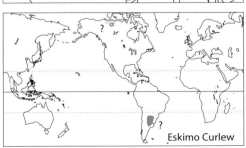

Eskimo Curlew

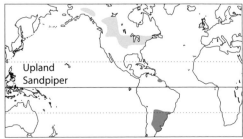

Upland Sandpiper

Plate 65 **WHIMBREL AND BRISTLE-THIGHED CURLEW**

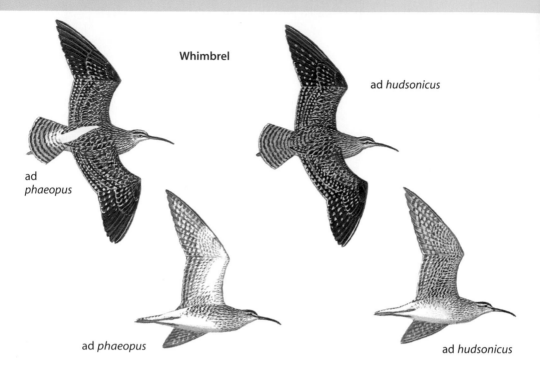

Whimbrel

ad *hudsonicus*

ad
phaeopus

ad *phaeopus*

ad *hudsonicus*

Whimbrel

Numenius phaeopus   See also plate 24

Key ID features W 214–278mm. A medium-sized curlew species, with variable plumage according to race. Nominate has a white rump and V on back; and largely white underwing-coverts.

Behaviour The circling display flight is performed higher in the sky than that of Eurasian Curlew.

Flight action Flies strongly with more rapid wing-beats than larger curlew species, closer to those of Bar-tailed Godwit.

Voice Flight call is a far-carrying, rippling *whi-whi-whi-whi-whi-whi-whi*. Bubbling display song is very similar to that of Eurasian Curlew.

Distribution The nominate race *phaeopus* nests in northern Europe and Russia, winters Africa and NW India, vagrant to Atlantic coast of North America; *hudsonicus* breeds in Alaska and north Canada, winters south to South America, vagrant to western Europe; *variegatus* breeds eastern

Siberia, winters Pacific islands and Australia, regular spring and autumn migrant to western Alaska.

Racial variation The 'Hudsonian Whimbrel' *hudsonicus* has a cinnamon-buff barred-brown tail, rump and back; with buff underwing-coverts barred brown; *variegatus* has dark brown upperparts, a heavily brown-barred white rump and back; and white underwing-coverts barred brown.

Confusion species Flocks of Bar-tailed Godwit (plate 62), particularly at a distance, look very similar, though the upperparts are paler and their bills are straight or slightly upcurved; the eastern race *baueri*, which lacks the white rump and lower back of the nominate race, has upperparts similar to the *hudsonicus* and *variegatus* races of Whimbrel. Compared with Slender-billed Curlew (plate 64), the upperwing of Whimbrel never shows the marked contrast and the Whimbrel underwing shows far less white. Bristle-thighed Curlew lacks the barred rump of 'Hudsonian Whimbrel' and has richer cinnamon underwing-coverts. Far Eastern Curlew (plate 66) appears similar to *variegatus* but is larger and generally longer-billed.

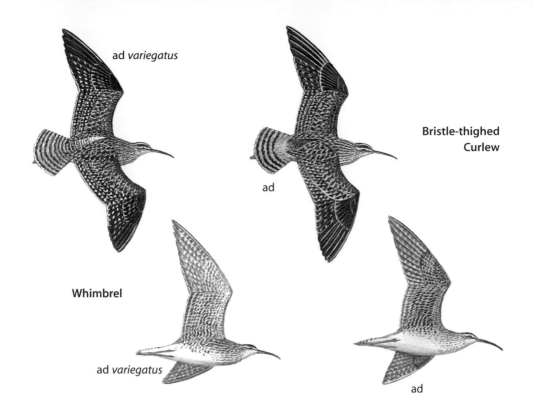

ad *variegatus*

Bristle-thighed
Curlew

ad

Whimbrel

ad *variegatus*

ad

Bristle-thighed Curlew
Numenius tahitiensis   See also plate 24

Key ID features W 225-260. The warm–brown innerwing-coverts and mantle, and the mainly dark brown flight feathers, contrast with the unbarred bright cinnamon lower rump, uppertail-coverts and tail, the last distinctly barred brown; the underwing-coverts and axillaries are also cinnamon, barred brown.
Behaviour Performs a spectacular soaring display flight, uttering a variety of complex notes.
Voice Quite unlike Whimbrel; a far-carrying, insistent *teeoip*, remarkably like a human attention-attracting whistle.
Distribution and status VULNERABLE. Vagrant to S Alaska, Vancouver I., Washington and Japan.
Confusion species 'Hudsonian Whimbrel' has a similar cinnamon tail, rump and back, all of which are barred; the unbarred uppertail-coverts and lower rump of Bristle-thighed Curlew are diagnostic.

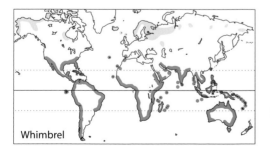

Whimbrel

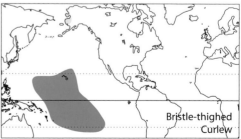

Bristle-thighed
Curlew

Plate 66 LARGER CURLEWS

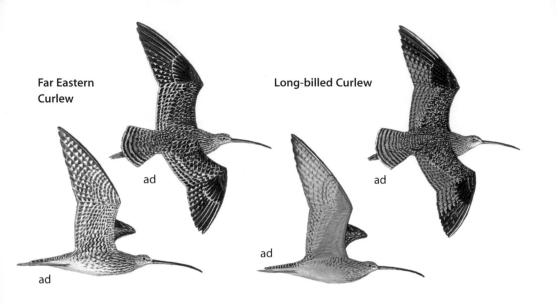

Far Eastern
Curlew

Long-billed Curlew

ad

ad

ad

ad

Far Eastern Curlew
Numenius madagascariensis   See also plate 25

Key ID features W 290–338mm. The largest curlew, with almost entirely brown upperparts, but secondaries and inner primaries notched buffish-white; barred brown underwings and very long bill.
Behaviour A bubbling courtship display song is delivered in flight with downcurved wings.
Flight action Flocks often fly in line or V formation.
Voice A plaintive *curr-ee* call similar to that of Eurasian Curlew but flatter. When alarmed makes a strident *ker ker-ee-ker-ee*.
Distribution Vagrant to British Columbia, more regular in western Alaska in spring.
Confusion species Eastern race of Eurasian Curlew *orientalis* is similar but has a white rump and lower back and almost white underwing-coverts and axillaries. The cinnamon colour of Long-billed Curlew is diagnostic. Could be confused with the *hudsonicus* race of Whimbrel (plate 65), but this and the eastern race of Whimbrel, *variegatus*, are considerably smaller and shorter-billed and show a cleaner white belly and undertail-coverts; *variegatus* also has barring on the white lower back and rump.

Long-billed Curlew
Numenius americanus   See also plate 25

Key ID features W 257-308mm. A large, cinnamon plumaged curlew, with a very long bill.

The outer primaries and greater primary-coverts are dark brown; the upperwing-coverts are mottled dark brown and buff; the secondaries, inner primaries, lower back, rump and tail are cinnamon, heavily barred brown; the underwing is a uniform, bright cinnamon.
Behaviour Performs spectacular roller-coaster display flights, with slow-flapping and gliding, covering a large territory.
Flight action Slow wing-beats are more goose-like.
Voice Usual flight call is a loud, rising *cur-lee*.
Distribution The breeding range of the northern race *parvus* extends from northern USA into Canada, with the nominate race *americanus* nesting in the Midwest states.
Confusion species Apart from the distinctive upcurved bill shape, the Marbled Godwit (plate 63), though smaller, appears very similar, but the secondaries and inner primaries are a brighter cinnamon and not heavily barred like the Long-billed Curlew.

Eurasian Curlew
Numenius arquata   See also plate 25

Key ID features W 268–326mm. A large curlew, with long downcurved bill and conspicuous white back and rump; the white underwing-coverts and axillaries are barred brown.
Behaviour Male performs a shallow, gliding display flight, with wings held above the horizontal.
Flight action Wing-beats are slower than those of Whimbrel, noticeably similar to large gulls.

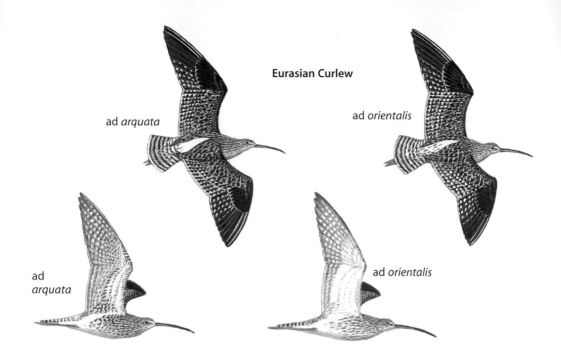

Eurasian Curlew

ad *arquata*

ad *orientalis*

ad *arquata*

ad *orientalis*

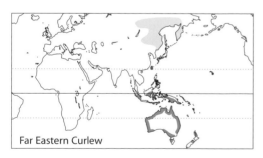

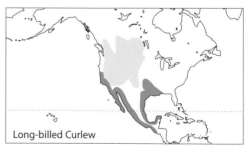

Voice   An onomatopoeic *cour-lee*, with the accent on the first syllable, rising and far-carrying. Song, also heard during the winter, is a sequence of bubbling phrases that accelerate and rise in pitch.

Distribution   The nominate race *arquata* is resident in Europe east to the Urals, some winter north to Iceland and south to West Africa; *orientalis* breeds east of the Urals and is more migratory, wintering from the coasts of Africa to southeast Asia and Japan. Vagrant to the Atlantic coast of North America.

Racial variation   The eastern race *orientalis* is typically larger, with a longer bill; the lower rump has obvious brown streaks; and the underwing is virtually white.

Confusion species   Long-billed and Far Eastern Curlews lack the white rump and back of Eurasian and have darker underwings, the latter with dark brown barring and the former noticeably cinnamon. The Whimbrel (plate 65) is smaller and shorter-billed, with darker upperparts. Slender-billed Curlew (plate 64) has white underwing-coverts.

Far Eastern Curlew

Long-billed Curlew

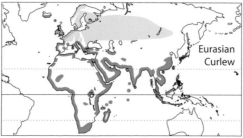

Eurasian Curlew

Plate 67   GREENSHANKS, SPOTTED REDSHANK AND MARSH SANDPIPER

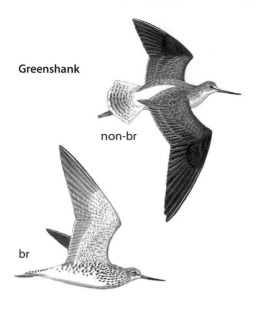

Greenshank

non-br

br

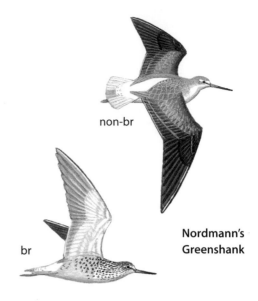

non-br

br

Nordmann's
Greenshank

Greenshank
Tringa nebularia   See also plate 27

Key ID features W 177–200mm. The dark grey-brown upperwing primaries and primary-coverts and slightly paler innerwings, contrast with the white V back, rump and uppertail, which is finely barred centrally; the axillaries and underwing-coverts are white, finely barred brown; and there is a moderate toe projection.
Behaviour In display, the male performs a song dance, flying to a great height: sometimes the pair will perform in unison, turning and swerving in perfect harmony. The male also performs giant, typical *Tringa* 'switchbacks' while singing.
Flight action Powerful, often twisting and turning erratically.
Voice Attention often drawn by loud call, a rapid, ringing and far-carrying triple *teu-teu-teu*, similar to Greater Yellowlegs. On the breeding grounds the song is a repeated, melodic *too-hoo-too-hoo-too-hoo*.
Distribution Vagrant to Newfoundland and Alaska.
Confusion species Nordmann's Greenshank, being shorter legged, has toes that only just project beyond the tail-tip. Greater Yellowlegs (plate 68) has a dark back, a square white rump, dark bars across the full width of the tail, while the yellow toes project further beyond the tail-tip. Marsh Sandpiper is smaller, with narrower wings and the toes project well beyond the tail-tip.

Nordmann's (Spotted) Greenshank
Tringa guttifer   See also plate 32

Key ID features W 169–183mm. The dark upperparts contrast with the white V back, rump and pale grey tail; the axillaries and underwing-coverts are pure white contrasting with the grey flight feathers; the toes just project beyond the tail-tip.
Voice A distinctive, loud *gwaak*, reminiscent of a Gull-billed Tern.
Distribution and status ENDANGERED. On migration occurs in Japan, South Korea, Taiwan and China. Vagrant to Assam and Burma.
Confusion species Extremely similar to Greenshank but stockier, with broader wing base; toes only just project beyond the tail-tip, the underwing-coverts are pure white, rather than finely barred and the tail is less barred. Marsh Sandpiper is smaller, with narrower wings and toes that project well beyond the tail-tip.

Spotted Redshank
Tringa erythropus   See also plate 26

Key ID features W 158–180mm. Has a fairly uniform black or grey mantle and wings; an elliptical white patch restricted to the back; a sleek, attenuated shape, with dark red toes that clearly project beyond the tail-tip - on rare occasions they may be tucked into the body.
Flight action Flight typically fast and direct, with shallow wing-beats.

non-br

Marsh Sandpiper

non-br

Spotted
Redshank

br

br

Voice A diagnostic, far-carrying, fluty *chu-it* with rising inflexion. Has various songs on the breeding grounds, including a fairly rapid *tee-u-wee tee-u-wee tee-u-wee*.

Distribution Vagrant to North America.

Confusion species Redshank (plate 70), which has a distinct white trailing edge to the secondaries and inner primaries. American dowitchers (plate 62), on the rare occasions when the Spotted Redshank retracts its legs and toes.

Marsh Sandpiper
Tringa stagnatilis See also plate 27

Key ID features W 128–148mm. In contrast to the dark upperwings, shows a distinctive, narrow white V back, rump patch and uppertail-coverts, with fine central barring on the rest of the white tail; axillaries and underwing-coverts are largely white; greenish toes project well beyond tail-tip.

Flight action Typically fast and free.

Voice Migrants when flushed usually utter a sharp *tew*, sometimes repeated and not unlike that of Greenshank, but thinner and higher-pitched. Alarm call on breeding grounds or in winter is a sharp *chip*, sometimes repeated, when it sounds similar to the call of Wood Sandpiper.

Distribution Vagrant to W Europe and Aleutian Islands.

Confusion species Greenshank is larger, more heavily built, with just its toes projecting beyond the tail-tip. Lesser Yellowlegs (plate 68) is similarly proportioned but has a dark back, a squarish rump-patch, and the underwing-coverts are barred, compared with white on Marsh Sandpiper. Wood Sandpiper (plate 69) is also dark-backed, with a white rump-patch and has a more heavily barred tail. Wilson's Phalarope (plate 77) is superficially similar, but also lacks a white back and toes only project a little beyond the tail-tip.

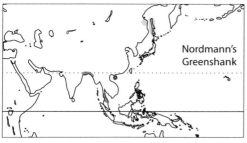

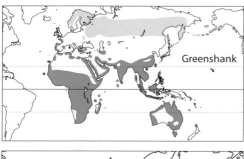

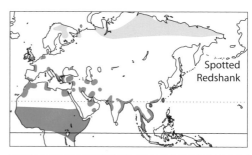

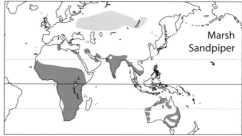

Plate 68 YELLOWLEGS AND TATTLERS

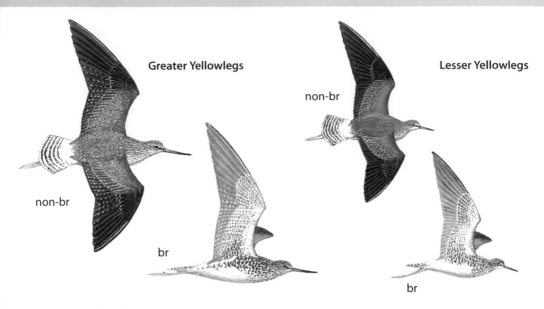

Greater Yellowlegs · non-br · br

Lesser Yellowlegs · non-br · br

Greater Yellowlegs
Tringa melanoleuca   See also plate 28

Key ID features W 181–210mm. A large *Tringa* species, with a square white rump; the blackish-brown secondaries and inner primaries have small white notches; and the bill is considerably longer than the projecting toes.
Behaviour Performs lengthy rising and falling 'switchback' display flights.
Voice A clear, descending three or four note *whew-whew-whew* very similar to that of Greenshank. During display flights makes a loud *whee-oodle whee-oodle*.
Distribution Vagrant, scarcer than *flavipes*, to Greenland, Iceland, western Europe and Japan.
Confusion species Apart from the larger size, the white-spotted secondaries and inner primaries, though difficult to see, distinguish this species from Lesser Yellowlegs. The white on the similarly sized Greenshank (plate 67) extends up the back.

Lesser Yellowlegs
Tringa flavipes   See also plate 28

Key ID features W 149–170mm. A medium-sized *Tringa* species, with a square white rump; the uniformly blackish-brown flight feathers are unmarked; and the bill and projecting toes are similar in length.
Behaviour Performs typical *Tringa* 'switchback' display flights.
Flight action Lighter than the larger Greater Yellowlegs with more rapid wing-beats.
Voice Most typical flight call is a two or three

note *tu-tu*, shorter, sharper and not descending as in Greater Yellowlegs.
Distribution Vagrant to Iceland, western Europe east to Israel, and Japan.
Confusion species The unmarked secondaries and primaries, though difficult to see, distinguish this species from Greater Yellowlegs. Also note comparative lengths of bills and projecting toes. The Wood Sandpiper (plate 69) has a similar square white rump, but the upperparts are brown, rather than brownish-grey, with white speckling across the innerwing-coverts – it is best separated by call. The Marsh Sandpiper (plate 67) has a whiter tail, with the white extending up the back. Wilson's Phalarope (plate 77) has a similar upper-part pattern but the underparts are essentially white. At a glance, the upperparts of Stilt Sandpiper (plate 74), particularly non-breeding birds, are also similar, but the underwing-coverts are white, rather than barred and in breeding plumage the body is dark.

Grey-tailed Tattler
Heteroscelus brevipes   See also plate 28

Key ID features W 154–175mm. Grey-brown upperparts, with slightly paler tail and uppertail-coverts.
Behaviour More often seen flying alone than with other waders.
Flight action Fast and effortless, with rapid wing-beats, gliding on bowed wings Common or Spotted Sandpiper-like.
Voice A disyllabic, rising *tu-eet* given in flight and at rest is reminiscent of Semipalmated Plover

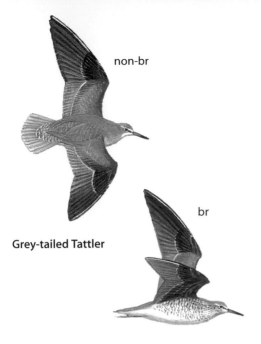

non-br

br

Grey-tailed Tattler

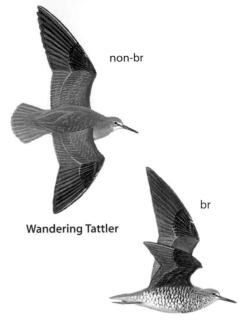

non-br

br

Wandering Tattler

(plate 55). Anxiety call, a Greenshank-like *tuu tuu tuu* but softer.

Distribution Vagrant to Alaska, California and Britain.

Confusion species The fairly uniform greyish upperparts and dark underwings are unique to the two tattler species.

Wandering Tattler

Heteroscelus incanus   See also plate 28

Key ID features W 163–186mm. Uniform slate-grey upperparts.

Behaviour As with Grey-tailed, more often seen flying alone than with other waders.

Flight action Fast and effortless, like Grey-tailed. Also, is capable of climbing rapidly, with zigzagging flights to avoid predators.

Voice Quite distinct from Grey-tailed: a plaintive, rippling trill of six to ten *pu-tu-tu-tu-tu-tu-tu* notes, like a subdued Whimbrel.

Distribution Also known to breed in Chukotka, Eastern Siberia. Vagrant to Manitoba, Ontario, Massachusetts and the Texas coast; more regular to Japan.

Confusion species If seen in profile, Grey-tailed Tattlers lack the grey flanks of Wandering in non-breeding and juvenile plumages.

Greater Yellowlegs

Grey-tailed Tattler

Lesser Yellowlegs

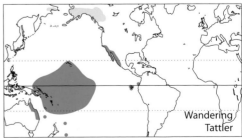

Wandering Tattler

Plate 69 WOOD, SOLITARY AND GREEN SANDPIPERS

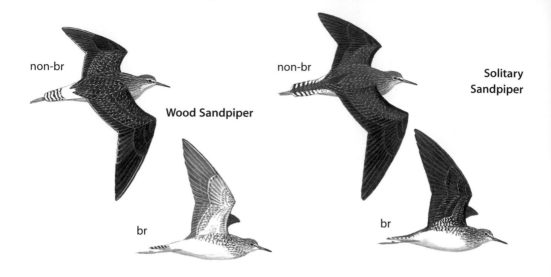

non-br

Wood Sandpiper

non-br

Solitary
Sandpiper

br

br

Wood Sandpiper
Tringa glareola   See also plate 29

Key ID features W 120–134mm. The upper-parts are brown, with variable whitish speckles on the mantle and innerwing-coverts; distinctive white rump and uppertail-coverts, with a finely barred tail; the underwing is whitish and the toes project beyond the tail-tip.

Behaviour The display comprises rising with sharply angled-back wings to perform a circling flight; followed by a typically *Tringa* 'switchback-flight', with rapid fluttering wing-beats, rising higher, gliding up and forward on stiffly arched wings, with tail spread and legs dangling. Delivers song while gliding down before repeating upward fluttering.

Flight action Uses a fluttery action, with a fast wing-beat; when flushed typically 'towers' high, with remarkable acceleration.

Voice Flight call is a shrill, whistled *chiff-iff-iff*. On breeding grounds utters a song comprising repeated *whirrru-whirrr-whirrru* notes.

Distribution Vagrant to Iceland, Greenland and N America. Has bred in Alaska.

Confusion species Lesser Yellowlegs (plate 68) is slightly larger and greyer on mantle. Green Sandpiper has much darker upperparts, appearing almost black-and-white, and has dark as opposed to pale underwings. Solitary Sandpiper lacks a white rump. Common and Spotted Sandpipers (plate 70) are smaller, show clear white wingbars and have a different manner of flight. The white rump may cause momentary confusion with

Curlew Sandpiper and Stilt Sandpiper (plate 74) and Wilson's Phalarope (plate 77), but the more uniform upperwing, and barred tail pattern of Wood Sandpiper are diagnostic.

Solitary Sandpiper
Tringa solitaria   See also plate 29

Key ID features W 125–146mm. The uniform dark brown upperwings are balanced by dark underwings and contrasting all-white underparts, apart from a streaked breast and finely barred axillaries. The dark rump and centre of the otherwise barred white tail are distinctive, and the toes project slightly beyond the tail-tip.

Behaviour During display flights, which are less spectacular than those of yellowlegs, the song is a repetitive series of whistled notes.

Flight action When flushed, often flutters up in a series of short ascents before dropping down again, but equally may 'tower'. However, when threatened by a predator, will use a snipe-like zigzag flight to escape.

Voice Similar to that of Green Sandpiper but quieter and less frequent. A single sharp *pit*, sometimes a disyllabic *twit-wit* or, more usually, a high *pleet-weet-weet* flight call.

Distribution Nominate race *solitaria* breeds in northern part of the range, from Alaska and northern British Columbia to Hudson Bay, and *cinnamomea* to the south, from southern British Columbia to Labrador. Vagrant to Bermuda, Greenland, Iceland and western Europe.

Confusion species Green Sandpiper has a

Green Sandpiper

non-br

br

distinct white rump. Wood Sandpiper has a white rump and a pale underwing. Spotted Sandpiper (plate 70) is smaller and has bold white wingbars and a very different wing-flicking flight.

Green Sandpiper

Tringa ochropus   See also plate 29

Key ID features W 136-155mm. The dark upperwings and broad, dark barred tail contrast with square white rump and uppertail-coverts; the dark underwing, streaked breast and white underparts create an almost black-and-white appearance, and the toes barely protrude beyond the tail-tip.

Behaviour Performs a 'switchback' display flight similar to Wood Sandpiper. On migration, most often flushed in ones and twos from small, freshwater habitats.

Flight action Rapid, with deep wing-beats and, to escape a predator, will use a snipe-like zigzag flight, sometimes towering before plummeting down.

Voice Noisy, particularly when flushed, uttering a loud *weet-tweet-wit-wit* call. Calls may be heard from migrants flying high overhead at night. On breeding grounds has a *tit-ti-tit* warning call and a melodious song consisting of variations on a loud, whistling *loo-tit-ti-lhit*.

Distribution Vagrant to N America.

Confusion species The contrasting black-and-white appearance is virtually diagnostic, but also see Confusion species for Solitary and Wood Sandpipers.

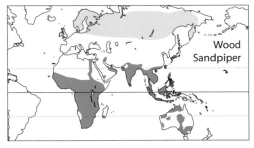

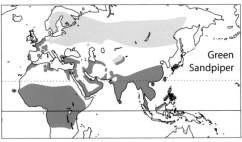

Plate 70 **SPOTTED, COMMON AND TEREK SANDPIPERS, AND REDSHANK**

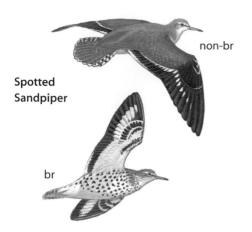

Spotted
Sandpiper

non-br

br

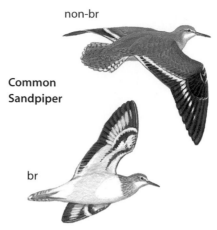

non-br

Common
Sandpiper

br

Spotted Sandpiper
Actitis macularia   See also plate 30

Key ID features W 99–113mm. Brown above, with a relatively short white wingbar on the inner-primaries and outer-secondaries only. White trailing edge to inner secondaries only. The breeding adults have distinctive spotted underparts.
Behaviour Performs similar display flights to Common Sandpiper.
Flight action Has a unique flickering flight, shared with Common Sandpiper. They make alternating bursts of stiff wing-beats and short glides, just above the surface of the water, with bowed wings. On migration they fly with regular wing-beats, more like calidrids.
Voice A sharp, faintly rising *weet weet* or *peet peet peet*, slightly weaker in quality than the similar call of Common Sandpiper.
Distribution Vagrant to western Europe. Bred in Scotland in 1975.
Confusion species Separated from Common Sandpiper by white wingbar falling short of inner-secondaries.

Common Sandpiper
Actitis hypoleucos   See also plate 30

Key ID features W 105–119mm. Brown above, with a bold white wingbar that stretches right across the inner secondaries onto the inner primaries. Broad white trailing edge to inner secondaries only. The underparts are mainly white in all plumages.
Behaviour Display flight may involve female chasing male, usually low over the water, with rapid bursts of very shallow wing-beats, interspersed with glides on bowed wings, often in tight

loops or figures-of-eight.
Flight action The unique manner of flight, shared with Spotted Sandpiper, is described under that species.
Voice Noisy on breeding grounds and often heard on migration. A thin, high-pitched and penetrating, descending *tseep-seep-seep*.
Distribution Vagrant to Alaska.
Confusion species Separated from Spotted Sandpiper by the bold white wingbar crossing the inner secondaries.

Terek Sandpiper
Xenus cinereus   See also plate 30

Key ID features W 126–142mm. Larger than *Actitis* species, with a diagnostic upturned, orange-based black bill; the uniform pale-grey upperparts, including back, rump, tail and mid-wing panel, contrast with the dark outer-wing and striking broad white trailing-edge to the secondaries.
Behaviour The male's display flight consists of flying up at an angle, hovering then gliding down.
Flight action Similar to *Tringa*, rapid and erratic, with deep wing-beats, but often flies low along tideline, with shallow, fluttering wing-beats on bowed wings, similar to *Actitis* species.
Voice Rich and full-toned; the flight call is a melodious rippling *huhuhuhu*, recalling that of Whimbrel but softer. Other variations include a fluty *twit-a-whit-whit-whit*. Display song comprises complex trisyllabic-sounding *per-rrrr-eeee* units, the last syllable rising.
Distribution Vagrant to western Europe and Pacific coast of N America.
Confusion species Unmistakable, once upcurved bill seen, also lacks white wingbar and white rump of *Actitis* and *Tringa* species respectively.

non-br

Terek
Sandpiper

Redshank

br

br

non-br

Redshank
Tringa totanus   See also plate 26

Key ID features W 149–176mm. The conspicuous white trailing edge to the secondaries and inner primaries is distinctive, and the orange toes project beyond the tail-tip.

Behaviour On alighting often holds the wings vertical. When displaying, the male performs a 'switchback' song flight, beginning with a steep climb, followed by a downward glide on depressed wings and succeeded by rising on rapidly quivering wings still kept below the horizontal.

Flight action Strong but erratic, both flickering and gliding with wings frequently held below the horizontal.

Voice Very vocal irrespective of season. The commonest call is a loud, familiar *tu-tuhu*, lengthened to *tutu-tutu-tutu* when alarmed. During the breeding season the display song comprises a repetitive *taludl*, or a harsh, squealing *tyee*.

Distribution Northern race *robusta* breeds in Iceland and the Faeroe Islands; vagrant to Greenland.

Confusion species Spotted Redshank (plate 67), which has a similar white back but lacks the distinct white trailing edge to the secondaries and inner primaries. Terek Sandpiper has a narrower white trailing edge, and grey upperparts, including back and rump. Dowitchers (plate 62) have a similar white back and rump, but only a narrow whitish trailing edge and longer bills.

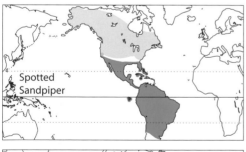

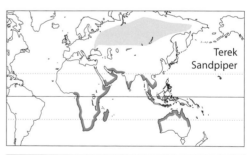

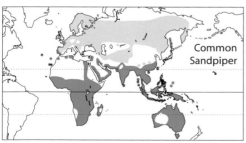

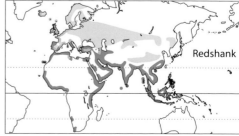

Plate 71 **TURNSTONES AND SURFBIRD**

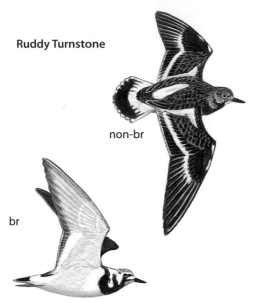

Ruddy Turnstone

non-br

br

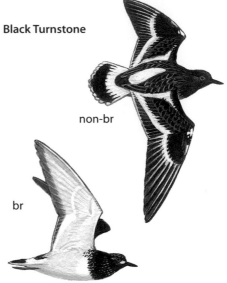

Black Turnstone

non-br

br

Ruddy Turnstone
Arenaria interpres   See also plate 31

Key ID features W 145–165mm. A chunky wader, vividly patterned, with a bold white wing-bar and white back, innerwing triangles and tail base, contrasting with a broad black subterminal tail band, brown rump and brown or chestnut wing-coverts, scapulars and mantle.
Behaviour Feeding flocks fly in small tight groups, but in loose lines when migrating. On the breeding grounds males circle over their territories with deep, slow wing-beats, making few calls. A more frequent aerial activity is the pursuit-flight in which several birds fly over the tundra in a rapid, jinking chase. After seeing off a potential predator, males may briefly tumble in the air before gliding back to their territories.
Flight action Strong and direct, often low, with stiff and shallow wing-beats.
Voice A clear, rapid, low-pitched *tuk-a-tuk-tuk* is the most common call. When disturbed may utter a sharp *tchit-ik*. Feeding birds have a low *tuk* contact call.
Distribution The nominate race *interpres* breeds from Ellesmere Island, across Greenland, northern Eurasia and Siberia to northwest Alaska and winters on coasts of western Europe south to Africa, across southern Asia and further south; also on the Pacific coast of North America from California to at least Mexico; *morinella* breeds from northeast Alaska across Arctic Canada and winters from South Carolina and Gulf of Mexico south.
Confusion species Black Turnstone appears entirely black-and-white, lacking the brown paler fringed upperpart feathers of Ruddy.

Black Turnstone
Arenaria melanocephala   See also plate 31

Key ID features W 147–162mm. Another chunky wader, with striking black-and-white upperparts.
Behaviour In the display flight the male climbs high before diving down like a snipe, producing an audible sound from tail-feather vibrations. Pursuit-flights include dashing zigzag chases.
Flight action As Ruddy Turnstone.
Voice A trilling *skirrr*, less harsh and higher-pitched than Ruddy Turnstone.
Distribution Vagrant inland to westernmost states and provinces, also Yukon Territory and Montana; and to Wrangel Island, Siberia.
Confusion species Ruddy Turnstone is very similar at a distance, but appears browner and paler

Surfbird

non-br

br

headed, particularly in breeding plumage. The white on the back and the coverts quickly separate it from similar rock-feeding species like Surfbird, Rock and vagrant Purple Sandpipers (plate 76); the range of the last named has not yet overlapped with Black Turnstone.

Surfbird

Aphriza virgata   See also plate 31

Key ID features W 169–185mm. The grey upperparts with conspicuous wingbar and a black

subterminal band on a white tail are distinctive.

Flight action Powerful with rapid wing-beats, as befits a long-distance migrant.

Voice Generally quiet but makes an occasional plaintive *kee-wee-ah* whistle. May also be heard uttering a low turnstone-like chatter.

Distribution Vagrant to Pennsylvania; occasionally in spring to Texas coast.

Confusion species Similar to Great Knot (plate 74) if the bill is not seen, but the broader white wingbar and contrasting black tail-band should quickly confirm the identification.

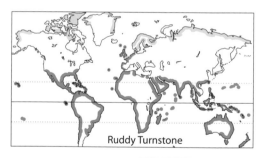

Ruddy Turnstone

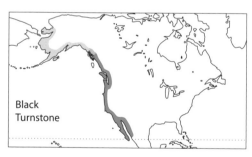

Black Turnstone

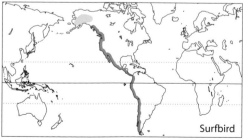

Surfbird

Plate 72 **STINTS AND SPOON-BILLED SANDPIPER**

Little Stint

non-br

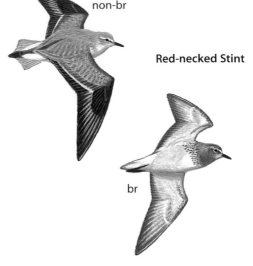

non-br

Red-necked Stint

br

br

Little Stint
Calidris minuta   See also plate 35

Key ID features W 91–104mm. A small calidrid, with a narrow white wingbar; the central rump and tail are dark brown; the sides of the rump and uppertail are white and the rest of the tail-sides grey.

Behaviour The display flight involves three different elements, accompanied by song and contact calls: exaggerated, slow wing-beats, with legs dangling and tail depressed; a brief period with quivering wings held in a V; and a glide, with the wings decurved below the horizontal.

Flight action Fast, with rapid wing-beats, jinking freely. May rise steeply, when flushed, but 'towers' less often than Temminck's and Long-toed Stints.

Voice Typical call is a sharp, squeaky *stit*, also makes a trilling call. Song is a repeated weak *svee-svee-svee*.

Distribution Vagrant to Canada, both coasts of the USA and Japan.

Confusion species Red-necked Stint, the call of which is diagnostic, but other calls overlap. Semipalmated and Western Sandpipers (plate 73) have similar upperpart patterns but are larger.

Red-necked Stint
Calidris ruficollis   See also plate 35

Key ID features W 94–112mm. Virtually identical to Little Stint but some individuals show extensive white on inner primaries.

Flight action The normal manner of flight differs little from other small calidrids.

Voice Normal flight call is a high-pitched *kreet, kreep* or *chreek*, either fairly straight or with a slight inflection of the *ee*. The song comprises harsh double whistles given methodically: *correk correk correk*.

Distribution Vagrant to both coasts of North America and western Europe.

Confusion species Little Stint, Semipalmated and Western Sandpipers (plate 73) all look similar in flight, but the latter two are larger.

Temminck's Stint
Calidris temminckii   See also plate 36

Key ID features W 94–105mm. The pure white outer tail feathers are most distinctive, particularly as the bird alights; the rump, uppertail-coverts and central tail feathers are a dull grey-brown; the white wingbar is indistinct.

Behaviour The male performs a long circular display flight, during which he hovers and may sing continuously for several minutes.

Flight action Has a rapid towering escape flight; also a low-flying fluttery flight, sometimes with wings bowed like Spotted or Common Sandpipers.

Voice The usual flight call is a rapid, trilling *tirirrir*. The song is a sustained reeling *kililililil*, given from the ground or during the display flight.

Distribution Vagrant to Alaska and British Columbia.

Confusion species Tail pattern and call are diagnostic, separating it from the similarly pale-legged Long-toed Stint and Least Sandpiper (plate 73).

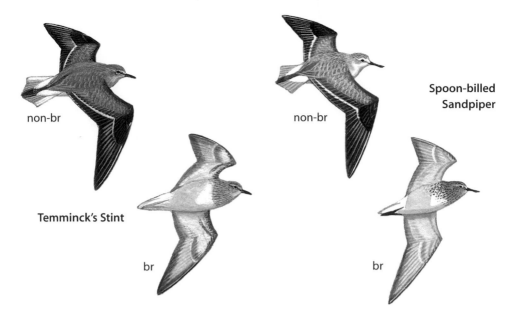

Spoon-billed
Sandpiper

non-br

non-br

Temminck's Stint

br

br

Spoon-billed Sandpiper
Eurynorhynchus pygmeus   See also plate 32

Key ID features W 98–106mm. The unique bill, which in profile is longish, may not be easy to see; the white wingbar is fairly prominent, as are the white sides to the uppertail-coverts.
Behaviour The male's display flight, when he sings, includes brief hovering, circling and rapid dives.
Voice Contact calls include a shrill *wheet* and a quiet rolled *preep*. The song, given in display flight, is a descending, buzzing *preer-prr-prr*, reminiscent of a cicada.
Distribution and status ENDANGERED. Vagrant to Alaska, British Columbia and Alberta. Main winter range unknown; small numbers recorded from several sites in South Asia. The largest wintering numbers recorded comprised more than 250 in Bangladesh in 1989.
Confusion species Easily confused with Red-necked and Little Stints unless the bill is seen.

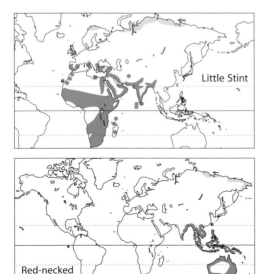

Little Stint

Red-necked Stint

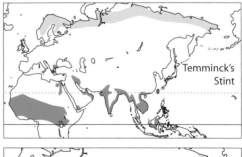

Temminck's Stint

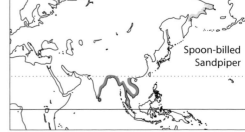

Spoon-billed Sandpiper

Plate 73 AMERICAN SANDPIPERS AND LONG-TOED STINT

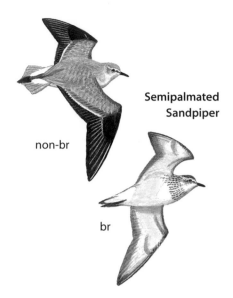

**Semipalmated
Sandpiper**

non-br

br

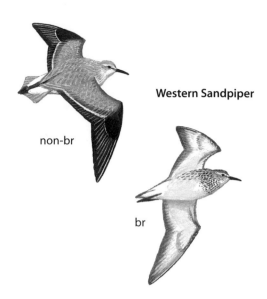

Western Sandpiper

non-br

br

Semipalmated Sandpiper
Calidris pusilla   See also plate 34

Key ID features W 93–104mm. Shows a moderately conspicuous white greater-covert wingbar; and the tail is black–centred with white sides.
Behaviour Like other gregarious calidrids, dense flocks may create extremely mobile clouds, as they fly to and from roosts, or evade predators.
Voice Typical call is a soft, thick *chewp* or *chirrup*. Song, given in display flight, is a monotonous repetition of *ree-ree-ree* or *di-jip-di-jip-di-jip*.
Distribution Regular migrant along Pacific USA. Vagrant to Greenland, Iceland and western Europe.
Confusion species From above, virtually indistinguishable from Red-necked and Little Stints (plate 72) and Western Sandpiper. Larger than Least Sandpiper, which has a similar upperwing pattern, but Least looks browner and darker above and also on the underside of the flight feathers.

Western Sandpiper
Calidris mauri   See also plate 34

Key ID features W 94–103mm. Shows a moderately conspicuous white wingbar, mainly across the greater covert tips; and the tail is black–centred with white sides.
Behaviour Flocks may perform spectacular aerial manoeuvres, like similar Semipalmated Sandpiper, Dunlin and larger Red Knot.
Voice A short, high-pitched, penetrating *dzheet*. Song consists of a few long buzzy trills that ascend, then drop at the end: *brr-eee brr-eee brr-eee*

breee-urrrr.
Distribution Vagrant to Lake Baikal in Siberia, Japan and western Europe.
Confusion species Virtually indistinguishable from Red-necked and Little Stints (plate 72) and Semipalmated Sandpiper, unless breast colour and bill length can be seen at close range. Larger than Least Sandpiper, which has a similar upperwing pattern, but appears browner and darker, with a less conspicuous wingbar, and is also darker on the underside of the flight feathers.

Least Sandpiper
Calidris minutilla   See also plate 36

Key ID features W 86–96mm. The smallest calidrid, with fairly uniform brown upperparts and an inconspicuous wingbar, but all the primary shafts show some white.
Flight action As befits its size, makes very rapid wing-beats. Has a fast 'towering' flight, as well as a snipe-like zigzag 'escape' flight.
Voice A high-pitched, two-syllabled *krree-eeet*. The song is a rhythmically repeated *breee breee breee*.
Distribution Vagrant to Alaska, Japan, Iceland and western Europe.
Confusion species When in flight with Western and Semipalmated Sandpipers, which have similar upperwing patterns, Least appears darker and smaller. Similar to Long-toed Stint, which has a shorter and even less conspicuous wingbar, but has white on only the outer primary shaft. Little and Red-necked Stints (plate 72) have more conspicuous white wingbars and whiter underwings.

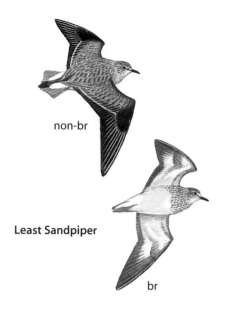

non-br

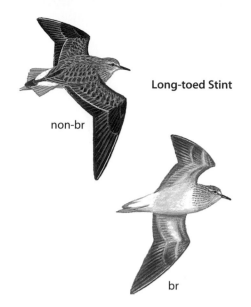

Long-toed Stint

non-br

Least Sandpiper

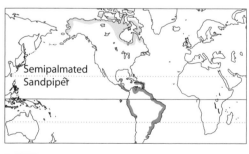

br

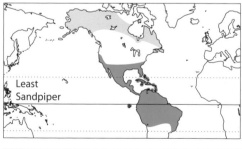

br

Long-toed Stint
Calidris subminuta   See also plate 36

Key ID features W 88-100mm. The white wingbar is indistinct and only the outer primary shaft is white. The underwing is extensively greyish-brown. The only calidrid, apart from Stilt and Curlew Sandpipers (plate 74), which shows toes projecting beyond the tail-tip, but only just.
Behaviour Flushed individuals may tower rapidly. During the display flight sings and circles high.

Flight action The wing-beats may appear weak and fluttery.
Voice Usual flight call is a rippling *chrrup*. Song is a slow *kroer-kroer-kroer*.
Distribution Vagrant to Alaska, Oregon, western Europe and Israel.
Confusion species Similar to Least Sandpiper, but toes project beyond tail-tip. Least Sandpiper has a slightly more obvious wingbar and shows whitish shafts to all primaries and whiter underwing-coverts. Temminck's Stint (plate 72) has conspicuous white outer-tail feathers.

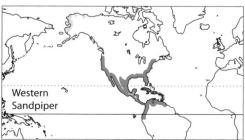

Semipalmated Sandpiper

Least Sandpiper

Western Sandpiper

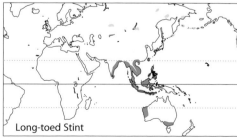

Long-toed Stint

Plate 74 **'WHITE-RUMPED' SANDPIPERS AND KNOTS**

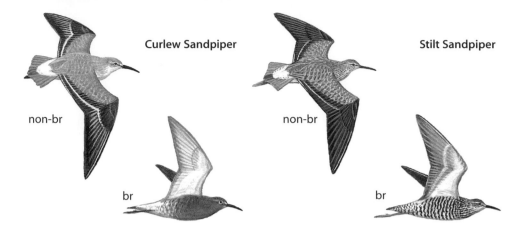

Curlew Sandpiper

non-br

br

Stilt Sandpiper

non-br

br

Curlew Sandpiper

Calidris ferruginea   See also plate 39

Key ID features W 125–139mm. Shows a distinct white patch on the lower rump and uppertail-coverts; an obvious white wingbar; a white underwing; and the toes just project beyond the tail-tip.
Behaviour The male song flight above its territory includes slow wing-beats and glides.
Voice A rippling *chirrup,* softer than the call of Ruddy Turnstone but with a similar rhythm.
Distribution Vagrant to North America.
Confusion species White-rumped Sandpiper has a shorter straight bill and narrower wingbar. Stilt Sandpiper lacks a distinct white wingbar and has toes that project well beyond the tail-tip.

Stilt Sandpiper

Calidris himantopus   See also plate 41

Key ID features W 124–140mm. Long wings and bill, and projecting toes create distinctly cross-like proportions. Grey-brown upperparts and indistinct white wingbar are uniform and contrast with white patch on the uppertail-coverts.
Behaviour Males advertise their territories with long song flights.
Voice An occasionally heard soft *tew* and a soft, rattling *krrrr.* In song flight utters a buzzy, rhythmically repeated trill *zuree zuree zuree* and a braying *heehaw heehaw heehaw.*
Distribution Vagrant to W Europe and Japan.
Confusion species Lesser Yellowlegs (plate 68) is slightly larger, but with a shorter rather than long droopy bill, a barred tail and no wingbar; Wilson's Phalarope (plate 77) is smaller, with a thin straight bill and little toe projection; Curlew Sandpiper has a clear white wingbar and toes that just project beyond the tail-tip.

White-rumped Sandpiper

Calidris fuscicollis   See also plate 37

Key ID features W 118-131mm. A long-winged calidrid with a prominent white band across the uppertail-coverts but an indistinct white wingbar.
Behaviour The hovering display flights may sometimes involve females.
Voice The flight call is a thin, high-pitched, mouse-like squeak. On the breeding grounds, utters a fishing-reel-like buzzing and a pig-like *oink* during display flight.
Distribution Vagrant to Pacific coast of USA; frequent vagrant to Iceland and NW Europe, east to Austria.
Confusion species Baird's Sandpiper (plate 75) lacks the white uppertail-coverts. Curlew Sandpiper has a broader white 'rump' and normally a more distinct wingba and longer decurved bill.

Great Knot

Calidris tenuirostris   See also plate 33

Key ID features W 170–189mm. Long-winged calidrid with obvious white uppertail-coverts; streaked back and innerwing-coverts; narrow but conspicuous white wingbar; dark primary-coverts; and mainly white underwing.
Behaviour Flying flocks are looser, less compact and more linear than those of Red Knot.
Voice Generally silent but has a low, disyllabic *nyut-nyut* call, not unlike that of Red Knot.
Distribution Vagrant to western Europe, Israel and Alaska.
Confusion species Non-breeding Red Knot, which looks shorter-winged and more compact, and lacks obvious white uppertail-coverts. Grey Plover (plate 54) in non-breeding plumage has a similar upperpart pattern but diagnostic underwing black axillaries.

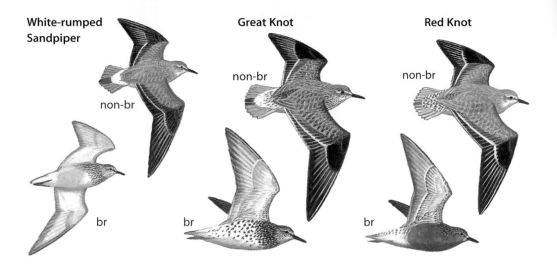

White-rumped Sandpiper
non-br
br

Great Knot
non-br
br

Red Knot
non-br
br

Red Knot
Calidris canutus   See also plate 33

Key ID features W 155–180mm. Narrow whitish wingbar; pale greyish innerwing, back, rump and tail, which contrast with the blackish primary-coverts and dark-grey flight feathers; underwing-coverts appear greyish.
Behaviour Flying to and from roosts, large flocks create fluid shapes, like abstract sculptures, as they swirl in the air.
Voice Generally quiet, the flight call is a slightly hoarse *knut* and the alarm call a sharp *veek-veek*. Display song is variable, including a fluty, melodious, rather mournful *poo-mee* or *whip-poo-mee*.
Distribution The nominate race *canutus* breeds in central Siberia and winters in Africa; *rufa* breeds throughout western Canada and Alaska, wintering

in the USA and S America; *islandica* breeds in northeast Canada and Greenland, wintering in western Europe; *rogersi* breeds in eastern Siberia and winters in Australia.
Confusion species Non-breeding Great Knot is larger (compare Key ID features). Grey Plover (plate 54) in non-breeding plumage is similar but larger, with diagnostic black axillaries.

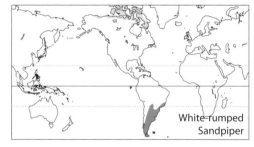

White-rumped Sandpiper

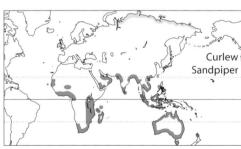

Curlew Sandpiper

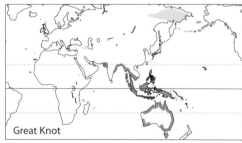

Great Knot

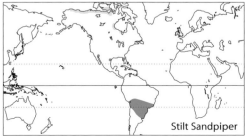

Stilt Sandpiper

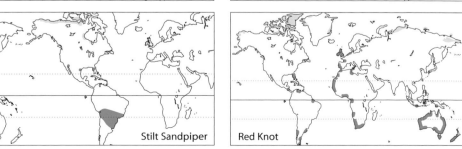

Red Knot

Plate 75 **'DARK-RUMPED' SANDPIPERS AND RUFF**

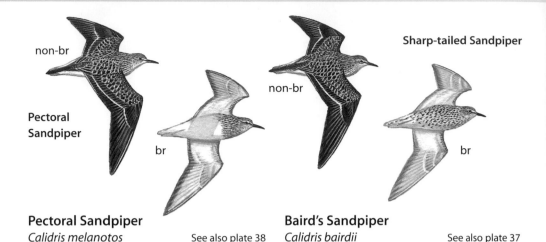

Pectoral Sandpiper — non-br — br

Sharp-tailed Sandpiper — non-br — br

Pectoral Sandpiper
Calidris melanotos   See also plate 38

Key ID features W 124–150mm. Dark brown upperparts; indistinct white wingbar; narrow trailing edge to the inner secondaries; and prominent white sides to the rump and uppertail-coverts.
Behaviour During the song-flight the inflatable sac in the breast is pumped up and down in time with the hooting call.
Flight action Uses a snipe-like zigzag flight to escape a predator, or when flushed alone.
Voice Usual call is a reedy *trrrt-trrrt* repeated irregularly, or a harsh *kreek*. The male also makes a rapid, foghorn-like hooting *oo-ah* during the song-flight.
Distribution Regular in autumn to western Europe and east to Israel and Egypt.
Confusion species Sharp-tailed Sandpiper (compare Key ID features). Ruff has a similar upperpart pattern but is larger and the white oval sides to the uppertail-coverts are more prominent. Baird's Sandpiper (compare Key ID features).

Sharp-tailed Sandpiper
Calidris acuminata   See also plate 38

Key ID features W 124–145mm. Dark brown upperparts, with a narrow white wingbar; the white lateral uppertail-coverts show some dark streaking.
Behaviour Song flight includes trilling calls, as the male glides down on upraised wings, following short ascents.
Voice A short twittering *pleep* or *tuwit* in sequence is reminiscent of Barn Swallow *Hirundo rustica*.
Distribution Regular in Alaska. Vagrant to Pacific coast of Canada and USA, and western Europe.
Confusion species Pectoral Sandpiper (see Key ID features above). Also similar to Ruff but is smaller and lacks prominent white tail sides

Baird's Sandpiper
Calidris bairdii   See also plate 37

Key ID features W 118–135mm. A long-winged calidrid, with a sometimes-inconspicuous white wingbar; back, central rump, uppertail-coverts and tail feathers dark brown; rump and uppertail-coverts edged off-white.
Behaviour Males are territorial and make circling song flights.
Flight action With its long wings flight is powerful, but wing-beats are perceptibly slower than those of the smaller stints.
Voice The usual call is a fairly low-pitched, rasping, trilling *krrrit*, most reminiscent of Pectoral Sandpiper. A guttural trilling song is given during the display flight.
Distribution Vagrant Japan, New Guinea, western Europe east to Poland.
Confusion species White-rumped Sandpiper (see plate 74) has distinctive white uppertail-coverts. Pectoral Sandpiper (compare Key ID features) is larger, with more obvious white sides to uppertail-coverts.

Buff-breasted Sandpiper
Tryngites subruficollis   See also plate 38

Key ID features W 124–140mm. Upperpart flight feathers dark brown, innerwing buffy-brown; white underwings contrast with buff underparts.
Behaviour Males take part in long aerial chases and vertical flights at the territory boundaries.
Flight action More graceful than other calidrines.
Voice Usually silent; the occasional flight call is quiet, a low *tu* or a short trill, reminiscent of Baird's Sandpiper or Ruddy Turnstone chatter. During the display flights makes soft *tic tic* sounds.
Distribution Vagrant to W Europe and Japan.
Confusion species Buff-breasted is smaller than other plain-backed species such as Upland Sandpiper (plate 64) and the three Golden Plovers

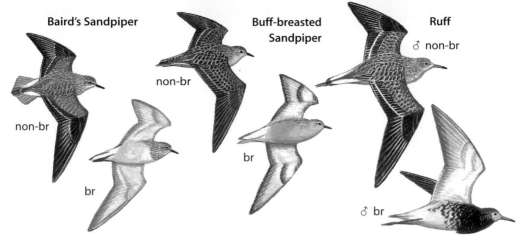

Baird's Sandpiper

non-br

non-br

br

Buff-breasted Sandpiper

non-br

br

Ruff

♂ non-br

♂ br

(plate 54); has a shorter tail than the sandpiper and an even more indistinct wingbar than the plovers. Smaller than Ruff, which has prominent white sides to the uppertail-coverts, a narrow but obvious white wingbar, lacks the dark crescents on the underwing primary-coverts and has toes that project well beyond the tail-tip. Eurasian Dotterel (plate 58) is similar but has conspicuous black-and-white tail-tip and prominent supercilia meeting on nape.

Ruff

Philomachus pugnax   See also plate 41

Key ID features W males 260-320mm; females 200-250mm. Variable grey-brown upperparts, with an indistinct wingbar and prominent white oval sides to the uppertail-coverts; toes project well beyond the tail-tip.

Flight action Powerful but also more casual at times, with deep wing-beats, mostly below the horizontal, gliding when coming in to land.

Voice Invariably silent. Makes an occasional low *kurr* while feeding, or a shrill, rising *hoo-ee* may be heard from migrating flocks.

Distribution Regular in Alaska. Vagrant to Iceland, USA and Canada.

Confusion species Pectoral and Sharp-tailed Sandpipers are similar but their toes do not project beyond the tail-tip. Buff-breasted Sandpiper also has a similar upperwing pattern but lacks the obvious white uppertail-covert ovals and the toes barely project beyond the tail-tip.

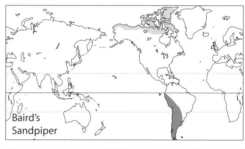

Baird's Sandpiper

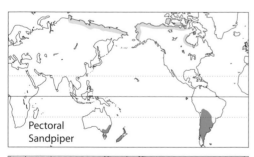

Pectoral Sandpiper

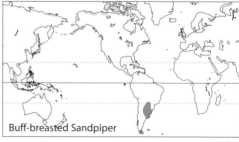

Buff-breasted Sandpiper

Sharp-tailed Sandpiper

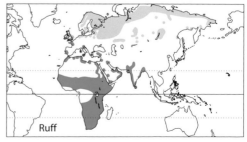

Ruff

Plate 76 **PURPLE, ROCK AND BROAD-BILLED SANDPIPERS, AND DUNLIN**

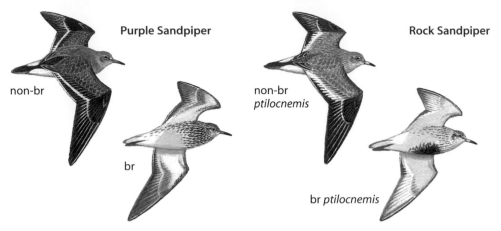

Purple Sandpiper

non-br

br

Rock Sandpiper

non-br
ptilocnemis

br ptilocnemis

Purple Sandpiper
Calidris maritima   See also plate 40

Key ID features W 123–142mm. The generally dark upperparts contrast with a distinct white wingbar, a narrow white trailing edge to the secondaries and the white sides to the uppertail-coverts. The underwing-coverts are whitish and the flight feathers dark grey.

Behaviour In the display flight the bird flies up with quivering wings and holds them above horizontal as it proceeds in wide circles, sometimes gliding with them held in a V; to land floats down with wings in a V giving moaning calls.

Flight action Invariably flies low over the water when disturbed.

Voice The usual flight call is a sharp *twit* or *wit*, sometimes a swallow-like *kwit-it-it-kwit*, but this species is generally quiet away from the breeding grounds, where a wide variety of trilling and wheezing phrases may be heard. Essentially a series of short elements, each strung together and repeated three or four times, e.g. *tullawhee tullawhee whee whee*; also a wheezy, trilling *prier-r-r-r-r* or *kryy-i kryy-i kryy-i*.

Distribution Vagrant to inland North America and eastern Europe, Italy and Malta.

Confusion species Non-breeding Rock Sandpiper (see Confusion species for that species).

Rock Sandpiper
Calidris ptilocnemis   See also plate 40

Key ID features W 112–145mm. Distinctly dark, with conspicuous white wingbar and tail sides, and narrow white trailing edge to secondaries.

Flight action Has a fluttering flight when displaying and, like Purple Sandpiper, generally flies low over water when disturbed.

Voice Similar to that of Purple Sandpiper.

Distribution Vagrant south to Los Angeles. The nominate *ptilocnemis* is mainly resident on the Pribilof Islands; *tschuktschorum* is migratory, breeding in eastern Siberia and western Alaska, winters south to northern California; *couesi* breeds on the Aleutian Islands and S Alaska; and *quarta* breeds on the Commander and Kuril Islands off Siberia.

Racial variation The generally paler nominate race *ptilocnemis* can be separated from *couesi* in flight, if good profile views are obtained, when respectively, the more solid black lower breast compared with the heavily black-spotted lower breast and flanks can be seen.

Confusion species Purple Sandpiper in non-breeding plumage is almost identical to three races of Rock Sandpiper, but differs from the nominate, which has generally paler upperparts, a broader white wingbar and all whitish underwings. The upperparts' pattern is similar to Dunlin though the Rock Sandpiper wingbar is more conspicuous.

Broad-billed Sandpiper
Limicola falcinellus   See also plate 40

Key ID features W 100–115mm. In non-breeding plumage, the blackish leading edge to the wing contrasts with the grey-brown median coverts and scapulars.

Behaviour The territorial song-flight of the male comprises flying slowly 10-20 metres above the ground, alternately shivering wings and gliding, while uttering the slow-flight song.

Voice A dry, trilling *ch-r-r-reet*, with a buzzing quality. The slow-flight song consists of a repeated rhythmic buzzing trill *dsrui-dsrui-dsrui*.

Distribution Vagrant to Aleutians and Iceland, scarce but regular to W Europe. The nominate breeds in Scandinavia and NW Siberia, migrating southeast to India and East Africa; *sibirica* breeds in NE Siberia and winters in SE Asia and Australia.

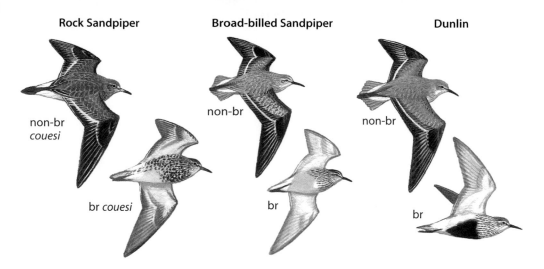

Rock Sandpiper

non-br *couesi*

br *couesi*

Broad-billed Sandpiper

non-br

br

Dunlin

non-br

br

Confusion species In non-breeding plumage, the smaller size and less obvious white wingbar separate it from Sanderling (plate 77) and the black leading edge to the wing distinguishes it from the larger Dunlin and smaller calidrids.

Dunlin
Calidris alpina
See also plate 39

Key ID features W 105–131mm. In breeding plumage black belly contrasts with white underwing. Has a narrow white wingbar, white sides to the rump and uppertail-coverts, and grey sides to the dark-centred tail.

Behaviour May form huge flocks, creating moving clouds in flight as they twist and turn in unison. Aerial display flights involve gliding and wing-quivering, with arched wings held just below the horizontal.

Voice A short, slightly rasping *treeep*. The breeding ground display song involves a long, throbbing buzz or descending trill, accompanied by harsh single or double notes.

Distribution The nominate race breeds in N Scandinavia and NW Siberia, and winters in western Europe, the Mediterranean and east to India; *sakhalina* breeds in NE Siberia and N Alaska, winters in China and Japan; *pacifica* breeds in W Alaska, winters along Pacific USA and in Mexico; *hudsonia* breeds in central Canada, winters SE USA; *arctica* breeds in NE Greenland, winters in W Africa; *schinzii* breeds in SE Greenland, Iceland, Britain and S Scandinavia, and winters mainly in W Africa.

Confusion species Rock Sandpiper has a more conspicuous white wingbar. In non-breeding plumage Sanderling (plate 77) is paler, with a bolder white wingbar and a shorter, straight bill.

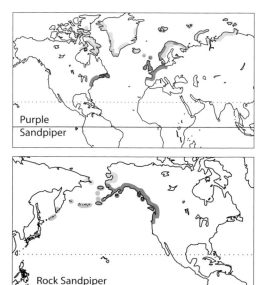

Purple Sandpiper

Rock Sandpiper

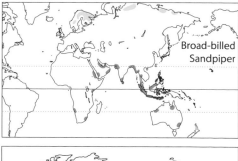

Broad-billed Sandpiper

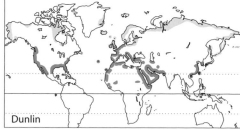

Dunlin

Plate 77 **PHALAROPES AND SANDERLING**

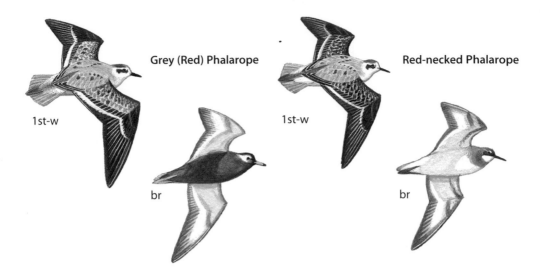

Grey (Red) Phalarope

1st-w

br

Red-necked Phalarope

1st-w

br

Grey (Red) Phalarope
Phalaropus fulicarius   See also plate 42

Key ID features W 122–141mm. In breeding plumage the chestnut underparts and dark upperparts with obvious white wingbar are diagnostic. Non-breeding birds have pale grey upperparts contrasting with mainly dark wings and a conspicuous white wingbar, which broadens on the inner secondaries. In profile view the black face-mask is distinctive.

Behaviour The females perform circle-flights over the breeding grounds, flying round in wide circles with rather slow wing-beats, sometimes tilting the body from side to side, like a displaying *Charadrius* plover, exposing the light underwing and calling constantly. A wing-whirr display, usually performed by the female, involves hovering low over the ground, with legs dangling, neck arched forward and tail vertically down, while the wings produce a loud whirring sound.

Flight action Powerful on longish wings, with slower wing-beats and less erratic than the following species.

Voice Flight call is a sharp, high-pitched *wit*, pitched slightly higher than that of Red-necked Phalarope and similar to Sanderling or Little Stint. An alarm call is usually a hard, piercing disyllabic *tweu-wit*.

Confusion species Sanderling, which shows a broader white wingbar, particularly across the inner primaries, and lacks the black face-mask. In non-breeding plumage a Grey Phalarope, flying over the sea, is paler and larger than Red-necked. Juveniles are more distinct, as Red-necked is initially dark-backed.

Red-necked Phalarope
Phalaropus lobatus   See also plate 42

Key ID features W 102–118mm. The grey upperparts of non-breeding birds contrast with darker wings and distinct narrow wingbar.

Behaviour On the breeding grounds the female performs an advertising-flight, which involves the wing-whirr display described for Grey Phalarope.

Flight action Rapid wing-beats, twisting and turning in swallow-like flight low over water.

Voice Usual contact call is a chirping *kirk* or almost disyllabic harsh *cherrp*. A variety of notes is given on the breeding grounds, including a mate-seeking *wedu-wedu-wedu* given by the female at the end of the advertising flight.

Confusion species Superficially similar to small calidrids, like Little and Red-necked Stints (plate 72), until the dark face-mask is seen. For distinction from non-breeding Grey Phalarope, compare Key ID features.

Wilson's Phalarope
Phalaropus tricolor   See also plate 42

Key ID features W 116-129mm. In non-breeding plumage, the upperparts are a fairly uniform grey-brown, contrasting with the white rump and uppertail-coverts; the toes project just beyond the tail-tip.

Behaviour Courtship involves frequent pursuit flights and aggression against intruding females.

Voice Generally silent, but may utter a quiet, nasal grunting *ergh*.

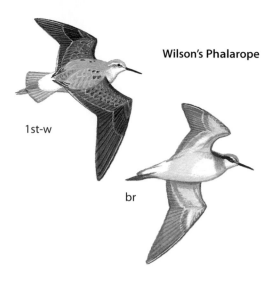

Wilson's Phalarope

1st-w

br

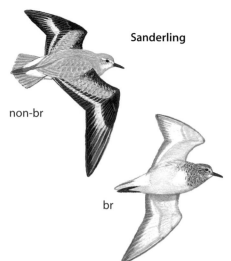

Sanderling

non-br

br

Distribution Vagrant to W Europe and Turkey.
Confusion species Distinguished from Lesser Yellowlegs (plate 68) and Stilt Sandpiper (plate 74) by its pale grey back, white breast and shorter toe projection.

Sanderling
Calidris alba   See also plate 33

Key ID features W 116-133mm. In non-breeding plumage, the black primary and lesser wing-coverts contrast with pale grey median coverts, scapulars and back. The bold white wingbar broadens across the inner primaries. The underwing is white.
Behaviour Display flights, mostly concerned with advertising for females, are usually at low levels, with the spread tail held level or depressed, the head drawn back, giving a hunched appearance, the bill pointing ahead or slightly down and moving from side to side; the wings are fluttered rapidly, followed by a brief glide with wings held slightly decurved. Also the male frequently hovers, with alternating rapid flutters and brief pauses.
Flight action Flies less erratically with slower wing-beats than Red-necked Phalarope.
Voice The flight call is a soft *twick-twick*. Feeding flocks utter quiet twittering calls. Song, given in brief bursts during display flight, is a complex churring, reminiscent at times of an alarm clock ring.
Confusion species Grey Phalarope (compare Key ID features). Compared to other calidrid species, the broader white wingbar is diagnostic.

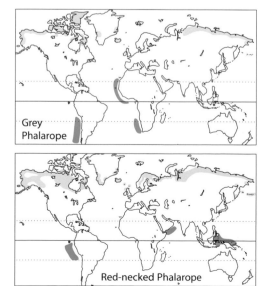

Grey Phalarope

Red-necked Phalarope

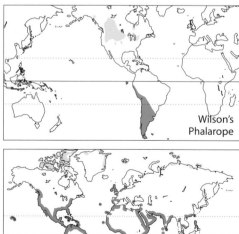

Wilson's Phalarope

Sanderling

ON MANY OCCASIONS IN THE FIELD a wader flies before it is seen at rest, and a rapid assessment of the visible features is required. As it flies away try to establish the pattern of the upperparts – the wings and tail. Is it uniform? Is there a pale or white area somewhere – on the wings or up the back, on the rump or the tail sides? A combination of wing and tail patterns can sometimes be sufficient to identify a wader. The three tables in Appendix A include (i) Nearctic species, (ii) Western Palearctic and (iii) Eastern Palearctic species, providing a quick reference source with which to compare your notes. Inevitably, some species will be included more than once, and possibly in all three tables, like the ubiquitous Dunlin.

Category explanations:

Wings

Plainish Essentially uniform, lacking any obvious wingbars or contrasting areas.

Indistinct wingbar Usually a narrow bar formed by pale tips to the greater coverts.

Moderate wingbar A more obvious, often white bar that can be seen from some distance – either on the tips of the greater coverts, or of the secondaries and inner primaries, when they produce a white trailing edge.

Distinct wingbar A broad, usually white bar, or bars, that may extend across the greater primary-coverts, or across the secondaries and inner primaries.

Contrasting pattern May refer to dark flight feathers contrasting with pale innerwing-coverts, or more vivid areas of black and white.

Tail

White back An obvious inverted white V stretching from the rump up the back.

White rump Often the lower rump; also includes white on the uppertail-coverts.

Plain or with fine bars A generally uniform colour, invariably similar to that of the wings.

Dark centre Rump and central uppertail-covert feathers usually a uniform darker colour.

White sides White outer tail-feathers.

Subterminal bar Obvious contrast between broad dark band, with narrow pale tips, and pale base.

WING \ TAIL	White back	White rump	Plain or with fine bars
Plainish	Black-necked Stilt	Greater Yellowlegs Lesser Yellowlegs Wilson's Phalarope	Black Oystercatcher American Woodcock Bar-tailed Godwit *(baueri)* Marbled Godwit Eskimo Curlew Whimbrel *(hudsonicus)* Bristle-thighed Curlew Long-billed Curlew Upland Sandpiper Grey-tailed Tattler Wandering Tattler Buff-breasted Sandpiper
Indistinct wingbar		Stilt Sandpiper	American Golden Plover Wilson's Snipe
Moderate wingbar	Short-billed Dowitcher Long-billed Dowitcher	Grey Plover White-rumped Sandpiper	Red Knot
Distinct wingbar		Piping Plover	
Contrasting pattern	Ruddy Turnstone Black Turnstone	Willet	Northern Jacana American Avocet Double-striped Thick-knee

Dark centre	White sides	Subterminal bar	TAIL / WING
Solitary Sandpiper			**Plainish**
Least Sandpiper Pectoral Sandpiper Ruff	Collared Plover		**Indistinct wingbar**
Lesser Sand Plover Semipalmated Sandpiper Western Sandpiper Baird's Sandpiper Dunlin Rock Sandpiper (*couesi*) Red-necked Phalarope	Wilson's Plover Mountain Plover	Wilson's Plover Mountain Plover	**Moderate wingbar**
Sanderling Rock Sandpiper (*ptilocnemis*) Grey Phalarope	Killdeer 'Snowy' Plover Spotted Sandpiper	American Oystercatcher Killdeer Piping Plover Hudsonian Godwit Surfbird	**Distinct wingbar**
		Ruddy Turnstone Black Turnstone	**Contrasting pattern**

WING \ TAIL	White back	White rump	Plain or with fine bars
Plainish	Black-winged Stilt Bar-tailed Godwit Whimbrel Slender-billed Curlew Eurasian Curlew Spotted Redshank Marsh Sandpiper Greenshank	Collared Pratincole Black-winged Pratincole Green Sandpiper Wood Sandpiper	Eurasian Woodcock
Indistinct wingbar			Jack Snipe
Moderate wingbar		Curlew Sandpiper	Eurasian Golden Plover Common Snipe Red Knot
Distinct wingbar	Redshank	Grey (Black-bellied) Plover	Senegal Thick-knee
Contrasting pattern	Ruddy Turnstone		Pied Avocet Spotted Thick-knee Cream-coloured Courser White-tailed Lapwing

Dark centre	White sides	Subterminal bar	TAIL / WING
	Little Ringed Plover	Northern Lapwing Dotterel	**Plainish**
	Three-banded Plover Great Snipe Pectoral Sandpiper Ruff		**Indistinct wingbar**
Little Stint Dunlin Broad-billed Sandpiper Red-necked Phalarope	Kittlitz's Plover Temminck's Stint Purple Sandpiper		**Moderate wingbar**
Sanderling Grey Phalarope	Ringed Plover Kentish Plover Common Sandpiper	Stone Curlew	**Distinct wingbar**
		Eurasian Oystercatcher Stone Curlew Spur-winged Lapwing Black-headed Lapwing Black-tailed Godwit Ruddy Turnstone	**Contrasting pattern**

WING \ TAIL	White back	White rump	Plain or with fine bars
Plainish	Eurasian Curlew (*orientalis*) Spotted Redshank Marsh Sandpiper Greenshank Nordmann's Greenshank	Oriental Pratincole Green Sandpiper Wood Sandpiper	Painted Snipe Eurasian Woodcock Amami Woodcock Solitary Snipe Latham's Snipe Wood Snipe Pintail Snipe Swinhoe's Snipe Bar-tailed Godwit (*baueri*) Little Curlew Whimbrel (*variegatus*) Far Eastern Curlew Grey-tailed Tattler
Indistinct wingbar			Pacific Golden Plover Jack Snipe Common Snipe
Moderate wingbar		Great Knot	Asian Dowitcher Red Knot
Distinct wingbar	Redshank		Ibisbill Terek Sandpiper
Contrasting pattern	Ruddy Turnstone	Little Pratincole	Pheasant-tailed Jacana Crab Plover Great Thick-knee White-tailed Lapwing

Dark centre	White sides	Subterminal bar	TAIL / WING
	Little Ringed Plover	Dotterel	**Plainish**
Oriental Plover Sharp-tailed Sandpiper Ruff			**Indistinct wingbar**
Long-billed Plover Lesser Sand Plover Caspian Plover Red-necked Stint Long-toed Stint Spoon-billed Sandpiper Broad-billed Sandpiper Red-necked Phalarope	Temminck's Stint		**Moderate wingbar**
Sanderling	Greater Sand Plover		**Distinct wingbar**
		Grey-headed Lapwing Red-wattled Lapwing Sociable Lapwing Ruddy Turnstone	**Contrasting pattern**

WADERS MAY FREQUENTLY BE SEEN flying overhead and, if a diagnostic call is not heard, a combination of features such as size, overall proportions, bill length, extent of feet or legs projecting beyond the tail-tip, and the plumage pattern, will often clinch the identification, or narrow it down to just a few species. From underneath, the patterns of the wings and body often differ from the upperparts: the characteristics listed concentrate on the most obvious - blacks, whites and reds. It was impractical to include the numerous species that appear to have fairly uniform pale underparts as they fly over, inevitably in their non-breeding plumages. Some species occur, and will be included in, more than one of the three main regions, but they are usually included where they are most regular and not where they occur as vagrants. Though the characteristics generally refer to birds in breeding plumage, they may also refer to non-breeding birds and juveniles; where necessary this is indicated as follows: B = breeding, N = non-breeding and J = juvenile.

Characteristic	Nearctic	Western Palearctic	Eastern Palearctic
all black	Black Oystercatcher		
mainly black body	American Golden Plover B Grey Plover B	Spur-winged Lapwing Eurasian Golden Plover B Grey Plover B Spotted Redshank B	Pacific Golden Plover B Grey Plover B
dark patch on belly	Rock Sandpiper B Dunlin B	Sociable Lapwing B Dotterel B Dunlin B	Sociable Lapwing B Dunlin B
black axillaries	Grey Plover	Grey Plover	Grey Plover
all dark underwing	Solitary Sandpiper Wandering Tattler	Cream-coloured Courser Temminck's Courser Green Sandpiper Black-winged Pratincole	Grey-tailed Tattler
dark-and-white underwing (cont. on p. 201)	American Oystercatcher Black-necked Stilt American Avocet Double-striped Thick-knee Hudsonian Godwit Spotted Sandpiper Willet	Eurasian Oystercatcher Black-winged Stilt Pied Avocet Stone Curlew Senegal Thick-knee Spotted Thick-knee Northern Lapwing Spur-winged Lapwing Black-headed Lapwing	Great Thick-knee Little Pratincole Northern Lapwing Grey-headed Lapwing Red-wattled Lapwing Sociable Lapwing White-tailed Lapwing Terek Sandpiper

Characteristic	Nearctic	Western Palearctic	Eastern Palearctic
dark-and-white underwing (cont.)		Red-wattled Lapwing Sociable Lapwing White-tailed Lapwing Black-tailed Godwit Common Sandpiper Terek Sandpiper	
mainly red-orange body	American Woodcock Long-billed Dowitcher B Hudsonian Godwit B Bar-tailed Godwit B Marbled Godwit Red Knot B Grey Phalarope B	Black-tailed Godwit B Bar-tailed Godwit B Red Knot B Curlew Sandpiper B Grey Phalarope B	Asian Dowitcher B
red/orange patches on body	American Avocet BJ Short-billed Dowitcher B Red-necked Stint B Wilson's Phalarope B Red-necked Phalarope B	Temminck's Courser Kittlitz's Plover B Lesser Sand Plover B Greater Sand Plover B Caspian Plover B Dotterel B Sanderling B Little Stint B Red-necked Phalarope B	Painted Snipe B Lesser Sand Plover B Greater Sand Plover B Caspian Plover B Oriental Plover B Red-necked Stint B Spoon-billed Sandpiper B Red-necked Phalarope B
buff to reddish axillaries/ underwing-coverts	American Woodcock Marbled Godwit Whimbrel (*hudsonicus*) Bristle-thighed Curlew Long-billed Curlew	Collared Pratincole	Oriental Pratincole Little Curlew
light underwing, dark body	American Golden Plover B Surfbird B Red Knot B Dunlin B Stilt Sandpiper B Buff-breasted Sandpiper	Eurasian Golden Plover B Grey Plover B Spotted Redshank B Red Knot B Dunlin B Ruff B Grey Phalarope B	Pacific Golden Plover B Dunlin B
dark underwing, light body	Black-necked Stilt Wilson's Snipe Hudsonian Godwit NJ Wandering Tattler NJ Solitary Sandpiper	Black-winged Stilt Cream-coloured Courser Collared Pratincole Black-winged Pratincole Green Sandpiper	Cream-coloured Courser Oriental Pratincole Little Pratincole Oriental Plover Grey-tailed Tattler

Characteristic	Nearctic	Western Palearctic	Eastern Palearctic
dark breast contrasts with white belly	American Oystercatcher Solitary Sandpiper Black Turnstone Surfbird NJ Semipalmated Sandpiper B Western Sandpiper B Least Sandpiper B White-rumped Sandpiper B Baird's Sandpiper B Pectoral Sandpiper	Eurasian Oystercatcher Northern Lapwing Red-wattled Lapwing Green Sandpiper Common Sandpiper B Ruddy Turnstone Sanderling B Temminck's Stint Dunlin N Purple Sandpiper Broad-billed Sandpiper B Ruff B Red-necked Phalarope B	Painted Snipe Crab Plover Black-headed Lapwing Grey-headed Lapwing Red-wattled Lapwing Lesser Sand Plover Greater Sand Plover Caspian Plover Oriental Plover Asian Dowitcher B Great Knot B Red-necked Stint B Long-toed Stint Spoon-billed Sandpiper B Broad-billed Sandpiper B
dark bands on breast	Semipalmated Plover Wilson's Plover Killdeer Piping Plover B 'Snowy' Plover	Ringed Plover Little Ringed Plover Three-banded Plover Kentish Plover	Long-billed Plover Kentish Plover

THIS SYSTEMATIC LIST COVERS ALL the wader species that have appeared within the region. Nomenclature and sequence follow Clements (2000), apart from a few preferred common names, with range information based on Dickinson (2003). Two species have been split in accordance with the recommendations of the American Ornithologists' Union: Black-necked Stilt *Himantopus mexicanus* from Black-winged Stilt *H. himantopus*, and Wilson's Snipe *Gallinago delicata* from Common Snipe *G. gallinago*.

All subspecies are included for each species in this systematic list (including those subspecies that are extralimital – these are marked with an asterisk). Breeding and wintering ranges are included (where these are known; the wintering distributions of some subspecies are poorly understood). Plate numbers are included for the reader's convenience; the first refers to the 'at rest' plate, the second to the 'in flight' plate.

The terms 'Critically Endangered', 'Endangered' and 'Vulnerable' occur on a number of occasions under 'Distribution and status' in the 'in flight' section of this book. These are categories of threat to certain species. The categories are defined in the 2004 IUCN Red List of Threatened Animals (see www.redlist.org) as follows:

Critically Endangered – A species is Critically Endangered when the best available evidence indicates that it faces an extremely high risk of extinction in the wild.

Endangered – A species is Endangered when the best available evidence indicates that it faces a very high risk of extinction in the wild.

Vulnerable – A species is Vulnerable when the best available evidence indicates that it faces a high risk of extinction in the wild.

The letters CR, EN and VU are appended to species in the list that fall into these categories.

Family JACANIDAE (jacanas)   Plate

Pheasant-tailed Jacana *Hydrophasianus chirurgus*   44, 46
    Pakistan east to SE and E China and south to Sri Lanka, Philippines and Greater Sundas; some winter E Arabia, S Asia

Northern Jacana *Jacana spinosa*   43, 46
    J. s. gymnostoma Mexico and Cozumel Island
    *J. s. spinosa Belize and Guatemala to W Panama
    *J. s. violacea Cuba, Isla de la Juventud, Jamaica, Hispaniola

Family ROSTRATULIDAE (painted snipe)

Painted Snipe *Rostratula benghalensis*   1, 46
    R. b. benghalensis Africa, Madagascar, Asia Minor through S Asia to Japan and Philippines, SE to Greater and Lesser Sundas east to Flores
    *R. b. australis N and E Australia

Family DROMADIDAE (Crab Plover)

Crab Plover *Dromas ardeola*   1, 47
    Coasts (mainly west) of Indian Ocean; winters south to SE Africa east to Andaman Islands

Family HAEMATOPODIDAE (oystercatchers)

Black Oystercatcher *Haematopus bachmani*   2, 47
    W coast of N America

American Oystercatcher *Haematopus palliatus*   2, 47
    H. p. palliatus Atlantic coasts of North America and the Gulf of Mexico
    H. p. frazari Pacific coast of North America
   * *H. p. galapagensis* Galápagos Islands

Eurasian Oystercatcher *Haematopus ostralegus*   2, 47
    H. o. ostralegus Iceland to NW European Russia, south to W Mediterranean; winters
      W and S Europe and W Africa
    H. o. longipes Balkans, Ukraine and Turkey to S and C European Russia and W Siberia;
      winters E Mediterranean, coastal E Africa, Arabia
    H. o. osculans Shores of Sea of Okhotsk and Kamchatka to Korea and NE China; winters
      E China and Korea

Family IBIDORHYNCHIDAE (Ibisbill)

Ibisbill *Ibidorhyncha struthersii*   1, 46
    Tien Shan, Pamir, and Tibetan Plateau to Shaanxi, Shanxi and W and N Hebei; winters
    S to N India, NE Burma

Family RECURVIROSTRIDAE (stilts and avocets)

Black-winged Stilt *Himantopus himantopus*   3, 48
    Mediterranean and sub-Saharan Africa to SE Asia and Taiwan

Black-necked Stilt *Himantopus mexicanus*   3, 48
    H. h. mexicanus W and S USA to N and C S. America, W Indies, Galápagos
    H. h. knudseni Hawaiian Islands

Pied Avocet *Recurvirostra avosetta*   4, 48
    C and S Europe to SW and C Asia, N, E, and S Africa; winters W Europe to NW India

American Avocet *Recurvirostra americana*   4, 48
> C and W North America, E USA, C Mexico; winters S and SE USA to N Honduras, Bahamas to Cuba

Family BURHINIDAE (thick-knees)

Stone Curlew *Burhinus oedicnemus*   5, 49
> *B. o. distinctus*: W Canary Islands
> *B. o. insularum*: E Canary Islands
> *B. o. saharae*: N Africa, Balearic Islands, Malta, Cyprus, Levant to SC Turkey and SW Iran; winters S Europe, N Africa, and Arabia
> *B. o. oedicnemus*: W and S Europe to N Balkans, Ukraine and Caucasus
> *B. o. harterti*: Volga delta, Transcaspia and NE Iran to W Pakistan and E Kazakhstan; winters NE Africa and SW Asia
> * *B. o. indicus*: C Pakistan, India and Sri Lanka east to mainland SE Asia

Senegal Thick-knee *Burhinus senegalensis*   5, 49
> Senegal to Sudan, Egypt, Ethiopia, N Uganda and NW Kenya

Spotted Thick-knee *Burhinus capensis*   5, 49
> * *B. c. maculosus* Senegal through C Africa to Ethiopia and Somalia, south to N Uganda and N Kenya
> *B. c. dodsoni* S Arabia, Eritrea and N Somalia
> * *B. c. capensis* South Africa and E Botswana to E and NW Angola, Tanzania and S Kenya
> * *B. c. damarensis* Namibia, Botswana, SW Angola

Double-striped Thick-knee *Burhinus bistriatus*   43, 49
> *B. b. bistriatus* S Mexico to NW Costa Rica
> * *B. b. dominicensis* Hispaniola
> * *B. b. pediacus* N Colombia
> * *B. b. vocifer* N Colombia to Guyana and N Brazil

Great Thick-knee *Esacus recurvirostris*   44, 53
> SE Iran to India, Sri Lanka, SE Asia and Hainan

Family GLAREOLIDAE (coursers and pratincoles)

Egyptian Plover *Pluvianus aegyptius*   6, 50
> Senegal to Nigeria, Sudan and W Ethiopia, south to N Angola, W and N Zaire, N Uganda

Cream-coloured Courser *Cursorius cursor*   6, 50
> *C. c. bogolubovi* SE Turkey to W Pakistan
> *C. c. cursor* Canary Islands and Sahara to Arabia and Iraq

C. c. exsul Cape Verde Islands
* *C. c somalensis* Eritrea, Ethiopia, N Somalia
* *C. c. littoralis* SE Sudan to N Kenya and S Somalia

Temminck's Courser *Cursorius temminckii*   6, 50
Sub-Saharan Africa

Collared Pratincole *Glareola pratincola*   7, 51
G. p. pratincola S Europe, N Africa to Pakistan; winters N tropical Africa
* *G. p. erlangeri* Coastal S Somalia, N Kenya
* *G. p. fuelleborni* Senegal to S Kenya, Congo, Namibia and E South Africa

Oriental Pratincole *Glareola maldivarum*   7, 51
C, E and SE Asia; winters south to Australia

Black-winged Pratincole *Glareola nordmanni*   7, 51
SE Europe and C Asia; winters S and SW Africa

Little Pratincole *Glareola lactea*   44, 51
India and Sri Lanka to S Indochina

Family CHARADRIIDAE (plovers)

Northern Lapwing *Vanellus vanellus*   8, 52
W Europe to China and Japan

Spur-winged Lapwing (Plover) *Vanellus spinosus*   8, 52
SE Europe, Middle East, sub-Saharan Africa south to Ghana, CAR and Kenya

Black-headed Lapwing (Plover) *Vanellus tectus*   45, 53
V. t. tectus Senegal and S Mauritania to Ethiopia, Uganda and NW Kenya
* *V. t. latifrons* S Somalia to E Kenya

Grey-headed Lapwing *Vanellus cinereus*   16, 53
NE and E China, S Russia Far East, Japan; winters Nepal to N Indochina, S China, S Japan

Red-wattled Lapwing *Vanellus indicus*   16, 53
V. i. aigneri Turkey to W Pakistan and NE Arabia
V. i. indicus C Pakistan, India, and Nepal to N Assam and Bangladash
* *V. i. lankae* Sri Lanka
* *V. i. atronuchalis* S Assam east to W Yunnan and S through mainland SE Asia to the Malay
   peninsula and N Sumatra

Sociable Lapwing (Plover) *Vanellus gregarius* VU   8, 52
SC Russia, Kazakhstan; winters NE Africa, Arabia, N India

White-tailed Lapwing (Plover) *Vanellus leucurus*   8, 52
Middle East through Iran to Kazakhstan; winters NE Africa to NW India

Pacific Golden Plover *Pluvialis fulva*   10, 54
NC and NE Russia, N Siberia, W Alaska; winters E Africa, India, SE Asia to Oceania, Australia and New Zealand

American Golden Plover *Pluvialis dominica*   10, 54
Alaska and N Canada; winters C South America

Eurasian Golden Plover *Pluvialis apricaria*   9, 54
P. a. apricaria British Isles to southern Sweden and Baltic States; winters W and S Europe
P. a. altifrons EC Greenland, Iceland, Faroe Is., Norway, and W and N Sweden to Taymyr; winters W and S Europe, N Africa and Middle East

Grey (Black-bellied) Plover *Pluvialis squatarola*   9, 54
Holarctic; almost cosmopolitan dispersal pot-breeding.

Ringed Plover *Charadrius hiaticula*   11, 55
C. h. hiaticula NE Canada and Greenland east to Scandinavia; winters Africa
C. h. tundrae N Eurasia; winters S Europe, S Africa and SW Asia

Semipalmated Plover *Charadrius semipalmatus*   11, 55
Alaska, N Canada; winters coastal N, C and S America, Bermuda, West Indies, Galápagos Is.

Long-billed Plover *Charadrius placidus*   16, 55
Russian Far East to NE and E China and Japan; winters E Nepal to S China and Japan

Little Ringed Plover *Charadrius dubius*   11, 55
C. d. curonicus N Africa, Europe, Asia (except SC and SE); winters Africa and S Asia to Indonesia and Philippines
* *C. d. jerdoni* India to S China and Indochina
* *C. d. dubius* Philippines to New Guinea and Bismarck archipelago; winters SE Asia to Australasia

Wilson's Plover *Charadrius wilsonia*   12, 56
C. w. wilsonia E USA to E Mexico and Belize
C. w. beldingi Baja California to C Peru
* *C. w. cinnamominus* Colombia to French Guiana, Dutch Antilles, Trinidad and Grenada

Killdeer *Charadrius vociferus*   12, 56
C. v. vociferus Canada, USA, Mexico; winters south to NW South America
* *C. v. ternominatus* Bahamas, Greater Antilles
* *C. v. peruvianus* Peru, NW Chile

Piping Plover *Charadrius melodus*   VU   13, 57
C and E North America; winters S USA, W Mexico, Bahamas, Greater Antilles

Kittlitz's Plover *Charadrius pecuarius*   45, 57
Egypt, Senegal to Sudan and Cape Province, Madagascar

Three-banded Plover *Charadrius tricollaris*   45, 57
C. t. tricollaris Ethiopia and E Africa to Gabon, S Zaire and South Africa
* *C. t. bifrontatus* Madagascar

Kentish Plover *Charadrius alexandrinus*   13, 57
C. a. alexandrinus W Europe, Atlantic islands and N Africa to NE China; winters
    N tropical Africa, S Asia, W Indonesia
C. a. dealbatus S Japan, E and SE China; winters S to Philippines and Borneo
* *C. a. seebohmi* S India, Sri Lanka
C. a. nivosus USA, Mexico, Bahamas, Greater and Dutch Antilles; winters south to
    Panama
* *C. a. occidentalis* Coastal Peru to SC Chile

Collared Plover *Charadrius collaris*   43, 56
WC Mexico to N Argentina and C Chile

Lesser Sand Plover *Charadrius mongolus*   14, 58
C. m. pamirensis W Tien Shan, Pamir and NW Himalaya to W Kunlun Shan; winters
    E and S Africa to India
C. m. atrifrons C and E Himalayas and S Tibetan Plateau; winters S China and Greater
    Sundas
C. m. schaeferi E Tibetan Plateau to S Mongolia; winters S China to Greater Sundas
C. m. mongolus Lake Baikal to Sea of Okhotsk; winters SE China and Taiwan to Australia
C. m. stegmanni NE Siberia, Kamchatka and Commander Islands; winters Taiwan,
    Philippines, New Guinea, E Australia and W and SW Pacific Islands

Greater Sand Plover *Charadrius leschenaultii*   14, 58
C. l. columbinus Turkey to SW Iran; winters Mediterranean, Red Sea and Persian Gulf
C. l. crassirostris E Transcaucasia and Transcaspia to Syr Dar'ya basin and WC Kazakhstan;
    winters shores NE and E Africa to W India
C. l. leschenaultii EC Kazakhstan and W China east to Mongolia; winters on shores of
    Indian Ocean (including E Africa), Indonesia, Philippines and Australasia

Caspian Plover *Charadrius asiaticus*   15, 58
Caspian Sea to E Kazakhstan and NW China; winters E and S Africa

Oriental Plover *Charadrius veredus*   16, 58
Tuva and Mongolia to SE Transbaikalia and N Mongolia; winters to Australia

Dotterel *Charadrius morinellus*   15, 58
N Europe and N Asia to E Russia; winters Mediterranean to W Iran

Mountain Plover *Charadrius montanus*   VU   15, 54
   W USA; winters SW USA to NE Mexico

Family SCOLOPACIDAE (sandpipers, curlews, snipe and phalaropes)

Eurasian Woodcock *Scolopax rusticola*   17, 59
   Palearctic; winters W and S Europe and N Africa to SE Asia

Amami Woodcock *Scolopax mira*   VU   17, 59
   C Ryukyu Islands

American Woodcock *Scolopax minor*   17, 59
   SC and SE Canada, E USA; winters SE USA

Jack Snipe *Lymnocryptes minimus*   19, 60
   N Europe and Baltic to Siberia E to Kolyma basin; winters W Europe south to W and E
   Africa, E to Indochina

Solitary Snipe *Gallinago solitaria*   18, 61
   G. s. solitaria Mountains of southern Siberia and perhaps N Mongolia; winters S, C and
   E Asia south to E Pakistan to Burma
   G. s. japonica NE Mongolia to NE China and Kamchatka; winters Amurland to
   Kamchatka, Korea, Japan, E China

Latham's Snipe *Gallinago hardwickii*   18, 61
   Russian Far East, S Sakhalin and S Kuril islands to N Japan; winters in E Australia,
   Tasmania

Wood Snipe *Gallinago nemoricola*   VU   18, 61
   Himalayas to Burma and SC China; winters India, Bangladesh, Burma, N Indochina

Pintail Snipe *Gallinago stenura*   19, 60
   NE European Russia to NE Siberia, S to N Mongolia and NE China; winters Saudi
   Arabia, E Africa and Aldabra Is. (W Indian Ocean), India to SE China and Taiwan, S to
   Philippines and W Indonesia

Swinhoe's Snipe *Gallinago megala*   18, 61
   C and SE Siberia, south to N Mongolia; winters India to N Australia

Great Snipe *Gallinago media*   17, 59
   N and E Europe to W and C Siberia; winters sub-Saharan Africa and Iran

Common Snipe *Gallinago gallinago*   19, 60
   G. g. faeroeensis Iceland south to Faroe Islands, Orkney and Shetland Islands; winters
   British Isles

G. g. gallinago   N and C Palearctic; winters W Europe and N, W and E Africa to S Japan and W Indonesia

Wilson's Snipe   *Gallinago delicata*   19, 60
N and C North America; winters NW and C USA to N South America

Short-billed Dowitcher   *Limnodromus griseus*   20, 62
L. g. caurinus   S Alaska and S Yukon; winters C USA to Peru
L. g. hendersoni   C Canada; winters SE USA to Panama
L. g. griseus   NE Canada; winters S USA to Brazil

Long-billed Dowitcher   *Limnodromus scolopaceus*   20, 62
Taymyr east to Chukotkiy and Koryakskiy Mountains of NE Siberia, W Alaska, N Yukon; winters W and S USA to Panama and French Guiana

Asian Dowitcher   *Limnodromus semipalmatus*   32, 62
S Siberia (patchy), N Mongolia and NE China; winters E India to Indochina, south to N Australia

Black-tailed Godwit   *Limosa limosa*   21, 63
L. l. islandica   Iceland to Shetland Is. and W and N Norway; winters British Isles and Netherlands to Iberia
L. l. limosa   W and C Europe to C Asia; winters Mediterranean and Africa to India
L. l. melanuroides   Lena Basin and Lake Baikal to Kamchatka; winters Indochina south to Australia

Hudsonian Godwit   *Limosa haemastica*   22, 63
NW Alaska to Hudson Bay; winters SE South America and SC Chile

Bar-tailed Godwit   *Limosa lapponica*   21, 62
L. l. lapponica   Iceland, Faeroe Islands and Shetlands; winters SW Europe
L. l. menzbieri   NE Siberia, from Lena delta to Chaunskaya Bay; winters SE Asia to NW Australia
L. l. baueri   NE Siberia to N and W Alaska; winters China to Philippines, Australia, New Zealand and Pacific islands

Marbled Godwit   *Limosa fedoa*   22, 63
L. f. fedoa   C Canada, NW USA; winters S USA to Panama and NW parts of South America
L. f. beringiae   Alaska; winters W USA

Little Curlew   *Numenius minutus*   23, 64
NC and NE Siberia; winters New Guinea, Australia

Eskimo Curlew   *Numenius borealis*   CR   43, 64
NC Canada; winters Uruguay, Argentina; probably extinct

Whimbrel *Numenius phaeopus*   24, 65
  N. p. phaeopus NW Palearctic; winters Africa and India
  N. p. alboaxillaris Steppes N of Caspian Sea; winters coastal Indian Ocean
  N. p. variegatus Siberia; winters India, Philippines, Indonesia and Australia
  N. p. hudsonicus Alaska to N Canada; winters S South America

Bristle-thighed Curlew *Numenius tahitiensis* VU   24, 65
  W Alaska; winters Marshall and Hawaiian Islands to the Society Islands

Slender-billed Curlew *Numenius tenuirostris* CR   24, 64
  SW Siberia and N Kazakhstan; winters NW Africa, Iraq and Persian Gulf

Eurasian Curlew *Numenius arquata*   25, 66
  N. a. arquata British Isles to the Urals; winters NW Africa
  N. a. orientalis E Russia and N China; winters Africa, SE Asia, Indonesia

Long-billed Curlew *Numenius americanus*   25, 66
  N. a. parvus SW and SC Canada to SW USA; winters SW USA to Mexico
  N. a. americanus WC USA; winters SW USA to Guatemala

Far Eastern Curlew *Numenius madagascariensis*   25, 66
  E Siberia and Russian Far East; winters Taiwan and Indonesia to Australasia

Upland Sandpiper *Bartramia longicauda*   23, 64
  C Alaska, C and S Canada, NC USA; winters Surinam, Paraguay and S Brazil to
  C Argentina

Spotted Redshank *Tringa erythropus*   26, 67
  N Europe, N and NE Siberia; winters W and S Europe, N, W and E Africa to SE Asia, SE
  China and Taiwan

Redshank *Tringa totanus*   26, 70
  T. t. robusta Iceland and Faroe Islands; winters British Isles and W Europe
  T. t. totanus N and W Europe from the British Isles and Spain to W Siberia; winters W
  Africa and the Mediterranean east to India, Indonesia
  T. t. ussuriensis S Siberia and Mongolia to E Asia; winters E Mediterranean and E Africa
  to India and SE Asia
  T. t. terrignotae S Manchuria, E China; winters SE and E Asia, ?Australia
  T. t. craggi Xinjiang in NW China; winters S Asia, SE Asia (to Australia?)
  T. t. eurhinus Tajikistan, N India, C and S Tibet; winters India to the Malay peninsula

Marsh Sandpiper *Tringa stagnatilis*   27, 67
  E Baltic and Ukraine to E Siberia and NE China; winters Mediterranean and sub-Saharan
  Africa to Indonesia and Australasia

Greenshank *Tringa nebularia*   27, 67
  T. n. nebularia W Palearctic; winters S Africa, S Asia, Australasia

T. n. glottoides Siberia to Kamchatka; winters Australasia

Nordmann's (Spotted) Greenshank *Tringa guttifer* EN   32, 67
Russian Far East; winters NE India to mainland SE Asia

Greater Yellowlegs *Tringa melanoleuca*   28, 68
S Alaska and E across C Canada to NE Nova Scotia; winters coastal and S USA, C and
South America

Lesser Yellowlegs *Tringa flavipes*   28, 68
Alaska to C Canada; winters S USA, West Indies, C and South America

Green Sandpiper *Tringa ochropus*   29, 69
N Palearctic; winters W Europe and Africa to Philippines and N Borneo

Solitary Sandpiper *Tringa solitaria*   29, 69
T. s. cinnamomea C and S Alaska to NE Manitoba; winters South America
T. s. solitaria E British Columbia to Quebec and Labrador; winters W Indies, Central and
South America

Wood Sandpiper *Tringa glareola*   29, 69
N Palearctic; winters Africa, S Asia, Philippines, Indonesia, Australia

Terek Sandpiper *Xenus cinereus*   30, 70
E Baltic area, Belarus and N Ukraine to NE Siberia; winters S and E Africa, Middle East,
S Asia, Indonesia to Australasia

Common Sandpiper *Actitis hypoleucos*   30, 70
Europe and N and C Asia; winters S Europe, Africa, and S and E Asia to Australasia

Spotted Sandpiper *Actitis macularia*   30, 70
Canada and N USA below Arctic Circle; winters W Indies, S USA to central South
America

Grey-tailed Tattler *Heteroscelus brevipes*   28, 68
NC and NE Siberia; winters Taiwan and Malay peninsula to Australia and New
Zealand

Wandering Tattler *Heteroscelus incanus*   28, 68
NE Siberia, S Alaska to NW British Columbia; winters SW USA and W Mexico, Ecuador
and Galapagos Islands, Pacific islands to E Australia and New Zealand

Willet *Catoptrophorus semipalmatus*   27, 63
C. s. inornatus SC Canada and NC USA; winters southern USA to northern South
America
C. s. semipalmatus SE Canada, E and S USA, West Indies; winters S USA, C America, West
Indies to S Brazil

Ruddy Turnstone *Arenaria interpres*   31, 71
  A. i. interpres NE Canada, Greenland and N Europe to NE Siberia and W Alaska; winters
    W and S Europe, Africa and S and E Asia, Australasia, Pacific islands, and W USA to
    W Mexico
  A. i. morinella NE Alaska and N Canada; winters S USA to South America

Black Turnstone *Arenaria melanocephala*   31, 71
  W and S Alaska; winters SE Alaska to NW Mexico

Surfbird *Aphriza virgata*   31, 71
  S and C Alaska and C Yukon; winters Pacific coast of N, C and S America

Great Knot *Calidris tenuirostris*   33, 74
  NE Siberia; winters E Arabia to Indochina, New Guinea and Australia

Red Knot *Calidris canutus*   33, 74
  C. c. canutus Siberia; winters South Africa and Australasia
  C. c. rogersi Mountains of Chukotka and Chukotskiy peninsula; winters Australasia
  C. c. roselaari Wrangel Island and NW Alaska; winters shores of Gulf of Mexico
  C. c. rufa N Canada; winters S South America
  C. c. islandica Islands off N Canada, N Greenland; winters W Europe

Sanderling *Calidris alba*   33, 77
  Holarctic; worldwide coastal distribution following post-breeding dispersal

Semipalmated Sandpiper *Calidris pusilla*   34, 73
  N Chukotskiy peninsula, W and N Alaska, N Canada; winters C and S America, W Indies

Western Sandpiper *Calidris mauri*   34, 73
  N and E Chukotskiy peninsula, W and N Alaska; winters coastal USA to N South
    America, West Indies

Red-necked Stint *Calidris ruficollis*   35, 72
  NC Taymyr, NE Siberia, W and N Alaska; winters SE Asia to Australasia

Little Stint *Calidris minuta*   35, 72
  N Europe and N Siberia; winters SW Europe and Africa to India

Temminck's Stint *Calidris temminckii*   36, 72
  N Europe, N Siberia; winters W and E Africa, S Asia to S China, south through mainland
    SE Asia to the Malay peninsula and Borneo

Long-toed Stint *Calidris subminuta*   36, 73
  SW to E Siberia; winters India and Indochina to Australasia

Least Sandpiper *Calidris minutilla*   36, 73
  Alaska and N Canada; winters S USA to N South America, West Indies

White-rumped Sandpiper *Calidris fuscicollis*   37, 74
NE Alaska and N Canada to S Baffin Island; winters S South America

Baird's Sandpiper *Calidris bairdii*   37, 75
Extreme NE Siberia, Alaska and NW Canada to NW Greenland; winters W and S South
America

Pectoral Sandpiper *Calidris melanotos*   38, 75
N Siberia, W and N Alaska, and N Canada; winters SE Australia, New Zealand, S South
America

Sharp-tailed Sandpiper *Calidris acuminata*   38, 75
NC and NE Siberia; winters New Guinea to Australia and New Zealand

Curlew Sandpiper *Calidris ferruginea*   39, 74
N Siberia (rarely N Alaska); winters Africa to Australasia

Dunlin *Calidris alpina*   39, 76
C. a. arctica NE Greenland; winters NW Africa
C. a. schinzii SE Greenland, Iceland and British Isles to S Scandinavia and Baltic; winters
SW Europe and NW Africa
C. a. alpina N Europe and NW Siberia to Yenisey River; winters W Europe,
Mediterranean, Africa and SW Asia to India
C. a. sakhalina Extreme NE Asia; winters E China, Korea, Japan, Taiwan
C. a. actites N Sakhalin; winters E Asia
C. a. kistchinskii N Sea of Okhotsk and S Koryakland to N Kuril Islands and Kamchatka;
winters E Asia
C. a. arcticola NW and N Alaska and NW Canada; winters China, Korea and Japan
C. a. pacifica W and S Alaska; winters W USA and W Mexico
C. a. hudsonia NC Canada east to Hudson Bay; winters SE USA

Purple Sandpiper *Calidris maritima*   40, 76
Holarctic on tundra; winters coastal E USA and NW Europe

Rock Sandpiper *Calidris ptilocnemis*   40, 76
C. p. quarta Kuril Islands, S Kamchatka and Komandorskiye Islands
C. p. tschuktschorum Chukotska peninsula to W Alaska; winters NW North America and
E Japan
C. p. ptilocnemis Pribilof, St Mathew and Hall Islands; winters Alaska
C. p. couesi Aleutian Islands and Alaska

Stilt Sandpiper *Calidris himantopus*   41, 74
N Alaska and N Canada; winters S USA, C South America

Spoon-billed Sandpiper *Eurynorhynchus pygmeus* EN   32, 72
Chukotskiy peninsula to N Kamchatka; winters SE India, Bangladesh, Vietnam, Thailand
and the Malay peninsula S to Singapore

Broad-billed Sandpiper *Limicola falcinellus*   40, 76
  L. f. falcinellus N Europe, NW Siberia; winters E and S Africa to W and S India
  L. f. sibirica NE Siberia; winters NE India to Australia

Buff-breasted Sandpiper *Tryngites subruficollis*   38, 75
  Extreme NE Siberia, N Alaska, N Canada; winters SC South America

Ruff *Philomachus pugnax*   41, 75
  N and C Europe and across N Siberia to Sakhalin; winters W and S Europe, Africa and
    S Asia east to India, more rarely SE Asia and Australia

Wilson's Phalarope *Phalaropus tricolor*   42, 77
  S Canada, NW and CN USA; winters W and S South America and subantarctic islands

Red-necked Phalarope *Phalaropus lobatus*   42, 77
  N Holarctic; winters pelagic areas off WC South America, Arabian Sea, Philippines,
    Wallacea to W Melanesia and Australasia

Grey (Red) Phalarope *Phalaropus fulicarius*   42, 77
  N Holarctic; winters pelagic areas off W South America and W and SW Africa and
    subantarctic islands

BIBLIOGRAPHY

Brazil, M. 1991. *The Birds of Japan.* Christopher Helm, London.

Byrkjedal, I. & Thompson, D. B. A. 1998. *Tundra Plovers: The Eurasian, Pacific and American Golden Plovers and Grey Plover.* T & A D. Poyser, London.

Chandler, R. J. 1989. *North Atlantic Shorebirds.* Macmillan, London.

Clements, J. F. 2000. *Birds of the World: A Checklist.* Pica Press, Sussex.

Couzens, D. 2003. *Birds by Behaviour.* HarperCollins, London.

Cramp, S. & Simmons, K. E. L. 1983. *The Birds of the Western Palearctic.* Vol. 3. Oxford University Press, Oxford.

del Hoyo, J., Elliot, A. & Sargatal, J. 1996. *Handbook of the Birds of the World* Vol. 3. Hoatzin to Auks. Lynx Edicions, Barcelona.

Dickinson, E. C. 2003. *The Howard and Moore Complete Checklist of the Birds of the World.* Christopher Helm, London.

Doherty, P. & Oddie, B. *Waders of Europe, Asia and North America.* Bird Images, Sherburn-in-Elmet [videotape].

Flegg, J. 2004. *Time to Fly: Exploring Bird Migration.* British Trust for Ornithology, Thetford.

Fitter, R. S. R. & Richardson, R. A. 1952. *The Pocket Guide to British Birds.* Collins, London.

Ginn, H. B. & Melville, D. S. 1983. *Moult in Birds.* British Trust for Ornithology Guide 19, Tring.

Gollop, J. B., Barry, T. W. & Iverson, E. H. 1986. *Eskimo Curlew: A vanishing species?* Saskatchewan Natural History Society, Regina.

Grant, P. J. & Mullarney, K. 1989. *The New Approach to Identification.* Published privately.

Gretton, A. 1991. *The Ecology and Conservation of the Slender-billed Curlew.* ICBP, Cambridge.

Hale, W. G. 1980. *Waders.* Collins, London.

Hammond, N. & Pearson, B.1994. *Waders: Hamlyn Bird Behaviour Guides.* Hamlyn, London.

Harrington, B. 1996. *The Flight of the Red Knot.* Norton, New York.

Harris, A., Tucker, L. & Vinicombe, K. 1989. *The Macmillan Field Guide to Bird Identification.* Macmillan, London.

Harris, A., Shirihai, H. & Christie, D. 1996. *The Macmillan Birder's Guide to European and Middle Eastern Birds.* Macmillan, London.

Hosking, E. & Hale, W. G. 1983. *Eric Hosking's Waders.* Pelham Books, London.

Hume, R. 1990. *Birds by Character: the fieldguide to jizz identification.* Macmillan, London.

Hayman, P., Marchant, J. & Prater, A. J. 1986. *Shorebirds: An identification guide to the waders of the world.* Croom Helm, Beckenham.

IUCN, 2004. *The 2004 IUCN Red List of Threatened Species.* http://www.redlist.org/

Nethersole-Thompson, D. 1973. *The Dotterel.* Collins, London.

Nethersole-Thompson, D. & Nethersole-Thompson, M. 1979. *Greenshanks.* T & A D Poyser, Berkhamsted.

Nethersole-Thompson, D. & M. 1986. *Waders: Their breeding, haunts and watchers.* T & A D Poyser, Calton.

Paulson, D. 1993. *Shorebirds of the Pacific Northwest.* University of Washington Press, Seattle and London.

Paulson, D. 2005. *Shorebirds of North America – The photographic guide.* Christopher Helm, London.

Prater, A. J., Marchant, J. H. & Vuorinen, J. 1977. *Guide to the identification and ageing of Holarctic waders.* British Trust for Ornithology Guide 17, Tring.

Richards, A. 1988. *Birds of the Tideline: Shorebirds of the Northern Hemisphere.* Dragon's World, Limpsfield.

Rosair, D. & Cottridge, D. 1995. *Photographic Guide to the Waders of the World.* Hamlyn, London.

Sibley, D. 2000. *The North American Bird Guide.* Pica Press, Sussex.

Svensson, L. & Grant, P. J. 1999. *Collins Bird Guide.* HarperCollins, London.

van Rhijn, J. G. 1991. *The Ruff.* T & A D Poyser, London.

Vaughan, R. 1980. *Plovers.* Terence Dalton, Lavenham.

INDEX

FIGURES IN PLAIN TEXT refer to page numbers, while those in **bold** text refer to the plate numbers. Figures in *italics* refer to Appendix C (systematic list). Species are indexed by common name (*i.e.* Plover, Ringed) and scientific name; specific and subspecific names are also indexed for convenience.